- Modern English Poetry -
From Hardy to Hughes

for various Greek friends and especially for George Dandoulakis, Manos Georginis and Fotini Prevedourou

- Modern English Poetry -
From Hardy to Hughes

A CRITICAL SURVEY

John Lucas

BARNES & NOBLE
Totowa, New Jersey

© John Lucas 1986

All rights reserved. No part of this publication
may be reproduced, in any form or by any means,
without permission from the Publisher.

First published in USA in 1986 by
Barnes & Noble Books
81 Adams Drive, Totowa, New Jersey 07512

Library of Congress Cataloging-in-Publication Data

Lucas, John, 1937–
Modern English poetry from Hardy to Hughes.

1. English poetry—20th century—History and
criticism. 2. English poetry—19th century—History and
criticism. 3. National characteristics, English, in
literature. I. Title.
PR601.L79 1986 821'.91'09   86–3529
ISBN 0–389–20629–6

Printed in Great Britain

Contents

Prefatory Note

This study of modern English poetry grows out of years of reading, teaching, talking and writing about the subject. Over so long a period I have inevitably discussed and argued about the problem of English poetry with numerous friends, colleagues and students, and, equally inevitably, they have helped to sharpen my sense of just how problematic the idea of English poetry is. I suspect that the following book owes far more to them than I can readily assess, which isn't to say that they are to be blamed for what it contains.

To speak of a 'problem' may seem unduly contentious. Yet I hope that in what follows I have made a case for regarding the idea of Englishness as decidedly problematic. This is why I begin with a prologue in which I discuss some of the work of a great and still disgracefully neglected or misunderstood poet, John Clare. Clare of course is not a modern poet. How could he be? He died in 1864. Nevertheless, he seems to me to raise or embody most of the difficulties to do with being English that later poets have either to confront or try to resolve, in ways that bring up further difficulties.

This is why I put the word English in quotation marks when discussing T. S. Eliot. For it isn't merely the fact that Eliot was American by birth and only chose to take out British citizenship in 1927 that leads me to regard him with a certain quizzicality. There is also the fact that his English identity – royalist, Anglo-Catholic – can hardly be thought of as exhausting the possibilities of Englishness, no matter how orthodox his decision might seem, or be so regarded by the majority of his commentators.

As it happens, I think Eliot's choice cuts him off from certain critical ways of thinking about Englishness, and one reason for devoting a long chapter to Yeats is that Yeats's forging of his identity seems, by contrast, both more committed and more liberating. Another reason is that Yeats's greatness has much to do with his readiness to intervene in the large cultural, social and political issues

7

to do with Irish consciousness. By comparison, the inability of nearly all English poets – with the exception of W. H. Auden – to make comparable interventions is instructive and revelatory about English poetry in the twentieth century.

To say this is, of course, to say that I think poetry ought to be an act of intervention, which is probably to say that I write as a socialist. Those who claim to uphold the Arnoldian tradition of sweetness and light will no doubt claim that in what follows ideological considerations cloud my perceptions. The truth is that the Arnoldian tradition is both ideological and deeply debilitating. It has had far too much influence over the ways we are supposed to discuss poetry, and I believe it to have had far too much influence over English poets themselves. The world of platonic ideas, pure and undefiled by 'the smoke of the market place', or by the 'corruptions' of idiomatic language, produces a poetry drained of any worthwhile life.

The charge that the following book is ideologically conditioned does not worry me. I am, however, alert to another possible charge –which is that my concern with Englishness is exclusively male. It is so. In Chapter Five I try to explain why I think that during the modern period there has been very little good work by English women poets, but I should perhaps add that it does seem that the best women writers chose not to commit themselves to poetry (or not primarily), probably because 'poetry' had become identified with 'maleness' (obviously matters are very different in America, where Marianne Moore and Elizabeth Bishop are among the greatest of modern poets), and also – in the context of this book – because 'Englishness' turns out to be a largely, or even exclusively, male affair. To say this is not merely tautologous, but it does reveal that women have been pushed to the margins of, or have been made invisible to, the areas of concern which the following book takes up. This is a fact of history. It is also a fact of history that matters are now changing and that if in twenty years' time I were to up-date my study I would need to find space to consider the achievements of women poets from the 1960s onwards, although the best of them – Sylvia Plath, Anne Stevenson and Fleur Adcock – are, significantly enough, not English-born.

John Lucas

SEPTEMBER 1985

8

- I -

Prologue: Poetry and Possession

'Get there if you can and see the land you once were proud to own.' I begin with the opening line of poem no. XXII of Auden's *Poems 1930*, because it prompts two important questions that will concern me for much of the book that follows. Who is or are 'you'? And what does Auden mean by 'own'? His poem takes for granted a knowledge of Tennyson's 'Locksley Hall', which it knowingly parodies; and it also takes for granted an England in which 'nobody is well', as he has someone say at the beginning of *The Orators*. It is thus both knowing about a tradition of Victorian poetry and mockingly disenchanted with what has happened to the England over which Tennyson had, in a sense, presided as Poet Laureate. Not that Tennyson was Laureate when he published 'Locksley Hall' in 1842, but it was precisely the kind of poem to gain him the Laureateship.

At first glance Auden's 'you' may seem to be the common reader. But on reflection this will hardly do. The common reader in 1930 could hardly be thought of as owning England. 'You' is therefore more likely to be the 'owners' of England, rentier capitalists, appropriators of land, possessors of culture, wealth, social status, and so on. Such persons, the poem suggests, were once proud to own an England whose values and beliefs were the orthodoxies of the Victorian and Edwardian periods. They would include the splendours of Empire, material riches derived from industry and, to a lesser extent, agriculture. They would also include various institutions such as the public schools, the civil service, an enfranchised male middle-class, Church, Army, Monarchy, all of which could be cited as official evidence and cause of England's greatness, and a fit reason for pride. Tennyson's spokesman had looked towards the future with bland confidence: 'Yet I doubt not through the ages one increasing purpose runs,/And the thoughts of men are widened with the process of the suns.' And the poem had allowed for a vision of lasting peace: 'Till the war-drum throbbed no longer, and the

9

battle-flags were furled/In the Parliament of man, the Federation of the World.'

I know there will be those who say that to make Tennyson the spokesman for this windily empty optimism is to be less than fair to him, and they have some right on their side. But my concern for the moment is with what was made of Tennyson in the 1920s, and the fact is that after the Great War had all but ruined Europe, had wiped out much of its industrial base, and had been at least the partial causes of the Russian and Irish revolutions, it is not surprising that Auden should invite those who had identified with the vision of England that 'Locksley Hall' endorses to look again: to look and see 'Smokeless chimneys, damaged bridges, rotting wharves and choked canals,/Tramlines buckled, smashed trucks lying on their side across the rails.' My point is this: that among those who read Auden's poem the only appropriate response would be to say, 'But you can't mean us. We never did own this land. It wasn't ours to possess, even if we wanted to acknowledge our commitment to it.' And this of course is Auden's point also. 'You' can't mean everybody.

The *Oxford English Dictionary* defines 'to own' as follows: *to have as one's possession. To confess, or admit; to acknowledge.* The ambiguities are crucial. In the period with which this book is concerned some people, poets among them, might feel that they possessed England; but many more were bound to recognize that although they wished to own 'the land' – and while Auden's 'land' isn't literally England it is certainly a phantasmagoric version of it – they could not do so. Dispossession is therefore my theme, quite as much as possession. Or, to put the matter differently, I might say that my interests are often centred on the questions: who owns England? who speaks for it? can England be seen in terms of a unifying meaning, a single coherent image? can 'you' ever come to mean 'all'?

The questions are prompted by my strong sense that in the period 1880–1914 a number of writers, politicians and intellectuals show an extraordinary degree of self-consciousness in their desire to identify England, to speak of 'inherent' English traits, in other words to stabilise an image, to make it clear to themselves and each other just what England, the English and Englishness are and are not; and to promote this identity wherever possible. (Which must mean that they are worried about whether it makes sense.) It is these promoters who are addressed as 'you' in Auden's poem, together with others who, looking back to the utter disaster of the Great War, tried to build a bridge between pre- and post-war society and so speak for continuity. And I should say here that the Great War will feature in much of what follows, simply because when you read the poetry that came out of it and after it you can be left in no doubt as to its traumatizing effect on English society. 'Get there if you can' is partly about that effect. It says, 'look at the detritus of a wrecked society. Whose fault is it and what is to be done?'

The second question must be left. It will occupy me when I come to write about Auden in more detail. As to the first, the fault surely has something to do with 'you'. For the detritus of this society isn't merely a matter of industrial wreckage. There is human wreckage, also. If there are possessors then there will also be the dispossessed, those who cannot speak for England or who are excluded from its orthodox modes of utterance. Such people are non-'you'. But how can we know of their existence? One way of answering this question is by looking back into the nineteenth century and attending to the voice of one of the dispossessed, John Clare.

I want to say a little about Clare, because to do so will help to bring the concerns of this book into focus. Whatever I say must be brief, in the first place because he died in 1864, so that in a strict sense he can hardly belong in a book on modern poetry; and in the second place because although he mattered to Edward Thomas, and others knew of his work I cannot pretend that he is an overt influence on much modern English writing. On the other hand, his example seems to me very important; and I also think that what he writes about and the way he writes about it makes him representative and, in some senses, an important reproof to those who come after and who lack his heroism, toughness, and clear-sighted understanding of how 'you' are capturing England. In Clare's own case the capturing was literal. He was the victim of enclosure. He was also the victim of patrons and editors, who conspired not to let him publish some lines about the evils of enclosure on the grounds that they smacked of 'radical slang'. The lines in question appeared in 'Helpston', one of the poems of his first volume, *Poems Descriptive of Rural Life and Scenery*, 1820:

> Oh who could see my dear green willows fall
> What feeling heart but dropt a tear for all
> Accursed wealth o'er bounding human laws
> Of every evil thou remainst the cause
> Victims of want those wretches such as me
> Too truly lay their wretchedness to thee
> Thou art the bar that keeps from being fed

And thine our loss of labour and of bread
Thou art the cause that levels every tree
And woods bow down to clear a way for thee[1]

It is hardly surprising that Clare's self-appointed patron, Lord Radstock, should insist that these lines be cut out. But this was not the only way he suffered. There are occasions when Clare's editors so alter his lines, his punctuation and his language, that he comes across as a tame 'peasant' poet. And there are other occasions when he conspires with this and produces trivial drawing-room ballads and pieces of nature observation that you can find ten-a-penny in the literary journals of Regency and Victorian England. This is not to be wondered at. Clare seems to me in this sense symptomatic of many later writers. For whom is he writing? Is he a literary man among equals, a natural genius who aspires to higher things, a poet content to waste his sweetness on the desert air, or a champion of the people? He can be all these things by turn and in this, and especially when in certain of his poems he upbraids the 'vulgar' talk of 'humble hinds', we catch a glimpse of that cultural divide which Dickens explored in *Great Expectations*, and which is in some senses perhaps the most central of all modern experiences. In short, there are occasions when Clare seems to identify with precisely that culture which is 'owned' by those who are in a position to destroy his sense of himself. For these are the enclosers, of language as well as of land;[2] and when Clare speaks of humble hinds he is using their language, trying to slip inside and become one of them.

I do not mean to suggest by this that Clare shared Pip's great expectations. On the other hand, he undoubtedly had *some* expectations, and it seems that they are at least partly responsible for elements in his poetry that betray or reveal his sense of unease with his possible and very different audiences. For whom is he writing? It is a question that haunts later poets, and the fact that many of them appear to be most secure when talking to themselves or to the dead again suggests that Clare's experiences and problems are a great deal more representative than have usually been allowed.

> The psychological unity of many selves in one community is bound up . . . with the consciousness of some lengthy social process which has occurred, or is at least supposed to have occurred. And the wealthier the memory of a community is, and the vaster the historical processes which it regards as belonging

to its life, the richer – other things being equal – is its
consciousness that it *is* a community, that its members are
somehow made one in and through and with its own life.

That passage comes from Josiah Royce's *The Problem of Chris-
tianity*.[3] Royce was a Harvard philosopher, and his notion of
community has the air of an essentially American dream of Europe
and, specifically, of England. At all events, it is very close in spirit to
the image of England which Henry James directed at W. D. Howells,
when he explained to him that novels of worth could only be written
from and about a community rich in 'manners, customs, usages,
habits, forms, upon all things matured and established . . .' It is an
image which has been sedulously fostered by certain of the English
themselves, and one of its most persuasive variations is the notion of
the 'organic community' developed by F. R. Leavis and *Scrutiny*.
This wished-for community has its roots in Carlyle's *Past and
Present* and Ruskin's famous section on 'The Nature of Gothic' in
The Stones of Venice; and Leavis may well have derived his own
version from such sources together with William Morris's *News
From Nowhere*. I can see the point of identifying with this, and I can
understand why the desire to believe in such a community was bound
to come about at a time of large, rapid and, as in some ways it had to
seem, catastrophic change. But the fact is that the 'organic community' is a myth, an imposition from the outside on the actual
historical process. At its grandest, this dream of community is a
dream of England, and we shall see later that different inventions of
this dream are an essential part of the period with which I am
concerned. But the dream breaks on hard, unignorable fact: that
those who own England and who therefore presume to speak for it,
are appropriators who exclude others, who write them out of
history, or who conspire to make them invisible, or who allow them
to become part of history on the condition that they adopt a voice
which denies their own sense of community and self. Hence Lord
Radstock's censorship. Hence Clare's use of such words as 'clown'
and 'hind'. And hence the fact that two of his greatest poems, 'The
Flitting' and 'To a Fallen Elm' are scarcely ever mentioned in
discussions of his work.

   It is true that both Mark Storey, in his *The Poetry of John Clare*,
and Edward Storey, in his biography, *A Right to Song*, say something
about 'The Flitting', but their accounts are woefully inadequate.
Both of them try to explain the poem in purely biographical terms. It

was written shortly after Clare had moved from Helpston to Northborough, and according to Mark Storey:

> The importance of home is crucial: at this stage (the poem's opening stanzas) the cottage at Northborough is not transformed into the house he had hoped for. Home is still Helpstone [sic]. . . . Home, like poesy, had the power to transform the ordinary into the magical. He dislikes what is new and strange. . . .

But then we are to understand that Clare manages to make a connection between 'the past, unseen things, what he has lost, and the power of poetry to live on'. As a result, he rejects all pomp and splendour for the 'poetry of nature' and 'turns his attention to the preservation of all living objects'. Every weed now means something to him:

> the realisation of this encourages the stoicism of the last two stanzas: parting is inevitable, as is change, but nature can 'make amends', because of the power of memory, related to the eternity of nature. Grandeur is seen to fade, but grass springs eternally. Here lies what hope there is for Clare, as his personal sorrow gives way to a comprehensive philosophy of the value of the poetry of nature.[4]

This account is not merely typical of the two Storeys, it fits in uncomfortably well with the prevailing attitude to Clare. The poetry of nature soothes away the hurts of the world, and Clare can be pensioned off to a modest but useful life as conservationist of little things.

One thing is obvious, to me at least. If Storey's account of 'The Flitting' is in any way accurate then the poem doesn't deserve much attention. He makes it sound like a branch line of that tradition which runs through (say) Langhorne's 'Country Justice', with its recommendation of 'the fair Vale, where REST, conceal'd in Flowers,/Lies in Sweet Ambush for thy careless Hours', and comes to rest with the Georgians. Storey in fact turns the poem into a proto-Georgian piece of soft, sentimental, evasive mush. Yet 'The Flitting' is a great poem, and although the move to Northborough may have triggered it off, it isn't about that at all. A moment's reflection is enough to prove this to be so. For you may know nothing about such a move and still find the poem completely intelligible.

'The Flitting' is about dispossession. It is a grieving, eloquent utterance of a sense of being denied ownership of or relationship with all that you feel most intensely to be yours, all that feels so intimately connected with you that it is integral to your sense of selfhood. Here is the first stanza.

> Ive left mine own old home of homes
> Green fields & every pleasant place
> The summer like a stranger comes
> I pause & hardly know her face
> I miss the hazels happy green
> The bluebells quiet hanging blooms
> Where envys sneer was never seen
> Where staring malice never comes

The home isn't merely a house, it composes a neighbourhood. By contrast, the new place is one of strangeness and thus strangers, it is a denial of familiarity. As D. W. Harding points out in *Social Psychology and Individual Values*, in homesickness 'it seems likely that although the conscious longing may be for familiar places and physical surroundings, the house, the village, the scenery and so on, these ultimately derive their value from associations with the people to whom we are attached; that very word "familiar" underlines the fact'. Whether Clare got on well or badly with particular Helpston neighbours is of no relevance whatsoever. For 'The Flitting' voices an experience that was and remains typical. It is not directly about the effects of enclosure, but it certainly registers the keen, wounding shock of being away from all that had been known and taken for granted. It could only have been written by someone who knew the dehumanizing effects of the kinds of removals which enclosure helped to bring about, and/or who could imaginatively grasp their meaning for those who were their victims. 'Envys sneer' and 'staring malice' do not refer to local detractors but to that world which the poem comes to associate with the city, or with fashions that are inevitably hostile or indifferent to particular kinds of worth, and yet which, also inevitably, have power over other peoples' lives. And in the last analysis this includes the power to enclose not only land, but also the language, and culture.

The former place is known intimately, is nameable: 'royce wood', 'Langley bush'. By contrast, in the new place 'The sun een seems to lose its way/Nor knows the quarter it is in'. You realize just how sharp Clare's sense of disorientation is as soon as you note that 'know' rather than 'knows' would be the expected word. As it is, the two lines take for granted a kind of matter-of-fact common sense ('seems' is a key-word in the poem), while at the same time recording a dislocation that feels entire.

Clare also makes a crucial and precise link between his loss and the world of fashion. For in an important sense 'The Flitting' is about knowing yourself to be at the mercy of values you despise and yet which have ultimate power over you, because they are endorsed by and are an intimate expression of those whose authority is everywhere: in matters of art, politics, law. They are the owners. It is worth noting that Clare attacks this subject in two sonnets on Bloomfield, only one of which appeared in *The Rural Muse*. As we might expect, it is the more conventional of the two. 'Sweet unassuming minstrel not to thee/The dazzling fashions of the day belong' it begins; and it ends by claiming that Bloomfield's 'gentle muse' will linger on when the proud streams of the fashionable are 'summer burnt & dry'. The other sonnet is much better: a hard, angry, proud poem, which lashes those who sail in 'that gay ship popularity':

> Let not their fancys think tis muses fare
> While feeding on the publics gross supply
> Times wave rolls on – mortality must share
> A mortals fate & many a fame shall lie
> A dead wreck on the shore of dark posterity

Stanza 7 of 'The Flitting' begins, 'Alone & in a stranger scene/Far far from spots my heart esteems'; and two stanzas later Clare returns to that word 'esteems' in rejecting the comfort of books:

> For books they follow fashions new
> & throw all old esteems away
> In crowded streets flowers never grew
> But many there hath died away

There is no need to read biography into these lines, or to assume that in them Clare is sadly musing over his own lost fame in London. The four lines speak with an epigrammatic terseness of the eddies of taste which wash lightly over matters of worth, and which deny its value even in the act of praising it; and they inevitably link with the opening of stanza 7 because they express a disenchantment that belongs as much to the stranger scene as to books. Both have been arranged/ordered by others. This is the world of Vanity Fair – except to put it that way is to ignore the subtle tact by means of which Clare links power processes that are hatefully opposed to all that's implied by 'esteem'. (Johnson defined the word as 'reverential regard', and this is the sense in which Clare uses it). Those who are ignorant of the feelings, values and relationships summed up in esteem compose a world of strangers: they are indifferent to the dear familiarity of a peopled place. 'Strange scenes mere shadows are to me/Vague unpersonifying things', Clare writes in stanza 12, and then, in the following stanzas:

> Here every tree is strange to me
> All foreign things where e'er I go
> Theres none where boyhood made a swee [swing]
> Or clambered up to rob a crow
> No hollow tree or woodland bower
> Well known when joy was beating high
> Where beauty ran to shun a shower
> & love took pains to keep her dry
>
> & laid the shoaf upon the ground
> To keep her from the dripping grass
> & ran for stowks & set them round
> Till scarse a drop of rain could pass
> Through – where the maidens they reclined
> & sang sweet ballads now forgot
> Which brought sweet memorys to the mind
> But here no memory knows them not

What is almost miraculously beautiful about those stanzas has something to do with the way Clare takes over Augustan abstractions and rescues them from the expected and the dull: 'Where beauty ran to shun a shower/& love took pains to keep her dry'. The tender eroticism of those lines is made firm by the carry-over into the next stanza's imaginative exactness of recall, including the easy, unforced use of colloquial words and ways of speaking. But then comes the bleak disenchantment of the last line, the expulsion from a world of familiarity. In the next stanzas the new, strange place contrasts with the old one, where 'every weed & blossom too/Was looking upward in my face/With friendships welcome "how de do" '.

Weeds, blossoms, grasses. The conventional language of pastoral poetry. But in 'The Flitting' they carry a remarkable weight of significance. First, and most obviously, they operate in contrast to the trappings of the city:

> Give me no highflown fangled things
> No haughty pomp in marching chime
> Where muses play on golden strings
> & splendour passes for sublime
> Where citys stretch as far as fame
> & fancys straining eye can go

'Golden strings'. As the context makes clear, Clare's sardonic use of the cliché links poetry with money, power, class-bound assumptions of superiority. '& splendour passes for sublime'. This is art set upon a bough to sing: tame, lacquered, contemptible.

Art in a formal garden wants the weeds away. Clare nurses 'A love for every simple weed'. He calls it 'an ancient neighbour'. Johnson defined weed as a 'herb: noxious or useless', and thus makes clear the fact that the word has no botanical meaning. 'The Flitting' ends:

> Time looks on pomp with careless moods
> Or killing apathys disdain
> – So where old marble citys stood
> Poor persecuted weeds remain
> She feels a love for little things
> That very few can feel beside
> & still the grass eternal springs
> Where castles stood & grandeur died.

Where in these lines is the stoicism that Storey refers to? What first strikes me is the wit. Time will behave with exactly the same insolence towards Pomp as the Pompous have done towards those over whom they lord matters, whose lives they have displaced, whose art they have derided. Moreover, by the end of the stanza the 'poor persecuted weeds' have become 'grass', and are clearly metaphoric of the people displaced by pomp. The well-tended fields of enclosure weeded out tenant-smallholders just as surely as they weeded out groundsel and shepherd's purse. Clare knew that, how could he *not* know? And he would been aware of the kind of destruction of a community typified by the first Lord Milton, when he had the entire town of Milton Abbas moved because it was spoiling his view. It is not an isolated incident.

In *Man and the Natural World*, Keith Thomas remarks that towards the end of the eighteenth century a botanical society in Lichfield produced a *System of Vegetables . . . translated from . . . the Systema Vegetabilium of the Late Professor Linnaeus*, in which the Vegetable Kingdom was divided into tribes and nations, 'the latter bearing titles which were more sociological than botanical: the grasses were "plebeians" – "the more they are taxed and trod upon, the more they multiply." '[5] *This* is the context in which to think of the last stanzas of Clare's great poem. I do not see how you can read those stanzas without recognizing that they work towards a generous, even exuberant political affirmation, one which takes for granted and deliberately exploits the idea that to the owners of England its people are weeds or grass. Storey's obtuse and sentimental condescension to Clare – the recommendation of his 'stoicism' – misses the point about as completely as is possible. Clare's lines celebrate an act of reclamation that is radical. The grass *springs* where castles *stood* and grandeur *died*. This is an invading army, and the present tense shows that again and again rights will be asserted and won over those who denied them. So that the past tense of 'stood' has grandeur dying in the act of defending those castles that the grass overwhelms. And although I would not claim for the end of the poem a re-visiting of the spirit of 1789, it is surely not improper to note in this context the activities of Captain Swing and of George Lawless and his companions. At the very least, the placing of the word 'springs', and the continuous affirmation of energy it releases, ought to prevent us from reading the close of the poem as a stoical exercise about coming to terms with the poetry of nature.

Much the same is true of that other great poem, 'To a Fallen Elm'. It begins with the affectionate familiarity of companionable talk:

> Old elm that murmured in our chimney top
> The sweetest anthem autumn ever made
> & into mellow whispering calms would drop
> When showers fell on thy many coloured shade.

As we shall see later in this book, the elm becomes at this time something of an unofficial symbol of England, and although it has not that status in Clare's poem, it is obviously somehow an expression of neighbourliness, and can be linked to the language of community. For 'murmured' has about it the accent of speech that is characterized by unforced, loving acquaintance, familiar, intimate. (It's worth comparing Clare's use of the word with Hardy's, in 'Friends Beyond', where the 'Squire and Lady Susan, murmur mildly to me now', and contrasting their use with Tennyson's 'murmur of innumerable bees', for there the word, apt as it is, is nonetheless empty of those implications of human utterance which give it its richness in the use that Clare and Hardy make of it).

But 'To a Fallen Elm' is not a melancholy meditation on the 'principle of change' which defenders of the picturesque allege will explain why, during the period 1750–1850, there are so many poems and paintings dealing with ruin and decay. Clare's elm has not fallen because of old age, nor does he mourn for it in a manner that anticipates Hopkins's grief at the thoughtless despoliation of a sweet, especial rural scene. This was *intended*. 'Self interest saw thee stand in freedoms way/So thy old shadow must a tyrant be'. The cutting-down of the elm becomes the occasion for Clare to voice a passionate, pointed anger, directed through the poem's last 40 lines at those who claim ownership over the lives and circumstances of others. It is impossible to quote from 'To a Fallen Elm' without doing it the gravest injustice, because quotation severs the poem's driving pulse: its fierce, scornful anger. The voice of English radicalism sounds clearly through the poem, and in a way that is not often heard in subsequent English poetry. It is the voice of Byron and Cobbett, whose work Clare knew, and of others with whom he will have been familiar. Here he is, attacking the abuse of the term 'freedom':

> It grows the cant term of enslaving tools
> To wrong another by the name of right
> It grows a liscence with oer bearing fools
> To cheat plain honesty by force of might
> Thus came enclosure

'Thus came enclosure'. The only way to dodge the hammer-blow insistence of that is by avoiding the entire poem. And that is what usually happens. 'To a Fallen Elm' is even less often discussed than 'The Flitting'.

Clare's is or ought to be an immediately recognizable English voice. Nevertheless, he does not presume to speak for England. Nor, as we shall see, does Hardy, not often, anyway, and never when he is at his best. But Hardy and the poets who were his contemporaries as well as those who come after him often create visions of a community which seem meant to be or are offered as 'ideal communities', and even suggest a secret 'heart' of England. As with Clare, these later poets feel themselves to be somehow excluded from the visions they produce, no matter how they produce them – whether through memory, momentary glimpses, or other, more ghostly apprehensions. They are on the outside looking in, or in a chill present looking back to a warm past. Paradoxically, it is the American, T. S. Eliot, who summons up an inclusive vision where 'History is now and

England', although I shall suggest that what he sees is as elusive and probably illusory as the notion of community summoned up by Josiah Royce. It is a dream image imposed on the complex actuality of history, although this is not often admitted because it makes its appeal to many who wish to identify with its particular concept of Englishness.

The only modern English poet who seems fully to have grasped the problems that Clare faced and out of which he wrote is W. H. Auden. This has nothing to do with whether Auden knew much about Clare himself. It has everything to do with his understanding of the issues which, as it happens, Clare's great poetry often confronts. Auden writes from within the cultural orthodoxy, of 'castles and grandeur', as it were. But he does so as its enemy. Whether poets coming after him could profit from his intensely liberating example is a subject I leave for my final chapter.

Further Reading

The best writing about Clare is in John Barrell's *The Idea of Landscape and the Sense of Place*, 1974. Unfortunately, Barrell does not really discuss the issues that most engage us here. It is fascinating – revealing and betraying – to note that hardly any studies of either Romanticism or of nineteenth-century poetry make room for or know what to do about Clare. He will not fit. At the risk of making myself a hostage to fortune, I will – tentatively – suggest that readers may find something of interest in my essay 'Prospects and Dwellings: Some aspects of landscape poetry' in *The Experience of Landscape*, ed. Cosgrove and Daniels, 1986. A good recent study is by Tim Chilcott: '*A Real World & Doubting Mind': A Critical Study of The Poetry of John Clare* (1985).

- 2 -

Thomas Hardy: Voices and Visions

I

As has often been remarked, Thomas Hardy began the serious business of publishing volumes of poetry only after he had effectively finished with the novel. *Jude the Obscure* was published in 1895. Three years later Hardy published his first volume of poems, *Wessex Poems and Other Verses*. He was then nearing sixty. By the time of his death, in 1928, he had published six further volumes and another was to be published posthumously. If we also take into account *The Dynasts*, his great verse narrative of the Napoleonic Wars, this amounts to a prodigious collection of work. It also helps to affirm what some, including myself, believe: that Hardy was at least as natural a writer of poetry as of prose, and that although he apparently started late he was really always a poet. As indeed he was. For of course many of his poems were written at the time when he was earning his living as a novelist, and many episodes in his novels make better sense, or feel more natural, if you imagine them as prompted by the ballad tradition which ran so strongly in his veins.

He once told the amazed Robert Graves that he rarely revised a poem. There is some exaggeration in the remark, but it does tell us how easily poetry came to him. Too easily, we may think, looking at the sheer bulk of the *Complete Poems*, and there are undoubtedly some very slight pieces scattered among its thousand-odd pages. But this should not be taken to mean that Hardy's seemingly effortless spontaneity lacked craft. As Donald Davie has remarked, Hardy was formidably skilled and knowledgeable about matters of prosody. There is scarcely a metre he does not use, from dipodic through to trochaic octameter, and as late as the posthumously published *Winter Words* he is still experimenting with the dramatic hendeca-syllabics of 'Aristodemus the Messenian', a poem which must have been more fun to write than it is to read. He was equally resourceful in his use and invention of a wide variety of stanza forms, although such resourcefulness was fairly common among the Victorian poets whom he admired. And as with them – I think in particular of Browning and the much less important Meredith – Hardy occasionally gives the appearance of daft ingenuity. But such excesses are pardonable. They do not seem to me to amount to the kind of misplaced, rigid mechanisms which Donald Davie accuses Hardy of turning out from his poetry factory. For Davie, Hardy is a poet of the machine age, and his poems are to be compared to the Gothic structures beloved of Victorian engineers.[1] This will not do. Hardy, I repeat, is naturally a poet, and although without formal skills you will never be a poet, skill alone will not suffice. One way into the secret of Hardy's naturalness – and greatness – as a poet is via a poem called 'The House of Silence'. It is not one of his great poems, but it is a very instructive one. Two voices speak in it, one of a boy and the other of a man, who is also a poet. The boy says

> 'That is a quiet place –
> That house in the trees with the shady lawn'

and he adds that he sees nobody there. The man replies

> '– Ah, that's because you do not bear
> The visioning powers of souls who dare
> To pierce the material screen.
>
> Morning, noon, and night,
> Mid those funereal shades that seem
> The uncanny scenery of a dream,
> Figures dance to a mind with sight,
> And music and laughter like floods of light
> Make all the precincts gleam.'

'A mind with sight' may strike us as a slightly awkward phrase, but it also tells us a good deal that we need to know about Hardy. Of course, he had unusually keen powers of perception, as Tom Paulin in particular has shown. Even slight or poor poems may be momentarily redeemed by a visual image of piercing or arresting accuracy, as in the opening of 'The Prospect', 'The twigs of the birch imprint the December sky/Like branching veins upon a thin old hand', or as in the image in the first stanza of 'The Pedigree', where Hardy describes the moon in its old age: 'And green-rheumed clouds were hurrying past where mute and cold it globed/Like a drifting dolphin's eye seen through a lapping wave' – an image

which, if it tells us how often Hardy's perceptions were attuned to
and sharpened by moonlight, also tells us that he has probably at the
back of his mind some marine painting or other. (Hardy's interest in
and use of paintings is by now familiar knowledge.) Other poems
depend almost entirely on visual effects, as in the much-anthologized
'Snow in the Suburbs' or the finer 'Overlooking the River Stour',
where the obsessive accuracy of noting the minutiae of natural
occurrences, of a moorhen 'Planing up shavings of crystal spray', for
example, is psychologically telling, because it is only by fixing his
gaze on what's before him that the poet escapes from taking due note
of the woman in the room behind him. I might also note that Hardy is
preoccupied with physical grotesqueness, as in 'The Pedestrian',
where it is said of a fat man that "Twas as if his corpulent figure
slopped/With the shake of his walking when he stopped', or in the
greater 'The Convergence of the Twain', to which I shall return.

But 'A mind with sight' is not about ordinary powers of
perception, no matter how keen. What it *is* about becomes clearer
once we link it to the lines about 'The visioning power of souls that
dare/To pierce the material screen'. The lines echo Shelley's sonnet
'The Painted Veil'. Shelley the Platonist appealed to Hardy because
he shared the Romantic poet's belief in a world of forms that lie
behind the world of sensible appearances. As we shall see, Hardy
makes crucial use of the word 'forms'. In 'The House of Silence' he is
doing what he so often does, 'vision' people and voices who,
although dead, are present to 'a mind with sight'.

There is however an obvious problem about this. As everybody
knows, Hardy lost his religious belief while still a young man. He
then spent the rest of his life regretting the fact and trying to explain
or come to terms with a universe in which 'the Immanent Will'
pursued purposes which were at best indifferent to human needs. In
'Nature's Questioning' natural phenomena 'wonder, ever wonder,
why we find us here!'; and in the more famous 'The Impercipient',
Hardy finds himself cut off from believers at a Cathedral service:

> I am like a gazer who should mark
>   An inland company
> Standing upfingered, with 'Hark! Hark!
>   The glorious, distant sea!'
> And feel, 'Alas, 'tis but yon dark
>   And wind-swept pine to me.'

As the echoes of Wordsworth and Matthew Arnold indicate, 'The
Impercipient' is a self-conscious performance. It feels very much the

kind of poem that you would write in order to establish your credentials as an honest doubter, and it may be linked to a whole series of others which, late and soon in his career, Hardy produced as evidence of his taking 'a full look at the Worst'. (The phrase comes from 'In Tenebris II', one of three poems which are perhaps Hardy's most impressive achievements in the way of voicing the philosophical pessimism of his age.)

It is also worth saying at this point that Hardy's representative status as honest doubter led him to write the kind of poems that slide easily enough into anthologies. 'The Darkling Thrush' is a case in point, as is 'To An Unborn Pauper Child'. And it is worth noting further that there are occasions in Hardy's career as poet when he takes on public themes, almost as though he sees himself as spokesman for his age, even if not its official laureate. Hence, I suggest, the series of very unpleasant poems he wrote about the Great War. Hence, and much more justifiably, his great 'The Convergence of the Twain', where he exposes the vulgar materialism of the Edwardian era and sets the sinking of the *Titanic* in a perspective that grimly exposes human vanity and the rage for possessions.

> Over the mirrors meant
> To glass the opulent
> The sea-worm crawls – grotesque, slimed, dumb, indifferent.

'The Convergence of the Twain' comes immediately after 'Channel Firing', another very fine poem, in which Hardy places 'gunnery practice out at sea' in the context of a history which denies such practice its presumed unique value. The poem ends:

> Again the guns disturbed the hour,
> Roaring their readiness to avenge,
> As far inland as Stourton Tower,
> And Camelot, and starlit Stonehenge.

The opening up of history in the last two lines is both chilling in its awareness of the extent of the guns' bestial roar, and sadly wise in its reminder that violence and vengeance have always been part of human affairs.

Poems such as 'The Convergence of the Twain' and 'Channel Firing' show how good an occasional poet Hardy could be. There are the elegies to his fellow-writers and there are 'Drummer Hodge' and 'In Time of "The Breaking of Nations" ', which in their different ways establish perspectives against which to measure the horrors of war. 'Drummer Hodge' in particular is a sly, almost elusive poem, which may be thought to claim some kinship with Wordsworth's 'A Slumber Did My Spirit Seal', but which remains very much the poem that only Hardy could create, because only Hardy would see, deep down, the comic possibilities of Hodge's breast and brain growing to some southern tree.

Nevertheless, Hardy is less the poet of occasion than pre-occupation. Above all, he is preoccupied with 'visioning power'. Most of his great poems and many others, good, bad and indifferent, are the products of a mind with sight, of one who finds that 'Music and laughter like floods of light/Make all the precincts gleam'. Hardy's mind was lit by vision, and such vision for him is nearly always connected with moon- or candle-light. 'Nebulous' is one of his favourite words, both in his prose and poetry. Tom Paulin has shown its importance to Hardy the poet and I have elsewhere suggested its significance for Hardy the novelist.[2]

But what strikes me as powerfully suggestive about the lines from 'The House of Silence' is that music and laughter – the sounds of human voices at their most familiarly convivial – themselves achieve visionary status. They are like floods of light, are every bit as good as the visionary gleam. The visions by which Hardy's mind was lit were very often indistinguishable from, were in fact known through, sounds: of voices, music, song, laughter, murmurings. And it is as though poem after poem is a prompting of sounds from which he seeks release by the act of transcription. (I use that word in its sense of 'a representation in writing of the actual pronunciation of a speech sound'.) Such transcription repeatedly moves towards the condition of music or dance. It is noticeable that as the man in 'The House of Silence' begins to describe his vision so his speech rhythm becomes anapaestic:

> And músic and laúghter like flóods of líght

This movement towards the anapaestic occurs so often in Hardy's poetry that it requires some explanation. In order to try to provide this I will take one of his most familiar poems, 'The Oxen'.

> Chrístmas Eve, and twélve of the clóck.
>   'Nów they are áll on their knées',
> An elder sáid as we sát in a flóck
>   By the émbers in heárthside eáse.

> We pictured the meék, mild creátures where

They dwélt in their stráwy pén,
Nor díd it occúr to oñe of us thére
To doúbt they were knéeling theñ.

So fáir a fañcy féw would wéave
    In thése yèars! Yét, I feél,
If someone sáid on Chrístmas Ev́e,
    'Cóme; see the ox́en knéel

'In the lónely bar̃ton by yoñder coómb
    Our chíldhood uśed to kñow',
Í should gó with him iñ the gloóm,
    Hopíng it mígħt be śo.

                                              1915

Hardy did not always date his poems. The fact that he put the date at the end of 'The Oxen' is therefore important, and in some ways it makes the poem look an occasional one. 'It is not just modern times that make the old superstitions impossible to think of, it's the gloom of wartime' might be a gloss on the poem's meaning. But there is more to it than just that, and to see what else this apparently slight poem will yield I think it worthwhile analysing it in some detail.

The first two stanzas run with a dance-like ease and without any medial pauses. Moreover the metric tug is towards the anapaestic, and this ballad-metre is reinforced by the fact that the poem is written in the stanza form called common measure, which was often used in hymns and ballads alike. The poem's pivotal word is obviously 'then'. At first it seems to mean 'At midnight on Christmas Eve'. But you realize it also means 'all those years ago'. And as the apparently unbridgeable gap between past and present opens up so the cadences of the poem abruptly change. The third stanza is heavily iambic, its movement clogged and impeded both by the hectically enforced alliteration (as though the poet is desperately trying to hang on to the spirit of the first two stanzas) and by the broken second line, with the exclamation marks and commas entirely breaking the untroubled ease of utterance that had marked the previous stanzas. In the last line of the third stanza there is a kind of flutter of anapaest, but clearly the rhythms of the opening stanzas are not to be recovered: the gloom sees to that. But the major point I want to make is this: that the voice of the past, of the community, of 'we', is balladic, running smoothly into and out of the anapaestic; the voice of the present, isolated, hesitant, uneasy, is predominantly iambic. Yet memory is so strong for Hardy, voices make themselves so insistently present to him, that as the poem begins you cannot tell whether he is in the present or the past. For the first line has no verb: the voice starts out of silence. Past and present are in fact elided into the one, and as they are so the voice that emerges is that of the community, of shared, song-like utterance.

It is crucial that we register this fact, because otherwise we shall miss something of equal importance: that Hardy is the natural poet of a community whose natural modes of utterance are song and dance. Hardy loved dance, partly because of the physical exuberance it released, partly because it undoubtedly imaged the idea of community, of harmony between people. Merely naming the old dances gives him pleasure, as you can see in any number of his poems, for example 'Reminiscences of a Dancing Man', and perhaps especially in the very fine 'The Dance at the Phoenix', about an ageing woman who, lying in bed at night, hears the sounds of music coming from an inn. They recall the days of her youth when she had danced with soldiers, and so she once more takes herself off to the dance:

> The favourite Quick-Step 'Speed the Plough' –
> (Cross hands, cast off, and wheel) –
> 'The Triumph', 'Sylph', 'The Row-dow-dow',
> Famed 'Major Malley's Reel',
> 'The Duke of York's', 'The Fairy Dance',
> 'The Bridge of Lodi' (brought from France),
> She beat out, toe and heel.

The woman's name is Jenny, which tells us that she is no better than she should be. (Rossetti's famous poem, 'Jenny', about a prostitute, had linked name and profession.) Hardy's Jenny isn't a harlot but he makes it clear that in her youth she had been sexually involved with soldiers, especially the men of the King's Own Cavalry; and it is their successors who throw the dance to which, as a fifty-year-old matron, she now goes. There is even a hint that once again she has sex with soldiers, for when she finally returns to her sleeping husband's side – he had married her knowing nothing of her past – 'She felt she would give more than life/To be the single-hearted wife/That she had been erstwhile . . .'. As it is, her heart stops, and when the husband awakes to find her dead

> His doubts remained unstirred.
> His Jenny had not left his side
> Betwixt the eve and morning-tide:
> – The King's said not a word.

Hardy has many poems about misalliances: the wife makes the wrong marriage, or there is a man in her past whose memory or actual presence returns to plague her. Or it may be that the husband is the one who marries without love. Or lovers meet again after many years and regret their lost opportunities. With the exception of a handful – among which 'The Revisitation' stands out for its prodigious technical accomplishment – I do not think that these are among Hardy's best poems. And what is often of most interest in the poems, to us and I suspect to Hardy, is not so much the tale itself as the way it is linked to circumstances. In the case of 'The Revisitation' it is a particular landscape. With 'The Dance at the Phoenix' it is the dances.

It might even be possible to stretch a point and say that with 'The Rash Bride' it is Mellstock Choir and its music that most engages Hardy's attention. 'The Rash Bride' is a typical Hardy tale. The choir is out at Christmas and calls at the house of a young widow. One of the choir members loves her and plans to marry her. She comes to the window as they play and sing for her and then a man appears behind her. It is the kind of vision that Hardy repeatedly uses in his novels; here it leads to her death by suicide, since her new husband discovers that she had 'jilted' her other lover. The poem ends in the graveyard:

Our old bass player, as I recall – his white hair blown – but why recall! –
His viol upstrapped, bent figure – doomed to follow her full soon –
Stood bowing, pale and tremulous; and next to him the rest of us. . . .
We sang the Ninetieth Psalm to her – set to Saint Stephen's tune.

The point is that even more than dance Hardy responds to ballads, ballad-tunes, psalms, hymns, and church music generally. Hence the poems about the Mellstock choir and hence, of course, those subtle shifts of accent that occur in most of his poems and which attest to the keenness of his hearing, his sense of how to dramatize, bring alive voices, utterances. Just occasionally this produces a kind of epiphanic poem, where a tiny incident constellates rich meanings and implications. One of the finest examples of this is 'At the Railway Station, Upway'.

'There is not much that I can do,
    For I've no money that's quite my own!'
    Spoke up the pitying child –
A little boy with a violin
At the station before the train came in, –
'But I can play my fiddle for you,

And a nice one 'tis, and good in tone!'
The man in the handcuffs smiled;
The constable looked, and he smiled, too,
    As the fiddle began to twang;
And the man in the handcuffs suddenly sang
    With grimful glee:
    'This life so free
    Is the thing for me!'
And the constable smiled, and said no word,
As if unconscious of what he heard;
And so they went on till the train came in –
The convict, and boy with the violin.

It may be worth noting that Hardy is the first poet to use railway waiting-rooms and train journeys as images of intersecting lives caught for a moment in harmony, providing fleeting visions, togetherness, before they separate out. And of course it's the fact that you know the lives must break apart that gives to the 'frail travelling coincidence' its especial poignancy. (I use Philip Larkin's phrase because it helps to pinpoint the extent to which, in 'The Whitsun Weddings', he is in Hardy's debt.) Perhaps Hardy's most famous poem in this respect is 'In A Waiting-Room', but I confess to feeling about this rather as I do about the 'Darkling Thrush': it's somehow written to order. 'But the words of the child in the squalid gloom/ Had spread a glory through the gloom.' Hardy at his best doesn't need to nudge us in the ribs to make sure that we don't miss the significance of his tale. There's no such anxious attentiveness in 'At the Railway Station, Upway' and the poem is all the better for it.

II

But although Hardy makes use of the voices of strangers, he is more usually conscious of voices of friends, loved ones, old acquaintances. They 'murmur mildly to me now' he says in the wonderful 'Friends Beyond'; and indeed murmuring is the condition to which all these voices move. In the previous chapter I remarked that Clare used the word 'murmur' in a manner that implied loving familiarity, the voice at its most intimately communicative. But I have to add that Clare typically feels himself cut off from such communication. Not Hardy, however. Again and again his poems start out of speech rhythms that drift near to song, or they begin with metric regularity and then modulate into cadences that imply speech, words used 'in all their intimate accents'. A perfect example of that occurs in the last stanza of 'On a Midsummer Eve'.

> I idly cut a parsley stalk,
> And blew therein towards the moon;
> I had not thought what ghosts would walk
> With shivering footsteps to my tune.
>
> I went, and knelt, and scooped my hand
> As if to drink, into the brook,
> And a faint figure seemed to stand
> Above me, with the bygone look.
>
> I lipped rough rhymes of chance, not choice,
> I thought not what my words might be;
> There came into my ear a voice
> That turned a tenderer verse for me.

It is the last stanza, even the last line, that authenticates this little poem. For it is invaded by another voice: the shift towards anapaestic is at one with the way 'turned' turns into 'tenderer'. To take another example. 'To Lisbie Browne' may lie on the page as though it is a fairly routine late-Victorian exercise in making a sentimental drawing-room ballad, but you have only to begin to read it aloud to know how wonderful it is: the voice tender, affectionate, gently mocking, loving. And to say this leads to a further point.

In *Social Psychology and Individual Values*, D. W. Harding remarks that neurosis may take the form of a person's wanting to identify through a 'free flow of social feeling' with people whose life-styles may be seen as supportive of that person's aspirations. (Film and pop-stars are obvious examples.) But, Harding goes on, 'the many possibilities of using imaginary companionship in a neurotic way do not alter the fact that social support from sub-groups of people long dead may be one of the most effective and valuable contributions of tradition to the living individual'. Harding has professional subgroups particularly in mind here, but even so his words seem to me remarkably applicable to the heart of Hardy's poetry. For as everyone who reads that poetry recognizes, Hardy loves talking to the dead, or allowing them to talk to him. Hence 'Friends Beyond' or the equally fine 'Voices from Things Growing in a Churchyard', whose 'murmurous accents seem to come/Thence hitheraround in a radiant hum'. And hence a whole body of minor but effective poems, among which 'Paying Calls' and 'The Dead Quire' deserve special mention.

Hardy's intimate sense of possessing the past has, of course, to do battle with his sense that the past *is* the past, that in rational terms it can come no more, that it is dead and done with. For a variety of reasons nineteenth-century writers become preoccupied with the past, even one might say obsessed with it; and the predominant reason is quite simply that the present feels different. Change becomes the only constant, and a sense of exclusion from a past that guaranteed community, family relationships, shared assumptions, is common to many writers, Clare being the first of them. Hardy is too intelligent to indulge in a dream of a timeless, idyllic past, a golden world from which he has been thrust out onto the cold hillside. His novels everywhere show his awareness of the social process which dismantles such a dream. So, occasionally, do his poems. 'The Self-Unseeing', for example.

> Here is the ancient floor,
> Footworn and hollowed and thin,
> Here was the former door
> Where the dead feet walked in.
>
> She sat here in her chair,
> Smiling into the fire;
> He who played stood there,
> Bowing it higher and higher.
>
> Childlike I danced in a dream;
> Blessings emblazoned that day;
> Everything glowed with a gleam;
> Yet we were looking away!

The wry drop of tone in the last line shows that each of the participants in that blessed day was in fact wrapped in dreams of self-absorption. Indeed, in context the poem feels a good deal more sardonic than when it is read on its own. For the two previous poems, 'The Tree' and 'Her Late Husband', are about betrayals within marriage, so that when we come to 'The Self-Unseeing' it is quite possible to interpret the woman's smile as hinting at a secret love affair, and perhaps detect the same thing in the man's rapt absorption. Even the fact that the boy is included in 'looking away' tells us something about the process that is, for example, at the deep heart of *Great Expectations*, where Pip yearns to leave the 'happy valley' of childhood for the city, and a new, more ambitious life.

Yet against all this we have to set the vision. Betrayed or not, its vitality is beyond doubt: it is 'here' in the emphatic, alliterated lines of the last stanza; and as we have seen and will do again, *glow* and *gleam* are essential elements in Hardy's visioning. The gleam is usually that of moon- or candle-light, the glow is usually of fire-light. It is so in the fine poem, 'Logs on the Hearth', where, burning an old tree, Hardy recalls how he climbed it when he was a boy and

> My fellow-climber rises dim
> From her chilly grave –
> Just as she was, her foot near mine on the bending limb,
> Laughing, her young brown hand awave.

And it's as though, for a moment at least, a flame on the hearth has actually become the girl's hand; she has been summoned up by the warmth of the fire from the chill of the grave.

What can Hardy mean by such poems? Although he once said that he would give ten years of his life to see a ghost, he was an unbeliever. Moreover, he has poems where the absolute pastness of the past may not be denied. In 'The Self-Unseeing' we have to notice that the 'ancient floor' is 'footworn and hollowed and thin', and if this suggests the usage which Hardy always felt gave meaning to objects, it also calls attention to the fragility of timeworn things. The floor is about to disappear, along with those emphatically 'dead feet'. The finality of death helps to explain the particularly sharp feeling of 'The Photograph', where, burning a picture of 'a woman long hid amid packs of years', Hardy watches in appalled fascination until 'the flames had eaten her breasts, and mouth, and hair'. And yet that way of putting it shows with exact and deeply unsettling directness Hardy's sense of the woman's reality, almost of her presence. If you take seriously what he says, as you must surely do, then you are forced to recognize that he is responding not just to the destruction of the photograph, but to the woman herself.

> 'Thank God, she is out of it now!' I said at last,
> In a great relief of heart when the thing was done
>   That had set my soul aghast . . .

Hardy would not have written that last line unless he had meant it; and indeed the poem as a whole is quick with the intense feeling of being aghast. So it comes almost as a relief when he says that 'I felt as if I had put her to death that night'. The prosaic explanation, the saving 'as if': between them they modify an otherwise almost unbearable acuteness of discomfort.

And it is here that we come to the heart of the matter. For although

as a rational non-believer Hardy accepts the finality of death and the
necessary obliteration of the past, another and equally convincing
element in him feels differently. More than any other poet Hardy is
the poet of memory, and memory, Philip Larkin has said, 'links us to
our losses'. I do not know whether Hardy was at all in his mind when
he wrote those words, but he may have been, for Hardy is Larkin's
favourite poet. And according to Larkin, Hardy's truest poems are
characterized by 'the authority of sadness'. The very keenness of his
memory summons up all he has lost. Take, for example, 'In the Small
Hours', where the ageing man lies in bed and dreams that 'tunes flew
back to my fingers/I had melodied years ago'.

> And soon anon came crossing
>   The chamber in the gray
> Figures of jigging fieldfolk –
>   Saviours of corn and hay –
> To the air of 'Haste to the Wedding',
>   As after a wedding-day . . .
>
> It seemed a thing for weeping
>   To find, at slumber's wane
> And morning's sly increeping,
>   That Now, not Then, held reign.

The intensity of memory is strong enough to elide past and present: it
isn't 'as if' the figures return, the syntax actually places them there, in
the present, in the old man's chamber. Then they go, and 'It seemed a
thing for weeping'.

III

This is perhaps the best point at which to introduce a discussion of
the sequence of poems which Hardy wrote after the death of his first
wife, Emma. I regard a handful of them as among the great poems of
the language. They are not, however, exceptional, if by that is meant
that we would not have expected them of Hardy. When he was led to
speak of these poems he said that his old brain became vocal; and it is
as though he was invaded, taken over, by sights and sounds before
which he was powerless. In a fine poem about Hardy, called 'The
Birthplace', Seamus Heaney speaks of the 'unperturbed, reliable/
ghost life he carried, with no need to invent', and while, as we have
seen, the remark can apply to many of Hardy's poems, it bears
especially on the poems I want now to discuss.

It is an odd feature of these great poems that although they are works of art they hardly feel to be that. As you read them, you are aware of the absolute transparency of the medium that Hardy uses, and in this they are very unlike his great poem of failed vision, 'Neutral Tones', with its self-conscious, deadly awareness of a world blighted by the failure of a love-relationship.

> We stood by a pond that winter day,
> And the sun was white, as though chidden of God,
> And a few leaves lay on the starving sod;
>   – They had fallen from an ash, and were gray.
>
> Your eyes on me were as eyes that rove
> Over tedious riddles of years ago;
> And some words played between us to and fro
>   On which lost the more by our love.
>
> The smile on your mouth was the deadest thing
> Alive enough to have strength to die;
> And a grin of bitterness swept thereby
>   Like an ominous bird a-wing. . . .
>
> Since then, keen lessons that love deceives,
> And wrings with wrong, have shaped to me
> Your face, and the God-curst sun, and a tree,
>   And a pond edged with grayish leaves.

The appalling, flat rhythms, which have been well discussed in a famous essay by F. R. Leavis, and which are so utterly unlike the shifting cadences of most of Hardy's poems, enact a frightening blanking-out of the spirit. The chill seems final.

It was a chill that undoubtedly conditioned the later years of his marriage to Emma. I am not, however, going to embark on biographical speculations about that marriage, the reasons for its failure, or who was to blame. All relationships are in an integral sense opaque to the outsider; we are forced to see through a glass darkly and it distorts what we see. To say that the marriage failed because Hardy was unsympathetic, or cold, or self-preoccupied, seems to me merely impertinent. What is true is that in the year following Emma's death he wrote some fifty poems to do with her or their courtship and marriage; and in the following years he wrote at least as many again that take up the same subjects.

Nobody who writes about Hardy as poet can avoid mentioning these poems. Yet the vast majority of commentators wish to locate their power in the psychological truthfulness that Hardy brings to them. The poems become statements of stoic grief or bleakly explored suffering. That is true of some, but it is emphatically not true of others – the greatest; and this has been made clear in an essay which I think far and away the finest ever written on Hardy as poet: 'Hardy's Virgilian Purples', by Donald Davie.[3]

Davie draws attention to the importance of the Virgilian tag that Hardy uses as epigraph for the entire sequence of *Poems of 1912–13* that deal with Emma. *Veteris vestigia flammae*: ashes of an old fire. Hardy, as Davie remarks, was far more deeply read in the classics than he let on, or than he was given credit for. (James's 'good little Hardy' was after all assumed to be a faltering autodidact.) The evidence for his reading of and absorption in Virgil does not merely come from the epigraph, it is also there in a key moment in 'Beeny Cliff' – which is subtitled 'March 1870–1913'. Hardy is recalling how he and Emma rode along the Cornish cliff-tops in their courting days:

> A little cloud then cloaked us, and there flew an irised rain,
> And the Atlantic dyed its levels with a dull misfeatured stain,
> And then the sun burst out again, and purples prinked the main.

It is in Book VI of the *Aeneid* that we come upon the purple light. The phrase occurs at that moment where Virgil has entered the underworld and arrived at the abode of the blest. Dryden translates the moment as

> These holy rites performed, they took their way,
> Where long extended plains of pleasure lay,
> The verdant fields with those of heaven may vie,
> With aether vested, and a purple sky –
> The blissful seats of happy souls below:
> Stars of their own, and their own suns, they know.

Hardy would certainly have read that, because his mother gave him a copy of Dryden's version for his eighth birthday. But then he also knew the original. Davie's point is this:

> Virgil's *purpureus* describes a light that is not any terrestrial light, however preternaturally radiant and keen; it is preternatural through and through, the light of an alternative cosmos, lit by another sun by day and other stars by night. And it is this light, no other, that Hardy, agnostic and scientific humanist, claimed to see from Beeny Cliff when 'purples prinked the main'.

36

Davie also goes on to suggest that Hardy may well have been influenced by the fact that in the *Purgatorio*, at the very moment when Dante meets the honoured shade of Beatrice, Virgil's *veteris vestigia flammae* is quoted. 'And so when Hardy meets the dead Emma in "After a Journey", in the shadows which they cast not only does Aeneas meet the dead Dido but Dante meets the secret and transfigured Beatrice.' Davie further points out that Dante's precise sense of topography would have been certain to appeal to Hardy.

> And so, if we say that the landscapes presented so insistently in
> 'Poems of 1912–13' are so many stations in a personal
> purgatory, we can mean something quite precise: we mean that
> each locality – and there are three of them, Dorset round Max
> Gate, Plymouth, and North Cornwall round Boscastle – is
> presented as the location, the haunt and the habitat, of some one
> moral proclivity or principle. Max Gate is the landscape of
> treason, Boscastle (Beeny Cliff, St Juliot) is the landscape of
> loyalty and love. . . . The half-way house of Plymouth is the
> questionable, the problematic location.

If this is true, and I am certain that it is, it follows that when in 'A Dream or No', Hardy says:

> But nought of that maid from Saint-Juliot I see;
>   Can she ever have been here,
>   And shed her life's sheen here,
> The woman I thought a long housemate with me?

the answer is, no. For Hardy is speaking in Wessex, and what the poem invites us to consider is Emma's having left her 'sheen' in Cornwall. Or, to put it more tactfully, Hardy's sense of Emma's presence, his vision of her, belongs to the Cornish countryside where they met and courted. The sequence of poems therefore takes him from present Wessex to Cornwall.

'The Going' is the first poem in the entire sequence.

> Why do you make me leave the house
> And think for a breath it is you I see
> At the end of the alley of bending boughs
> Where so often at dusk you used to be;
>   Till in darkening dankness
>   The yawning blankness
> Of the perspective sickens me!

The weary despair of the last lines is so powerful that we might want to think the poem one long discharge of *accidie*. Yet the more urgent

rhythms of the opening lines forbid this interpretation, just as –
absurd as it may seem – they imply the presence of a woman whose
absence is firmly attested. And the early poems in the sequence all, in
different ways, and as they play off against each other, speak both of
despair, of the finality of death, and yet cannot let the matter rest
there. 'Well, well! All's past amend,/Unchangeable. It must go' he
says in the last stanza of 'The Going'. But it does not go. 'The Going'
is the first poem in the sequence, not the last. The next poem, 'Your
Last Drive', also seems to settle for finality – its closing line is 'You
are past love, praise, indifference, blame' – and yet the poems nag
away at her possible presence. The poem which follows, 'The Walk',
ends with his feeling 'that underlying sense/Of the look of a room on
returning thence'. *What* look, we want to know? But he cannot tell
us, for it is 'forms', 'presences', as in 'Old Furniture', who supply the
look of a room, and here there is only absence.

Or is there? 'Rain on a Grave' tries to settle for a kind of
Transformation: 'Soon will be growing/Green blades from her
mound,/And daisies be showing/Like stars on the ground,/Till she
form part of them'. . . . But no, he can't rest with that. In 'I Found
Her Out There' he wonders whether her shade (a Virgilian term)
may creep away from its burial place 'Till it catch the sound/Of that
Western sea'. But the fancy fades. 'Without Ceremony' and 'Lament'
accept that she is 'Wholly possessed/By an infinite rest'.

Yet the next poem, fanciful, odd, is spoken by her ghost: 'What a
good haunter I am, O tell him!'. It is not a great poem but it is
followed by one that is. Hardy dates 'The Voice' (December 1912),
and so perhaps wishes us to understand that the process of tracking
Emma down – for that's how the sequence as a whole seems to work
– is not a chronological one, but is subject to occlusions, doubts, the
sudden access to voice and vision, and their just-as-sudden disappearance. 'The Voice' is about all these things.

> Woman much missed, how you call to me, call to me,
> Saying that now you are not as you were
> When you had changed from the one who was all to me,
> But as at first, when our day was fair.
>
> Can it be you that I hear? Let me view you, then,
> Standing as when I drew near to the town
> Where you would wait for me: yes, as I knew you then,
> Even to the original air-blue gown!
>
> Or is it only the breeze in its listlessness
> Travelling across the wet mead to me here,

You being ever dissolved to wan wistlessness,
Heard no more again far or near?

Thus I; faltering forward,
Leaves around me falling,
Wind oozing thin through the thorn from norwood,
And the woman calling.

There is no criticism that can be adequate to this poem. This is art without art and yet known only through art. Those last, grieving, stumbling lines work because of the absolute contrast they make with the lines that have gone before: lines which have been dominated by a blend of trochaic and anapaestic, by a confidence, then urgency, then downward-curving sadness. Douglas Brown objected to Hardy's substituting 'wan wistlessness' for the original 'existlessness', but this seems to me mistaken. For as the poem's last line makes clear, Emma cannot be thought of as without existence. The voice emerges at the very last as 'calling'; and the implied peremptoriness of that word has to be respected. You could not write the poem unless you meant it. This includes meaning the doubts – even the beautifully honourable starts and hesitancies of the second stanza, their honesty, eagerness, fear. The way the lines swing round to pause and then apparently exult on 'yes' – as though he has seen her. 'Yes, there you are.' But of course he doesn't quite say that, although the breathtaking last line of the stanza suggests a vision that blends her into the air of the Cornish coastline.

And having half-gained, faltered towards that vision, Hardy sets out for Lyonnesse once again, and in 'After a Journey' and 'At Castle Boterel' writes two more great poems about arriving at the vision of Emma. As with 'The Voice', both of these poems seem to me beyond criticism. I will say, however, that in 'After a Journey' the voice is his, and it is one of such tender directness of address that I cannot see how anyone could argue that Hardy was fooling himself. As Davie remarks of 'At Castle Boterel':

> The crucial word is 'quality'. [Davie has quoted the poem's last four stanzas, beginning with 'It filled but a minute. But was there ever/A time of such quality, since or before,/In that hill's story?']. . . . For the qualitative has no existence outside of a mind that registers it. And quality is therefore invulnerable to time, since the 'rote' by which Time works is mindless. . . . if the 'time of such quality' persists indestructible in a metaphysical reality, then it is *truly* indestructible – because a man's mind survives the death of his body, or because quality exists as

perceived by a Divine Mind, or. . . The poet does not have to
decide these matters; he does not have to decide the mode in
which the quality will persist after his death, it is enough for him
to affirm his conviction that persist it will. And here, as I read
the poem . . . Hardy makes that affirmation.

This seems to me definitively true and it will also apply to 'After A
Journey'.

> I see what you are doing: you are leading me on
> To the spots we knew when we haunted here together,
> The waterfall, above which the mist-bow shone
> At the then fair hour in the then fair weather,
> And the cave just under, with a voice still so hollow
> That it seems to call out to me from forty years ago,
>   When you were all aglow,
> And not the thin ghost that I now fraily follow!

It may look as though after the first two lines he's lost contact with
her and has become caught up in his own memories. But of course the
excitement at rediscovering the place is for her, he shares or wants to
share with her: so that drop from the wonder of 'it seems to call out
to me from forty years ago' to 'When you were all aglow' is both
tribute to her, to her continuing vitality and his recovered vision
(glow/gleam) and honest admission of time passing, of 'the thin
ghost that I now fraily follow'.

In 'At Castle Boterel' he sees her as 'one phantom figure' who will
always be there.

> I look and see it there, shrinking, shrinking,
> I look back at it amid the rain
> For the very last time; for my sand is sinking,
> And I shall traverse old love's domain
>   Never again.

No doubt Douglas Brown is right to note that in the language of this
final stanza Hardy allows us to feel that what happens to him
happens to all men: 'my sand is sinking' generalizes his condition
through its easy, commonplace nature. Yet at the same time the
vision remains: the phantom woman is not to be thought of as a
psychological trick, a mere matter of projection.

Of course in later poems the return to a psychological explanation
occurs. It even does so in final poems of the sequence itself. And in
other poems, such as 'Penance' and 'Overlooking the River Stour'

Hardy confronts the pain that stays with him because of his guilty feelings over his relationship with Emma. In the first he blurts out these feelings to an interlocutor, sitting at the harpsichord where Emma had once played:

> and the chill old keys,
> Like a skull's brown teeth
> Loose in their sheath,
> Freeze my touch; yes, freeze.

In the latter, gazing obsessively at a scene in front of him, he refuses to turn to the guessed-at human misery behind him. Both poems are very painful, both exact a full look at the worst. There are others. But they do not take precedence over – indeed they are only made possible by – those visions and voices which for Hardy had an undeniable reality, no matter how impossible it might be to explain.

To deny Hardy's poems the authority of sadness would be absurd. And some, such as 'The Broken Appointment', have about them the dignity of contained pessimism which certainly justifies the claim that he had exacted a full look at the worst. Yet we need also to recall his remark to Edmund Gosse that as a whole the critic tribe did not understand that a mood could exhaust itself in the writing of a poem. We need further to bear in mind Hardy's second wife's remark to a visitor that Hardy was upstairs writing a miserable poem and thoroughly enjoying himself. And we also need to note that Hardy's poems can have about them an authority very different from that of sadness.

In the first place he can be very funny. Everybody knows 'The Ruined Maid', fewer are familiar with 'The Levelled Churchyard', about the reordering of bones and memorial tablets so that

> Here's not a modest maiden elf
> But dreads the final Trumpet,
> Lest half of her should rise herself,
> And half some sturdy strumpet!

And there are other, equally comic, equally delectable, sardonic or outrageous poems. I would not put 'Ah, Are You Digging on My Grave?' in quite the same category, but its wryly mordant note – a kind of revisiting of 'The Unquiet Grave' – clearly belongs in the same range as these others. It ends with the mistress, in her grave, thinking her dog at least has remained true to her, has come to pay his respects. But

'Mistress, I dug upon your grave
　To bury a bone, in case
I should be hungry near this spot
When passing on my daily trot.
I am sorry, but I quite forgot
It was your resting place.'

A poet who can write like that is not to be thought of as merely a
glum or inertly melancholic product of the late nineteenth century.

Moreover, if memory links us to our losses it can also provide
access to sudden, unexpected strengths: of gratitude, love, fellow-
feeling. There are a number of poems where memory operates as a
strong, positive force, as in 'A Church Romance'. A girl in church
turns to see a young viol player, whose playing 'seemed to throw/A
message from his string to her below,/Which said: "I claim thee as
my own forthright!" '

Thus their hearts' bond began, in due time signed.
And long years thence, when Age had scared Romance,
At some old attitude of his or glance
That gallery-scene would break upon her mind,
With him as minstrel, ardent, young, and trim,
Bowing 'New Sabbath' or 'Mount Ephraim'.

The lovely, rhythmic springiness of the last two lines, and particularly the final rhyme, provide an imaginative flush of joy that is
more than merely psychological. And, without stretching a point too
far, you could bring into consideration here 'The Last Signal', in
which Hardy walks to the funeral of his friend and fellow-poet,
William Barnes, and notes something flashing in the fire of the sun: it
is Barnes's coffin, and 'Thus a farewell to me he signalled on his
grave-way,/As with a wave of his hand'.

What characteristically strengthens the hold of memory for Hardy
are the connections between people and places. William Barnes, on
his grave-way, is linked to the landscape: 'he who in his prime/
Trudged so many a time from that gate athwart the land', so that
familiarity of man and that spot of earth helps to explain Hardy's
familiar, companionable feeling as he registers the last wave of his
old friend's hand. (It also explains, of course, the pleasure he takes in
fashioning a poem which uses internal rhyme: Barnes, too, was a
keen student of unexpected rhyme schemes.) Hardy reads a landscape, not as a casual observer might, nor as would be done by a
traveller or artist in search of the picturesque. As with Wordsworth

and Clare, landscape for Hardy matters because of its human associations. And so he writes 'The Lost Pyx', which could be characterized as his version of the 'White Doe of Rylestone', since it is 'A Mediaeval Legend', to which Hardy adds a footnote:

> On a lonely table-land above the Vale of Blackmore, between High Stoy and Bubb-Down hills, and commanding in clear weather views that extend from the English to the Bristol Channel, stands a pillar, apparently mediaeval, called Cross-and-Hand, or Christ-in-Hand.

Hardy is keen, in other words, that we should not think this an imaginary landscape, just as he is keen we should register the names of people and buildings mentioned in the poem he regarded as his personal favourite, 'A Trampwoman's Tragedy'. Accordingly, he provides a long footnote to that poem, telling us of pubs mentioned and of 'Blue Jimmy', a 'notorious horse-stealer of Wessex'. Certainly, the poem could not exist apart from the naming of names and places:

> Lone inns we loved, my man and I,
>   My man and I;
> 'King's Stag', 'Windwhistle' high and dry,
>   'The Horse' on Hintock Green,
> The cosy house at Wynyard's Gap,
> 'The Hut' renowned on Bredy Knap,
> And many another wayside tap
>   Where folk might sit unseen.

A peopled landscape is what sets Hardy's mind in motion, although very often the people themselves are dead or otherwise vanished. But without them the place is nothing. 'In a Eweleaze near Weatherbury' finds Hardy noting that 'The years have gathered grayly/Since I danced upon this leaze'; and it ends with his admission that were he to try to recover the thoughtless romanticism of youth, the girl with whom he had danced

> would not balm the breeze
> By murmuring 'Thine for ever!'
> As she did upon this leaze.

Human associations, especially love, redeem, hallow a landscape, 'Balm the breeze.' Who else but Hardy could have produced that astonishing phrase, so lifting above the ordinary what is otherwise a fairly conventional poem and giving the last line its gentle emphasis: 'As she did upon this leaze.' This leaze and no other: the spondee firms the rhythm, makes it *here* that she murmured words that warm and sweeten drab nature.

In this context it is inevitable that we should remember Hardy's famous remark about a beautiful landscape being unimportant beside the wear of a foot on a threshold. It brings us back to 'The House of Silence'. Hardy is the man who noticed such things as household possessions and their human meanings. In 'Her Death and After' he says that 'The rooms within had the piteous shine/That home-things wear when there's ought amiss', and we note that 'shine' is a variant of 'glow' and 'gleam', only here what is worn is perceived by the beholder to signify what's wrong. 'Wear' indeed implies borrowed light, and we may sensibly enough infer that the home-things borrow their shine from the man looking at them, that in other words he projects his sadness on to them. But it would be wrong to assume therefore that Hardy's vision of household furniture is one of trivial associationism. Anyone who looks at the interiors of the great seventeenth-century Dutch master, De Hooch, whom Hardy so admired, will see that his furnishings, tables, chairs, chests, pewter and glassware, are all touched by a subdued but firm, unifying light. In 'Old Furniture', Hardy says that

> I see the hands of the generations
> That owned each shiny familiar thing
> In play on its knobs and indentations. . . .
>
> Hands behind hands, growing paler and paler,
> As in a mirror a candle-flame
> Shows images of itself, each frailer
> As it recedes, though the eye may frame
> Its shape the same. . . .
>
> On this old viol, too, fingers are dancing –
> As whilom – just over the strings by the nut,
> The tip of bow receding, advancing
> In airy quivers, as if it would cut
> The plaintive gut.
>
> And I see a face by that box for tinder,
> Glowing forth in fits from the dark,
> And fading again, as the linten cinder
> Kindles to red at the flinty spark,
> Or goes out stark.

The shine of furniture comes from the fire, faces start out of it, hands are like candle-flame (and of course you can't tell whether there really is a flame in the room but, as in 'Logs on the Hearth', flame suggests – turns in a momentary vision – into hands). You could take the poem as an example of the projective imagination, wishing on to objects what is not 'really' there: but to rest content with that would be to cheapen it. For what Hardy sees is real enough, as vision; the grave, rapt movement of the lines proves it. It is therefore a more intense poem than 'Haunting Fingers', which, for all its touching and comic evocation of voices connected with particular instruments, Hardy takes care to subtitle 'A Phantasy in a Museum of Musical Instruments'.

IV

Yet phantasy itself is a word with strong and deep reverberations for Hardy. It is linked to phantoms, to ghosts – and to forms. At the end of another fine poem, 'The House of Hospitalities', about a home where he had long before enjoyed Christmas and New Year parties but which is now abandoned, and in decay, Hardy says

> Yet at midnight if here walking
>> When the moon sheets wall and tree,
> I see forms of old time talking,
>> Who smile on me.

Vision by moonlight, companions who talk and smile; and who are dead. But who are also 'forms of old time'. What does Hardy mean by the word? He may mean more or less the same as he does by the 'shape' of hands, in 'Old Furniture'. Nevertheless it is worth noting that when Wordsworth used the word, as he so often did, he was relying on that tradition of English philosophy in which the word 'form' could be taken to mean the essential properties of any object, and that he nearly always used the word when he was invoking the ways in which his memory kept alive the reality of past scenes. In 'Tintern Abbey' for example, he speaks of remembering the landscape features of the Wye, which are once again before him, and says

> these beauteous forms,
> Through a long absence, have not been to me
> As is a landscape to a blind man's eye;
> But oft, in lonely rooms, and 'mid the din
> Of towns and cities, I have owed to them,
> In hours of weariness, sensations sweet,
> Felt in the blood, and felt along the heart . . .

And there is the equally famous reference in Book One of *The Prelude* to those 'huge and mighty forms that do not live/Like living men'. 'Form' is the internalized, permanent essence of outward objects. I can see why Hardy might well have reached for the word. It was a way of both allowing for the possible projective nature of imagination – a throwing out of shadows so that they become forms – and at the same time a means of confirming their inner reality. He needed it, we may guess, because as the rational non-believer he had to find a way of coping with phenomena, or phantasies, that defied his rationalism. What Yeats came to call 'presences' Hardy called 'forms'; and his more philosophically acceptable word is there because he could not take refuge in the occultist religion that Yeats professed.

Forms are essential to his vision. Without them there could not be the hands and faces of 'Old Furniture'. Nor could there be the possible visions that provide one of his greatest poems, 'During Wind and Rain'.

> They sing their dearest songs –
> He, she, all of them – yea,
> Treble and tenor and bass,
>   And one to play;
> With the candles mooning each face. . . .
>   Ah, no; the years O!
> How the sick leaves reel down in throngs!
>
> They clear the creeping moss –
> Elders and juniors – aye,
> Making the pathways neat
>   And the garden gay;
> And they build a shady seat. . . .
>   Ah, no; the years, the years;
> See, the white storm-birds wing across!
>
> They are blithely breakfasting all –
> Men and maidens – yea,
> Under the summer tree,
>   With a glimpse of the bay,
> While pet fowl come to the knee. . . .
>   Ah, no; the years O!
> And the rotten rose is ript from the wall.
>
> They change to a high new house,
> He, she, all of them – aye,
> Clocks and carpets and chairs

On the lawn all day,
And brightest things that are theirs. . . .
Ah, no; the years, the years;
Down their carved names the rain-drop ploughs.

Because this great poem has been well and amply discussed by
Douglas Brown, Thom Gunn and Tom Paulin, I can afford to keep
my comments to a minimum.[4] I should, however, say that I disagree
with Brown's reading of the poem as essentially one that accepts
transience. Brown draws attention to the fact that each stanza is
composed of two kinds of ballads, broken at the repeated refrain,
'Ah, no'. And he rightly remarks that the images of each of the last
lines suggest, fittingly, the fact of time passing: the sick leaves and
rotting rose are properties of ballad tradition, and they are
appropriate images of decay with its promise of seasonal renewal.
This is so, but to stress this is to over-emphasize the poem's wise
acceptance of time passing.

In his account Thom Gunn also points towards the poem's
balladic nature, and he adds that it is not merely about a timeless past
versus the sudden, unlooked-for intrusions of time. For the poem
develops in compact ways the history of a family: from the shared
warmth of a fireside to activities by means of which every member of
that family works to keep the garden clear of the encroachments of
nature (although sooner or later Time will have his fancy), and then
to the move to a high new house, with its suggestion of material
possessions on show as a way of trying to defeat the depredations of
time. Again, I agree, but there is more to the poem than its enactment
of a family and its history, wonderfully though Hardy manages to
compress this into the four stanzas.

What more there is comes out in Tom Paulin's account. Paulin
emphasizes the continued vitality of the visions of the family.
(Significantly the visions start from a candlelight gleam which brings
with it that other source of gleam so common in Hardy's vision, the
moon – 'the candles mooning each face'.) The vision stays, no matter
how the ebullient cadences of the first part of each stanza are
ruptured by the sad and apparently final 'Ah, no'. The sense of
timeless vision balanced, precariously I will allow but balanced
nevertheless, against the steady progress of time – this is what
'During Wind and Rain' is about. It is a truly visionary poem. Not to
accept this is to set aside as unimportant Hardy's title for the volume
of poems in which 'During Wind and Rain' occurs. He called it
Moments of Vision and Miscellaneous Verses, and it seems to me

arrogantly thoughtless to assume that he had not pondered the meaning of such a title for his volume, especially since it includes 'On a Midsummer Eve', 'The Oxen', 'The Last Signal', 'The House of Silence', 'Old Furniture', 'Logs on the Hearth', and several more. Yet it is important to remark that although the volume may contain an exceptionally high number of very fine poems it is not exceptional for Hardy to be prompted by vision. Quite the contrary. This was why he needed poetry. For through poetry he was not only linked to his losses, he was able to turn the losses to gain.

V

Hardy is a great poet. Yet something is missing. In *Thomas Hardy and British Poetry* Donald Davie blames Hardy for putting up with the second best and encouraging later English poets to do the same. But this does not seem to me to be where the problem lies. It is more that his persistent locating of vision of community in the past can come perilously close to a disabling nostalgia or to a merely enervate sadness. 'The authority of sadness', Larkin says, by way of identifying the key quality of Hardy's poetry. The sadness is undeniable. But the authority? Always? The difficulty is that Hardy never offers any explanation for *why* the past is so different from the present. As we have seen, a few poems such as 'The Self-Unseeing' and 'During Wind and Rain' glance at this but they do not steadily confront it. Perhaps Hardy felt that this was not a matter for poetry, especially as he had written about it in his novels.

Or is there another explanation? Hardy after all was both secretive and ambitious, and he was often secretive about his ambitions, which included the desire to 'look away'. Perhaps there is nothing much to be done about this. We may say that Hardy's secretiveness is merely a version of that guilt which seems always to go with the desire, even though the desire is inevitable and is born from and testifies to the working of the social process, in ways that are at the heart of experiences out of which much English writing of the past 150 years has come. Nevertheless, Hardy's distancing himself from family and community will help to explain why, in his poems, the gap between past and present is so achingly recorded, but also why the process by which the gap is created is never much more than sketched in.

In other words, Hardy covers over the causes of those discontinuities out of which much of his poetry is made. As a result, these same discontinuities are presented as a fact. They cannot be protested against, as Clare protested. Hardy's position is quietist and ultimately mystificatory. The Immanent Will – or some other cosmic force – proposes and disposes. If this is less of a problem than might at first seem it is because the very intensity of Hardy's longing for community throngs his poems with voices and visions whose vitality keeps nostalgia at bay.

It is a remarkable fact that most of the poets I am concerned with in this book find that vision is the means of restoring or discovering community – although often, more grandly than Hardy, the community is England or what can be taken as a 'heart' of England. Hardy's pieties are more local. 'A certain provincialism of feeling is invaluable' he said, by way of rebuking Matthew Arnold's attack on provincialism; and we have seen that he did not often speak for England and that when he did – as in certain of his Boer and Great War poems – he did not produce good work. ('The Convergence of the Twain' and 'Channel Firing' are different matters, but then they are very 'unofficial' poems.) Later poets are more ambitious, or perhaps they feel themselves under greater strain to justify what Hardy may have thought he could take for granted. At all events, I think that their 'visions' are ways of trying to grasp a unity, a meaning, which can be grasped in no other way.

Further Reading

Apart from the books by Douglas Brown, Donald Davie and Tom Paulin, there are biographies by Robert Gittings and Michael Millgate. Of the two, the second is better because it is more tactful, less ready to rush to judgement. There is also the very important *Life of Thomas Hardy*, ostensibly written by Hardy's second wife, Florence, but in fact largely written by Hardy himself.

The best single volume of the Poems is that edited by James Gibson. A multi-volume edition is under way, edited by Samuel Hynes. The *Collected Letters* are being edited by Purdy and Millgate.

- 3 -

The Clerk's Dream of Poetry

I

Hardy's sense of history is essentially that it makes for separation, for the unbinding of communality. Like Clare, he knew what the social process did to people, although in his poetry he does not often focus on this. Unlike Clare, therefore, he develops a stoicism, by turns tough or wry, which allows him to recognize or accept an 'inevitability' about that process. But I put the word in inverted commas because I want to suggest that Hardy's way of coming to terms with this process is at once a way of limiting the damage and an indication of how he thinks it works. To assume that something is inevitable is to save yourself from the anger and outrage that Clare often shows, and at the same time it allows you to mark out a position of isolation for yourself. As we have seen, Hardy's isolation is both heightened and redeemed by his voices and visions, which are derived from the kinds of intimate knowledge and love for a place and its people. That can hardly be said of the self-conscious ruralists of the last years of the nineteenth century and of the Edwardian era.

One way of trying to focus on what was going on then is to consider the making of the Poet Laureate after Tennyson's death in 1892. Who was to succeed him? It could not be Swinburne, because although by now a reformed and utterly tame poet, in his flaming youth he had been a republican, an atheist and one of the 'fleshly school of poetry'. In the end Alfred Austin was appointed.

There have been one or two attempts to make a case for Austin, but the plain fact is that he is a ridiculously bad poet. Why then was he chosen? The answer has most to do with his politics. We can get an indication of what these were by looking at some lines from a poem called 'On Returning to England'.

> Let hound and horn in wintry woods and dells
> Make jocund music though the boughs be bare,

And whistling yokel guide his teeming share
Hard by the house where gentle Lordship dwells . . .
And though the throats of envy rage and rail,
Be fair proud England, proud fair England still.

It hardly needs saying that *this* evocation of community has nothing in common with Hardy's, let alone Clare's. Austin's lines provide a kind of myth of an 'ideal' England of feudal relations, of a revived Young England. Young England had been the dream of Austin's hero, Disraeli, and after his death in 1881 a group of admirers, some of them influential, did their best to revive the dream. They founded the Primrose League and they started the *National Review*. Both League and Review were in favour of chivalry and against modernity.

For at the heart of the dream of Young England is a belief that the purity of the stock is bound up with the maintaining or, it may be, recovering of those feudalistic relations that had made 'old' England so fine a place. From which it will be seen that the myth-making proportions of this dream are as large as they are difficult to take seriously. Yet they affected many people. In his formidably well-researched and suggestive study, *England and the Decline of the Industrial Spirit*, M. E. Weiner shows that during the 1890s much was written about the ways in which the 'pure' English countryside and its peasant stock was being infected, diluted and corrupted by the spread of industrial cities and their influence. I will add that, at the time this was going on, there seems also to have been a widespread and rather nasty attempt to throw off the Norman yoke and pretend that England and the English were still, at root, 'pure' Anglo-Saxon.

Consider the evidence. In 1894 the Journal of the Royal Society of St George put out a volume called *The English Race*. In the same year Grant Allen published *Anglo-Saxon Britain*. (Allen was a literary hack who obviously knew what was likely to sell.) In 1898 Edward Desmoulins produced his *Anglo-Saxon Superiority: To What Is It Due?* (the answer is, 'blood'); and the following year the *Anglo-Saxon Review* began publication. Some of its contributors, including W. H. Mallock, had contributed to the *National Review*, the first issue of which had carried Wordsworth's sonnet 'Merry England' and an essay by George Saintsbury on 'Young England'. It is also worth noticing that the National Trust was formed in 1895, and that *Country Life* began publication in 1898. What are we to make of all this?

Weiner argues that what we have here is a regression towards a myth of rural, peaceful and timeless England, and that this is part of a growing and ultimately fatal opposition on the part of the English to the industrial spirit. His suggestion that this is why the English still recruit top management from the squirearchy is interesting but not relevant to my present concerns. His identification of a particular myth certainly is. In the first place, there can be little doubt that the stress on purity of stock is linked to the need to insist on the health of the heart of Empire. The blood that circulates round the globe is pumped from a source whose untainted excellence may be taken for granted. (Of course, the hectic emphasis on this health, this excellence, suggests very different fears.) In the second place, and behind much of the insistence on purity of blood, is the fear of degeneracy. This requires some comment.

By the 1890s a largely bastardized social Darwinism had come to affect the way in which many people thought about English history. If every generation was engaged in the struggle for survival, the argument ran, it followed that those who survived must be the fittest so to do. They showed the greatest ability to adapt to changing circumstances. Very comforting, you might think. But the problem was this: suppose successful adaptation in fact meant learning to survive by adapting *down*? Where did people mostly live? In cities. What had an increasing number of surveys shown (the studies of Booth, Mearns and so on)? That people in cities were physically and often mentally degenerate. Yet they survived. In which case it followed that, given the conditions of city life, people learnt to survive more or less like rats. (Anyone who reads the 'city' novels of George Gissing or of Arthur Morrison will recognize the position outlined here.) In short, it was the least fit stock who adapted, or to put the emphasis differently, in learning to adapt the stock became less fit.

It should therefore come as no surprise to discover that those who argued this far also came to the conclusion that the highest – that is the 'purest', that is the 'Anglo-Saxon' – strain was to be found in rural England. But then another problem occurs. Because of the economic conditions of rural England many agricultural workers were being forced to look for employment in the cities. Once there, they would have to learn to adapt. The result would be more degeneracy of greater numbers.

I have of course telescoped a number of fears and arguments and it may look as though in the process I have reduced complicated matters to a grotesque parody of what really went on. But this is not so. In fact I have been doing very little more than paraphrase the main lines of Max Nordau's *Degeneration*, which first appeared in 1895, and which was treated with great seriousness by all sorts of people, including many who should have known better. The assertion of Nordau's that proved most arresting was that the city, the type of community of the modern world, forced the process of degeneration on to its inhabitants, whereas in the country the healthy continuation of the stock might be safeguarded.

It is this which explains much of the fervour of the self-conscious ruralism of the 1890s. And it is matched, opposed and in a sense no doubt feels itself vindicated, by the equally self-conscious decadence of those *fin de siècle* poets who write out of the experience of the city. Back to the land means trying to locate the true heart of England in the English countryside.

'The heart of England.' It is a phrase, even a cliché of the time. I do not know whether Richard Jefferies coined it, but he certainly intended to use it as the title for a novel which was eventually published in 1884 as *Hodge and his Masters*. The heart of this novel is in fact 'Fleeceborough', a small market town apparently based on Cirencester, and its mythical timelessness is in marked contrast to Hardy's Casterbridge. Fleeceborough is a repository and breeding place for all the true English values, and its health is threatened only by 'outsiders'.

You can find other such novels in the last twenty or so years of the nineteenth century. Yet towns may become cities, and so the heart of England became even more typically identified with a particular spot of earth, a patch of English soil rich, so we are asked to imagine, with the 'pure' English dead and from which, often enough, an elm would grow. For this is the moment at which the elm tree becomes an unofficial symbol of England. (Less contentious than the Royal Oak which had sheltered Charles II, or the sycamore under which the Tolpuddle martyrs met.) In 1889 William Morris (of all people, we might think) published an essay in his paper *The Commonwealth*, called 'Under the Elm-Tree: or Thoughts in the Countryside', in the course of which he remarks:

> What is the thought that has come into one's head as one turns round in the shadow of the roadside elm? A countryside worth fighting for, if that were necessary, worth taking the trouble to defend its peace.

53

Peace, you wonder, what peace exactly? Peace for Joseph Arch or for all those being forced off the land by economic depression and the new machinery?

But Morris's essay is symptomatic. Its stance helps to prepare the way for that eagerness with which young men went to war in 1914. They were fighting for England's hallowed 'earth' — or imagined themselves to be doing so. They also thought that they were fighting to defend, not merely the 'sad shires', but the houses to be found there. Such houses might not be where 'gentle Lordship dwells', but the sense of feudalism belonged as strongly to the image surrounding them. For these houses were seen as 'rooted' in one spot. There is of course nothing very new about this. A whole line of 'country-house' literature, starting with Ben Jonson's 'To Penshurst' and running through Carew, Marvell, Pope, Jane Austen and Dickens, provides various images of the country house as ways of reading the notion of 'Englishness', its social, political and cultural arrangements. Nor need we be surprised that the period with which I am concerned produced exactly the architect to create the new houses that would accrete to themselves the 'ideal' values of Englishness. Edwin Lutyens built deliberately 'quaint' houses, which absorbed various bits of the past: Anglo-Saxon, Gothic, Tudor, Queen Anne.[1]

As Mark Girouard has pointed out, such 'quaintness' was widely approved of, and 'quaint' became a vogue word of the period.[2] E. M. Forster's fictional house, Howards End, and Rudyard Kipling's Batemans have this much in common, that they are both 'quaint' and situated in the 'heart' of England. When Margaret Schlegel first sees Howards End she feels that she can 'realize England' from it. At Batemans, Kipling wrote *Rewards and Fairies* and *Puck of Pook's Hill*. *Rewards* was published in 1910, the same year as *Howards End*, and in the introduction, 'A Charm', Kipling writes:

> Take of English earth as much
> As either hand may rightly clutch.
> In the taking of it breathe
> Prayer for all who lie beneath —
> Not the great nor well bespoke,
> But the mere uncounted folk
> Of whose life and death is none
> Report or lamentation.
>   Lay that earth upon thy heart
>   And thy sickness shall depart.

The sickness Kipling has in mind is presumably that of modern society, and what he says here in a sense anticipates Rupert Brooke's turning from a world 'grown old and cold and weary'. This is a point I shall develop in the next chapter. Here, I want to make a rather different one, which is that Kipling is not really in touch with those 'mere uncounted folk' for whom he speaks. At all events, they do not speak through him as Hardy's folk speak through *him*, nor can they be thought of as like the folk Clare celebrates in so many of his poems. Instead, and very significantly, what we have here is the creation of an 'archetypal' Englishman, Hobden the Hedger, who is the link character in both *Rewards* and *Puck*, and of whom Kipling writes that

> His dead are in the churchyard – thirty generations laid.
> Their names were old in history when Domesday Book was made;
> And the passion and the piety and the prowess of his line
> Have seeded, rooted, fruited in some land the law calls mine.

The land to which Kipling refers is particularly Batemans, in Sussex, and it is worth noting that the heart of England is usually associated with the south. (It isn't tainted with industry, is somehow 'older' and happens to be where Lutyens built nearly all his houses. Besides, elms don't much grow in the north.)

Hobden is offered us as Anglo-Saxon in origin; and he is a much-repeated figure in the literature of the period. Hence Jefferies' Hodge and hence, we shall see in the next chapter, Edward Thomas's 'Lob' and Ivor Gurney's 'Lock Keeper'. Such figures underpin the mythicizing of a particular dream of England. There is a heart, which is usually a spot of earth. On it stands an old or 'quaint' house. A sort of tutelary spirit serves the house. And this is significant. Hodge, Hobden and the rest, like Miss Avery in *Howards End*, do not own the houses where their service is willingly given. Instead, their service implies that feudalistic structure which Alfred Austin and others offer as the ideal social-political arrangement.[3]

This brings us to an important point. For it must be obvious from what I have so far said that the poets of the period with whom I am concerned write about the heart of England in a very unfocused way. They have none of that detailed, exact knowledge that Clare and Hardy bring to their work. They are essentially weekend ruralists, living at a distance from what they write about, and although the distance is not always geographical it *is* always economic or social.

As a result the England they attempt to conjure up is socially regressive, evasive; and necessarily empty of human resonance. The actual is replaced by the mythic.

II

This is especially true of Walter de la Mare. De la Mare published four volumes of poetry before 1914. *Songs of Childhood* came out in 1902, *Poems* in 1906, *The Listeners and Other Poems* in 1912, and *Peacock Pie* in 1913. De la Mare is an interesting case because technically he is formidably well equipped and he has great gifts of ear: his sounds and cadences are, you might say, exquisite. And that, quite often, is the trouble. To read through the bulk of his poetry is a lowering experience. When you come upon any one of his poems you are bound to be impressed – delighted even – by its craft and its music. But after a while the persistent note of plangent sadness, of sugar-sweet melancholy, becomes merely tiresome. 'Tragedy should be a great kick at misery' Lawrence famously said, after reading and reacting against Bennett's *Old Wives' Tale*. The remark fits de la Mare far better. In a poem to Hardy, he speaks of

> a concourse of women and of men
> Whom his words had made living, long-suffering – they flocked
> to remembrance again;
> 'O Master,' I cried in my heart, 'lorn thy tidings, grievous thy
> song;
> Yet thine, too, this solacing music, as we earth folk stumble
> along.'

De la Mare's own poetry never does anything so clumsy or – I will say – humanly recognizable as stumble. It would be beyond him to see that Hardy's poetry is by no means always grievous, and I do not think he would recognize that it is saved from spineless melancholy by its firm connections with people and places, with community. De la Mare's own poetry is usually empty of human complications, of voices other than his own.

There is at least one exception. 'The Feckless Dinner Party' is a most interesting, ingenious and mordant poem about a rich, arrogantly silly collection of diners at a country house (I assume) who think they are being led into dinner by the butler 'Toomes', and in fact are being led the dance of death. As a satire on the glittering vulgarity of much that went on in Edwardian England 'The Feckless Dinner Party' is worth a great deal. But its welcome sharpness cannot finally do much to dispel the glutinous spread of sickly sweetness that is the *Collected Poems*.

De la Mare's skills, as I say, are considerable. Take, for example, 'All That's Past':

> Oh, no man knows
> Through what wild centuries
> Roves back the rose.

The haunting music, the mysterious quality of 'wild' which at the same time hints at loss of energy, of purpose; the sense of being in touch with a lost tradition of lyric poetry (for you can't read the lines without calling to mind the work of seventeenth-century poets such as Waller); these are the de la Mare hallmarks. Or consider so slight a poem as 'Martins: September':

> Unventured, trackless leagues of air;
>   England's sweet summer narrowing on;
> Her lovely pastures: nought their care –
>   Only this ardour to be gone.

Not bad, but even here an ardour 'to be gone' drains vitality out of the 'sweet summer' and 'lovely pastures'. Besides those epithets are so vague, so 'poetically' appropriate, that they seem to have been produced to order.

When war was declared de la Mare wrote of England that

> No lovelier hills than thine have laid
>   My tired thoughts to rest:
> No peace of lovelier valleys made
>   Like peace within my breast.

Well, a great many poets wrote rather silly poems in the autumn of 1914 (Hardy included), and de la Mare's is by no means the worst. Most of the poets I have in mind chose to see England as a place of pastoral beauty, even though a moment's reflection should have made them aware how absurd that was, especially as the majority of soldiers were bound to come from the great industrial cities. What England were *they* fighting for? But what is especially irritating about de la Mare's poem is the inevitability, so it feels, of 'lovelier' ('lovely', 'lovelier', 'loveliest': the words are strewn about his poems like blobs of icing sugar). This isn't really England at all. It is, if anything, a mythic land of lost content, a dream of sun-drenched hills and valleys, happily emptied of people. It is, at best, an adult's dream of the safe, cosy world of childhood.

This is why de la Mare wrote so much and, in his way, wrote so well for children. *Peacock Pie* is undoubtedly a minor classic of its kind. Still, it is typical of the period that so much writing *should* have been devoted to children, because leaving aside market forces – publishing houses were perhaps even more keenly aware of children as a target audience than they had been during the Victorian period – you feel that much of the writing directed at children is meant to make the world safe for them. (I am speaking of middle- and upper-class children, of course.).

In his *Images of Childhood in Literature* Peter Coveney writes perceptively about the regressive sentimentality of much children's literature of the Edwardian age, and as we might expect *Peter Pan* is a principal whipping-boy. But I do not think Coveney sufficiently understands the reasons for this regressiveness. My own very strong feeling is that middle-class writers of the period nurtured a deep, largely unvoiced, suspicion that all was far from well with their society. It was, they feared, degenerate. As a result they either invented (it is hardly too strong a word) an England which would look the – feudalistic – picture of health or they turned their backs on the complications of their age and wrote of a stable world where nothing would change. *Peacock Pie* after all presupposes that the children who read it will have a garden, probably a nurse, a governess, some servants; and that when they go to the shops the shopkeepers will be unfailingly deferential. This is, in other words, the solid surburban world that C. E. F. Masterman wrote so brilliantly about in *The Condition of England* (1909), and it can also be found in *The Wind in the Willows*, where Badger, Ratty and Mole form part of a hierarchically structured society which even Toad, in his mad, Ponderevo desire for expenditure, cannot destroy. The wild wooders may try to take over Toad Hall, but they will be put to flight. The council estates, those stand-ins for the degenerate cities, are not to threaten – not in literature, at least – the 'rootedness' of English society.

Literature is therefore a compensatory dream for what, deep down, many writers feared was actually happening in England, or likely to happen. In de la Mare's case this means creating a vision of England which is both 'archetypal' and unreal. You could no more walk about his valleys than you could shake by the hand his shepherd

'Nod', that whimsical variation on Hodge and Hobden. Nor could he, of course. Hence the persistent melancholy.

III

Yet the fact that de la Mare's England was for ever out of reach did not prevent people from trying to reach it. They bought houses in the country or, better still, had them built, they took excursions – motor-cars for the rich, trains, buses, bicycles and hiking clubs for the less well-off; one way or another they wanted to possess the coloured counties. And it is this that leads to what I call the clerk's dream of poetry.

In 'Thirty Bob a Week' John Davidson had written a powerful, bitter poem about the plight of the kind of man who was trapped in a life he could neither escape from nor enjoy. The city clerk is in fact an interesting literary phenomenon of the times. His first appearance is probably as 'The Shabby Genteel Gentleman' in one of the *Sketches by Boz*, and thereafter Dickens makes a good deal of use of him. But by the end of the nineteenth century he is to be found in much writing, poetry as well as prose, although he is probably best known for his appearance as Kipps or Mr Polly.[4] The clerk is not one of Nordau's degenerates, but as a type of city worker, oppressed and depressed, he becomes a familiar symbol of the conditions of work above the poverty line – just, but below all those comforts and pleasures that a life of work was supposed to provide. He is, in the words of E. M. Forster, writing in *Howards End* about his fictional clerk, Leonard Bast, poised precariously above the abyss. In order to escape from his stultifying life Bast goes in for culture; and he also dreams of life on the open road. One night he walks as far as Wimbledon.

Howards End was published in 1910. Two years earlier W. H. Davies had published his *Autobiography of a Super-Tramp*, and the work was to be reissued five times before 1920. Davies's memoir provided exactly that compensatory dream of the free life which was denied to those millions of clerks, who were pent in cities dim. By the time the *Autobiography* appeared Davies was known as a poet. In 1905 he had published *The Soul's Destroyer*, two years later came *New Poems*, then *Nature Poems and Others* (1908); and there were to be other volumes before 1914. Davies is a good, minor poet. He has genuine powers of observation and, if his technical skills are more limited than de la Mare's, his rhythms are nearly always more bracing. But he is of interest here because of the kind of vision he puts on offer, as in 'The Hill-Side Park'. The poem opens with the description of an ingenious formal garden. It ends as follows:

> This park, it was a miracle of care,
> But sweeter far to me the prospects there:
> The far beyond, where lived Romance near seas
> And pools in haze, and in far realms of trees.
> I saw where Severn had run wide and free,
> Out where the Holms lie flat upon a sea
> Whose wrinkles wizard Distance smoothed away,
> And still sails flecked its face of silver-grey.

Nobody would call that great poetry, but its pace is nicely judged, and the stresses do not follow metre so slavishly as to inhibit a speaking voice. But what I want particularly to draw attention to is that prospect of a wide sea. Davies does not pretend to be rooted in a dream of England. He is both a wanderer through it and beyond it. His vision of unfettered freedom is, I think, genuine; but it was bound to become popular with an audience that was typically fettered by city ways. And the fact is that during the Edwardian period a great deal of poetry was about unfettered existence.

I suggest that John Masefield's *Salt-Water Ballads* of 1902/3 is undoubtedly meant to minister to the trapped spirit of the city clerk. Masefield says that he writes out of a desire to speak for 'the dirt and the dross, the dust and the scum of the earth'. How he does so may be gauged from 'Bill', about a dead sailor:

> The mate came forward at seven bells and spat across the rail;
> "Just lash him up wi' some holystone in a clout o' rotten sail,
> 'N', rot ye, get a gait on, ye're slower'n a bloody snail!'

Masefield's efforts to imitate the argot of sailors' talk produces a kind of ventriloquism. It can also open up some decidedly unpleasant attitudes, as in 'Evening – Regatta Day', about the beating-up of a sailor who has cost his ship victory in one of the day's races:

> 'And Stroke is lashing a bunch of keys to the buckle-end of a belt,
> And we're going to lay you over a chest and baste you till you melt.
> The 'Craigie' boys are beating the bell and beating down the tier,
> D'ye hear, you Port Mahone baboon, I ask you, do you *hear*?'

Masefield might say that such poems were on behalf of the 'dirt and the dross' but the fact is that the speakers of his poems are presented for our admiration. And in their contempt for everything foreign and their red-blooded Englishness they are in fact a rebuke to the degenerates of the city. Masefield's sailors are, for all their swearing and sweating, a variation on the 'archetypal' Englishman found in other writing of the period with which I am now concerned.

Behind Masefield lies Newbolt, whose *Admirals All* was one of the most popular works of this period. And behind *Admirals All* lies an especially nasty kind of Imperialistic jingoism, with its appeal to 'manliness': to sport, clean living and cold baths, to the public-school ethos that is most famously captured in 'Vitae Lampada' ('Play up, play up, and play the game'), and which can be found in much other writing of the time. Consider for example, W. E. Henley's *Lyra Heroica*, an anthology of poetry for boys, first published in 1892 and frequently reissued over the next twenty or so years. Henley prefaces his book with the claim that

> To set forth, as only art can, the beauty and joy of living, the
> beauty and blessedness of death, the glory of battle and
> adventure, the nobility of devotion – to a cause, an ideal, a
> passion even – the dignity of resistance, the sacred quality of
> patriotism, that is my ambition here.

I hardly need to underline how such an ambition would help to create the spirit of 'Anglo-Saxonry' in which young Englishmen went to war in August 1914. But I do want to suggest that although such a spirit is thought to have been exclusive to the public schools it clearly spread wider than that. Or was meant to. *Lyra Heroica* was intended for clerks just as much as it was intended for captains. Henley's volume and many others of the period were clearly attempts to create or endorse both an undegenerate England and a particular kind of pure 'Englishness'. Clerks are to die defending an England of lovely valleys and sweet summers. (It is an interesting fact, by the way, that Edwardian summers were typically very wet and cold. Even the weather had to be invented.)

Masefield, Newbolt, Henley and others too numerous and unimportant to mention: behind them all looms the figure of Rudyard Kipling. *Barrack-Room Ballads*, first published in 1892 and thereafter seldom if ever out of print, is a work of genius, and I would not be fair to it if I did not say as much. Yet it seems to me essentially the genius of a propagandist. Kipling is the supreme ventriloquist, using voices that speak of a community, of soldiers, but with one eye on whom he is speaking to, just as much as on whom he is speaking for. *Barrack-Room Ballads* are reports from the front line, so to speak, and Kipling was first and perhaps last a journalist. Of course he had a great subject to hand: the ordinary British soldier fighting to defend Empire. And the soldier is not found wanting. Heart of Empire is healthy even if its owner speaks with a cockney accent. Kipling thus provides the clerk with a perfect dream of poetry, by offering the quickest way out of Manchester: to Mandalay, India, Africa.

Interestingly, when Kipling speaks in his own voice he is far less assured of the survival of Empire (without which, I think, he could not imagine England). This shows very clearly in the famous 'Recessional':

> Far-called our navies melt away –
> On dune and headland sinks the fire –
> Lo, all our pomp of yesterday
> Is one with Nineveh and Tyre!

The ruins of Nineveh, in Assyria, had been discovered by British archaeologists in the 1850s, so Kipling's reference is meant to offer a topical as well as a timely reminder to his audience: we will come to that. From which one may infer that Kipling's sense of Empire, of its rise and fall, has more reality about it than has his dream of England. For it is England's past that preoccupies him, and in those two children's books (for adults?) to which I have referred, as elsewhere, he visits that past as a kind of Wellsian time-traveller, or an archaeologist, who may want to emphasize continuity but who in fact betrays deep feelings of discontinuity, of how different it all was then, or of how remote he is from what he is writing about.

In a very real sense this discontinuity is England's 'sickness', and it is hard to see how it can be healed by the purely rhetorical gesture of taking up a fistful of earth. Although England's past may be somehow buried in that earth it is like Nineveh; cut off, dead, unavailable to the present. Different in temperament as Kipling and de la Mare undoubtedly are, they share a sense of lost community. Neither can 'realize' an England of the present as they would like it to be. Too honest to indulge in the kinds of silliness that characterize Austin's poetry, too much in love with their dream to want to renounce it, they are forced back into lamenting a land of lost content. What is lost includes, most importantly, language. There is nobody in English poetry at the end of the nineteenth century who can speak the language of the folk as Clare had been able to speak it;

and Hardy's intimations and echoes also belong to a losing moment. They are going into history. By contrast, the voices of Kipling's poetry are never far from pastiche. He pretends to the utterances of people from whom he is in fact remote. (The point is not affected by the fact that he was so imitable, even by those whose voices he had attempted to use: music-hall monologue and song is a variant on Kipling: it allows for those who employ it to be incorporated into orthodoxy's account of them, much as Irishmen would become stage-Irish or negroes play at being Uncle Tom.)

This is why C. K. Stead's claim that the Georgians were importantly trying to return poetry to the people will not wash. In *The New Poetic* Stead argues that Georgian poets wanted to break with the habits of previous generations – and especially of the 1890s – which had taken for granted not only that poetry would be remote from most people but that it ought to be. Art was a secret cult, to be served by a faithful few. The Georgians, Stead argues, wanted none of this. They actively sought an audience for poetry and their success in doing this can be measured by the steady sales of successive anthologies of *Georgian Poetry*. The first of these anthologies appeared in 1912, and its editor, Edward Marsh, claimed that 'English poetry is now once again putting on new strength and beauty'. According to James Reeves, 'the success of the anthology was immediate, and proved Marsh to have been right in assuming that there was a large public awaiting a particular kind of new poetry'. And in *Harold Monro and the Poetry Bookshop*, Joy Grant claims that Monro, who was a close friend of Marsh's and influential in setting up the anthology, wanted to take poetry out on to the streets 'in the manner of the Salvation Army: we should spout poetry at the street-corners, in public houses, and even in private houses'. Commendable enough no doubt, but you have only to look into them to see that the poets over whom Monro and Marsh enthuse and who fill the anthology's pages are characteristically locked into the kinds of stale perceptions and language which reveal that, no matter what the intention, Georgian poetry is quite without the force of connection to contemporary life and language that would make it of real value. It is noteworthy that during the years the anthologies were being published many people were affected by the large numbers of strikes and lock-outs, the poor wages and industrial unrest that were a feature of the years immediately before the first world war; others were involved in the Suffragette Movement, the campaign for Irish Independence, the desire to withdraw from Imperialism. None of these crucially important matters is ever more than glanced at by Georgian poets, and when they do so much as glance it is in a facetious manner. The one exception is Wilfrid Gibson, but his attempts to write about mundane, urban lives are fatally flawed by his reach-me-down language and contented use of jogtrot iambics. For the rest, what you have is an endless stream of poems about cottages, ducks, and country views. Is this what is meant by 'returning poetry to the people'? I do not see how weekend ruralism can claim to do any such thing, especially since it has no way – no voice, no procedure, no language – for addressing people and issues. It is, in short, one more sigh for the land of lost content.

IV

The phrase is of course A. E. Housman's, and before I end this chapter I need to say something about him, since he is the other considerable poet of the period under review. Like Hardy, Housman was a non-believer. In the useful introduction to his selection of Housman's poetry and prose, F. C. Horwood quotes from Arthur Balfour's *The Foundations of Belief*:

> Man will go down to the pit, and all his thoughts will perish.
> The uneasy consciousness, which, in this obscure corner, has,
> for a brief space, broken the contented silence of the universe,
> will be at rest. Matter will know itself no longer, 'imperishable
> moments' and 'immortal deeds', death itself, and love stronger
> than death, will be as though they had never been.

Horwood is surely right to note that such words were likely to meet with Housman's reluctant assent. But they would not have had Hardy's, I think. For though Hardy was a pessimist and a rational non-believer, he also nourished a vision that allowed for the possibility of survival. For Housman there is no such possibility. Like de la Mare, whose poetry he much admired, Housman is the onlooker at a paradise from which he has been effectively excluded.

> Into my heart an air that kills
>   From some far country blows:
> What are those blue remembered hills,
>   What spires, what farms are those?
>
> That is the land of lost content
>   I see it shining plain,

The happy highways where I went
And cannot come again.

This poem, which appeared as number XL in *A Shropshire Lad*, seems to have been written early in Housman's career. Yet it could easily have come much later. For once he had found his voice, his style and his subject-matter, he never really changed. Much of *A Shropshire Lad* derives, I think, from FitzGerald's lovely version of the *Rubá'iyát of Omar Khayyám*, and there are also echoes of Lucretius's *De Rerum Natura*. (It is significant that W. H. Mallock translated some of Lucretius in FitzGerald's stanza form: Persian melancholia and Roman scientific humanism come together to produce a typical late-nineteenth-century hybrid.)

A Shropshire Lad was not at first a success. Housman paid for its publication of 500 copies in 1896, and although a further 500 were published two years later the volume became a best-seller only with the advent of the Great War. Yet it is utterly characteristic of its period, and is different from its many competitors in being, for the most part, much better written. It could perhaps be argued that its melancholia is heightened by Housman's covert homosexuality and his hopeless love for Moses Jackson – and after all 'Uranian' poetry was much in vogue.[5] But I think it would be wrong to place the major emphasis on Housman's unhappy personal life. It is not *that* anguish which feeds into the majority of the poems. Yes, there are poems about defeated, unreturned or deadly love-affairs; but this is because the cast of the volume, you might almost say its strategy, is to evoke, ceaselessly, the days that are no more. Or, alternatively, the poems brood in lapidary manner on the inevitability of time passing, of civilizations going under. As, for example, in one of the best-known poems, which appeared as no. XXXI in *A Shropshire Lad*.

On Wenlock Edge the wood's in trouble;
    His forest fleece the Wrekin heaves;
The gale, it plies the saplings double,
    And thick on Severn snow the leaves.

'Twould blow like this through holt and hanger
    When Uricon the city stood:
'Tis the old leaves in the old anger,
    But then it threshed another wood.

Then, 'twas before my time, the Roman
    At yonder heaving hill would stare:
The blood that warms an English yeoman,

The thoughts that hurt him, they were there.

There, like the wind through woods in riot,
   Through him the gale of life blew high;
The tree of man was never quiet:
   Then 'twas the Roman, now 'tis I.

The gale, it plies the saplings double,
   It blows so hard, 'twill soon be gone:
To-day the Roman and his trouble
   Are ashes under Uricon.

It is not certain that this poem is meant as, among other things, a wry rebuke to those Anglo-Saxonries of the 1890s described earlier in this chapter, but it is entirely possible. At all events, Housman's introduction of the Roman in Britain works neatly to demolish those avowals of pure Anglo-Saxon blood which are so characteristic of the period. Suppose, however, we try to set Housman's poems against Hardy's 'Channel Firing', if only because Hardy's last line also opens history up in uncomfortable ways? What we find then is that Housman's Wenlock Edge is a much emptier place than Hardy's church. There are no voices, no presences that warm his perception of history. Or could we point to the English yeoman as one such presence? But who is he? Housman? If not, why is he introduced? If so, how can one possibly regard the author of this poem as any such thing? In fact the more you study the poem the emptier it becomes, simply because Housman has little grasp on the history of the place he is writing about. What preoccupies him is the general sadness of time passing, of how man comes and tills the field and lies beneath. In which case Wenlock Edge might be anywhere.

This brings me to another point. For if the poem lacks presences, it also lacks a speaking voice. Housman is a self-consumer of his woes. You can see that this is so if you try to speak the poem aloud. Where, for example, are you to put the stresses on the line 'When Uricon the city stood'?

When Uricón the cíty stóod.

What that draws attention to is that 'the city' is mere padding. After all, what else was Uricon but a city? But the plonking way you say the line would not have occurred to Housman, any more than the difficulty of sounding naturally the line 'The thoughts that hurt him, they were there.'

The thoúghts that húrt him, théy were thére.

No matter how you try to pace and place the stresses, that last phrase sounds unduly portentous. If it did not so sound to Housman the reason is that he never thought of the lines as being pressured by a human voice, even though he claimed to work his poems out by repeating them to himself. No doubt he did, but the fact remains that his poetry, fine in its elegiac way though it undoubtedly can be, remains a poetry empty of the reverberations of voice.

In addition, Housman's England is emptied of people. For all his references to 'lads' and, less often, 'lasses', there are no breathing presences in his poems. So his most famous and probably best poem, 'Tell Me Not Here', seems to offer a vision of England that is the counterpart of Paul Nash's pre-war landscapes. (The fact that Housman's poem was written in 1922 does not affect the point.) Its slightly unnerving melancholy has to do with its landscape being essentially vacant. Not only are people absent, you couldn't imagine them ever being present.

In 'Fare Well' Walter de la Mare had written

> Oh, when this my dust surrenders
> Hand, foot, lip, to dust again,
> May these loved and loving faces
>   Please other men!
> May the rusting harvest hedgerow
> Still the Traveller's Joy entwine,
> And as happy children gather
>   Posies once mine.
>
> Look thy last on all things lovely,
> Every hour.

In 'Tell Me Not Here', Housman writes:

> On russet floors, by waters idle,
>   The pine lets fall its cone;
> The cuckoo shouts all day at nothing
>   In leafy dells alone;
> And traveller's joy beguiles in autumn
>   Hearts that have lost their own.
>
> On acres of the seeded grasses
>   The changing burnish heaves;
> Or marshalled under moons of harvest
>   Stand still all night the sheaves;
> Or beeches strip in storms for winter
>   And stain the wind with leaves.

> Possess, as I possessed a season,
> The countries I resign,
> Where over elmy plains the highway
> Would mount the hills and shine,
> And full of pillared shade the forest
> Would murmur and be mine.

The debt is clear enough, and although there is not much doubt that Housman's is the better poem, both he and de la Mare have that slightly odd attitude to nature which suggests that on the one hand they possess it but that on the other it is being 'marshalled' to point up melancholy disenchantments, loss of human relationship (traveller's joy 'beguiles in autumn/Hearts that have lost their own'), or plain absence of people. This landscape is not known for the wear of a foot on a threshold. It is in fact a tourist's landscape, one to walk through rather than to know.

'Possess, as I possessed a season/The countries I resign', Housman says. Who is he talking to? And who, for the matter of that, is de la Mare talking to when he says 'Look thy last on all things lovely'? If you could call back the two poets' shades and put the question directly to them they would be puzzled. 'The reader,' they might say, 'we were addressing the reader.' But not any reader. If there is a particular reader in mind it must be of the future, someone who will 'possess' the countries that Housman resigns. Housman does not speak to the present and he cannot communicate with the past – or rather he can do so only as it appears in terms of the Roman, whose very unghostly previous existence is referred to in 'On Wenlock Edge'. He is simply cut off, seeing nature without having any sense of relationship to it. 'I know all her ways', he says in the last stanza of 'Tell Me Not Here'. All? Housman's knowledge is that of the jilted lover, forced to admit that he has been pushed out into the cold and that among the ways he never knew were the ways of work, of relationship, and perhaps above all, the ways of language – that is, of people. In short, Housman's poetry gives the lie to that dream of a peopled heart of England that I have been trying to identify in this chapter. In his poetry, even more than in de la Mare's, the country has become mysterious. Such poetry is both for the clerk and in a sense by him. It is a scholarly attempt to feed life into a dead myth. And what the poetry reveals is not knowledge – not the knowledge of Clare or Hardy – but bafflement.

In the *Preface* to the *Lyrical Ballads* Wordsworth had spoken of how the poet carries everywhere with him 'relationship and love'.

This is to offer poetry as a stay against changes and fragmentations within English society. It is also to make the poet a perhaps impossibly heroic, unifying force against such fragmentation: 'a rock of defence of human nature', in Wordsworth's own words. By the end of the nineteenth century, however, this heroic dream has gone. The best that poets can now do is to find a language not to be betrayed, to attest to forms and modes of utterance which, in their candid recognition of loss, tell how much would otherwise have gone 'silently out of mind'. At worst, poets are betrayed into a confession of separation – even of dispossession – which they cannot bring themselves to acknowledge.

The poets I have next to consider are even more immediately taxed over the matter of the language of relationship because, writing out of the experience of war, they find themselves faced with the agonising problem of trying to speak for and about an England whose apparently unitary nature is belied by especially troubling actualities.

Further reading

Apart from the books by Weiner, Masterman and Girouard, I recommend George Dangerfield's *The Strange Death of Liberal England*, Donald Read's *Edwardian England* and Paul Thompson's *The Edwardians*.

For literary matters two good books are C. K. Stead's *The New Poetic* and Richard Ellmann's *Edwardians and Late Victorians*, 1962. F. C. Horwood's *Selections from Housman* was published in 1971. His *Collected Poems* are widely available as are those of Kipling and de la Mare. There is no standard edition of Masefield or W. H. Davies, but editions of their work are easy enough to come by. Joy Grant's *Harold Monro and the Poetry Bookshop* was published in 1967.

See also the Penguin *Georgian Poetry*, selected and introduced by James Reeves, 1962.

- 4 -

Poetry and Pity

I

The story of what happened to English poetry during the Great War is familiar enough. It begins with the heady innocence of those public schoolboys who immediately volunteered for action and who were, many of them at least, dead by the time that the disasters of the Somme began to change the minds of others. From then on the poetry becomes marked by disillusionment, bitterness, aching sorrow for the soldiers themselves, and hatred for the Government and generals who were determined that the war should continue until the enemy had totally surrendered.

Rupert Brooke is the most famous of those who wrote of the 'innocence' of war. Claims have been made for his work, but it can hardly be thought of as serious poetry. Of course, it can be used as a way into the study of the spirit – perhaps even the diseased spirit – of Edwardian England. When for example Brooke speaks of gladly turning from a world 'grown old and cold and weary', it is possible to argue that he is turning his back on the vulgar materialism of his age. But it is equally possible to see in the words a soft-focus romanticism. War is to offer a renewal of the spirit. And although he also speaks of himself and others as 'swimmers into cleanness leaping', I am tempted to see in the image less an impulse to purge himself of the grime of materialism than the schoolboy's self-reminder that cold baths dispel hot thoughts. *Mens sana in corpore sano.*

This is not to say that I doubt the absolute sincerity with which Brooke and others went to war. Nor do I question the implied sense of relief that flickers through their desire to turn away from the society in which they had grown up. There was undoubtedly a great deal wrong with it. It *was* vulgarly materialistic, Imperialist jingoism *was* appalling, the gap between rich and poor *was* iniquitous. But in a sense Brooke claims to be fighting for precisely such a society. Or

70

rather its problems are all dissolved in the blur of the 'richer dust' which in some corner of a foreign field will be for ever England. Brooke does not mean this at all ironically. In so far as he can be said to have thought about the matter, he would probably have wished to assert that the heart of Empire was still sound.

So would Julian Grenfell. His one surviving poem, 'Into Battle', is almost emblematic in its desire for a 'clean' death. Grenfell is certainly a tragic figure but he is no sort of a poet. Very probably he wanted to die, and it is certain his mother wanted him to. (This will be developed in the chapter on Auden.) But death is a word for him, a gesture – or just possibly an escape from misery. (For her, it was the opportunity to appear in full consciousness of her heroic status – having sacrificed her son to the cause.)

> The woodland trees that stand together,
> They stand to him each one a friend;
> They gently speak in the windy weather;
> They guide to valley and ridge's end.

This stanza from 'Into Battle' is significant because it makes plain the fact that Grenfell sees war as a continuation of hunting across English shires. What waits at the ridge's end is, presumably, death, but death as high adventure. It will be gained in a cavalry war where gallant foes are pitted against each other. The idea that death could be 'gained', as you might gain a school prize, occurs in much of the early war poetry.

It is difficult not to fall into parody when speaking of such poems. For their language is that of faded chivalric gallantry: of G. A. Henty, Newbolt, E. Phillips Oppenheim, and those many other authors who wrote boys' fiction during this period and whose notion of chivalry is echoed in so much poster art of the Great War. (As Mark Girouard has shown in *The Return to Camelot*, although he seems not to recognize how offensive it is.) Consider Herbert Asquith's 'The Volunteer'.

> Here lies a clerk who half his life had spent
> Toiling at ledgers in the city grey,
> Thinking that so his days would drift away
> With no lance broken in life's tournament:
> Yet ever 'twixt the books and his bright eyes
> The gleaming eagles of the legions came,
> And horsemen, charging under phantom skies,
> Went thundering past beneath the oriflamme.

And now those waiting dreams are satisfied;
From twilight to the halls of dawn he went.
His lance is broken; but he lies content
With that high hour, in which he lived and died.
And falling thus, he wants no recompense,
Who found his battle in the last resort;
Nor needs he any hearse to bear him hence,
Who goes to join the men of Agincourt.

If Asquith were a better poet it might be possible to think that in the first stanza he is satirizing the clerk's dream of poetry: of escape from the city into a life of chivalry. But the second makes it clear that he shares the dream. *The Volunteer and Other Poems* was published in 1915, by which time it was becoming all too apparent that those men who went to war would not die with broken lances, nor lie content. The war had already settled down into a terrible stalemate of trench attrition, and the chewed-up no-man's land between the front lines made it absolutely certain that there would be no role for cavalry in the campaigns. The vague gesture in the direction of *Henry V* and the Tennysonian rhetoric of Asquith's poem (his 'halls of dawn' is a steal from 'Tithonus') are therefore simply ridiculous.

'The Western Line', another poem from the volume, is equally ridiculous.

Beyond the thunder of the guns,
  Beyond the flaming line,
Far from this sky of echoing bronze,
  The English valleys shine;
The gardens, moated in the wolds,
  By wind and water kissed;
And dainty girls, that England folds
  In sunshine and in mist.
The floods of battle ebb and flow,
The soldiers to Valhalla go! . . .

Above the clouds what lights are gleaming?
  God's batteries are those,
Or souls of soldiers, homeward streaming,
  To banquet with their foes?

It would be fatally easy to score cheap points against this kind of verse, which was being rushed on to the bookstalls throughout the war. I want to say only that the idea of the soldiers banqueting with their foes inevitably reminds you of tea after the rugger match, that what is here suggested as God's batteries in fact meant death or injury, often of the most disfiguring kind, for the soldiers who had to suffer them; and that an England of dainty girls and gardens moated in the wolds (more Tennyson) would have been quite unreal to the majority of men who had volunteered for service and who came from the towns and cities of industrial England.

And here we come to something of real interest. For as soon as war is declared there seems to be a general agreement among those who write anything that the England to be defended, championed, upheld, vindicated, is precisely that England of shining valleys which comparatively few people knew anything of and even fewer lived in. What are we to make of the fact that when Sir Maurice Yapp introduced the YMCA anthology of 1915, *The Old Country*, he spoke of the soldiers who would enjoy it, for each 'in imagination . . . can see his village home'? What of the fact that when Henry James explained to himself why he must support the allied cause, he spoke of his England as a countryside where trees sheltered cottages in which were bluey-white gathers of curtains at the windows? (In *Within the Rim*.) What had any of this to do with what England was actually like in August 1914?

The answer is, very little. And if we then ask why people claimed to be defending this rural paradise I think we must reply that it was the kind of image that, as so much Edwardian literature suggested, made the widest possible appeal. For which of those literate men – and some women – who spoke with such enthusiasm of the entry into war, could be expected to speak of the glory of defending Leeds or Manchester? And in this I see a deeper problem, or guilt. I see a veiled hope that the war might somehow restore England to that rurality, that dream of a pure 'heart', which I showed in the last chapter to have such a potent but debilitating force in Edwardian poetry. The dream was carried into the war. It was for the maintaining or restoring of *this* that men were supposed to be fighting. I do not of course suggest that the hope was a conscious matter; but I do think that the image of a chivalric war is inseparable from a dream of escape from modernity. What the war inevitably confirmed was that modernity could not be averted. The Great War was a machine war and men were ruthlessly fed to the machine.

We can understand why the poets of the first days of the war might not have understood this and why they dreamed of war as an escape into a world of Agincourt or Valhalla. To describe a totally new experience you need a totally new language and the writers did not have it. That is why the poets who come later – above all, Sassoon, Owen and Rosenberg – are commonly seen as succeeding where the previous ones failed. As the war dragged on, so the argument goes, it became evident that its horrors would need to be met by new modes of expression. And after the Somme, in particular, it would be insane to go on believing in the adequacy of those values and dreams which had launched men into the armed services in the autumn of 1914.

I do not disagree with the outline of this argument. But I am not so certain as most commentators appear to be that the later poets found a means of expression adequate to the horrors they encountered. In a sense this may not be a criticism. Could *any* writer hope to deal adequately with the events of that war? I think probably not, and indeed I am not sure that we have yet found a satisfactory way of talking about it, which may be why it continues to fascinate and at the same time appal. How can the mind cope with the statistics: as many as 9 million dead, many more wounded, the financial cost almost beyond reckoning. And then the follies, the horrors, the ignorance and stupidity of those in command. The fact that the British High Command never visited the front and that when one of them, Kiggell, actually got close, he burst into tears. 'I didn't know we were sending men to fight in this,' he said. And the young subaltern who was accompanying him said, 'It's worse further on up.'

No, I do not think we have the right to complain that the poets were not equal to accounting for all that went on in the Great War. But I do think there are flaws that have to be brought out into the open. I recognize how difficult this is to do without seeming merely insensitive. For those soldier-poets were heroes or died miserably or came home mad or in terrible anguish. How is it possible to criticize writers who went through such suffering? This is what Donald Davie no doubt had in mind when he remarked that the war poems are 'not poems at all, but something less than that and more; they are first-hand and faithful witnesses to a moment in the national destiny'.[1] This is generously meant but I cannot agree with it. In the first place, Owen and Rosenberg most certainly wrote genuine poems; in the second, the phrase 'faithful witness' seems to me to beg a number of questions. It is for this reason that I think we have to look more critically at the poems and poets who are usually thought to have produced the best work that came out of those terrible years.

My view is clearly shared by Jon Silkin. His influential *Penguin*

Book of First-World War Poetry has a long, combative introduction in which he singles out for criticism one of the most famous and cherished of all war poems, Wilfred Owen's 'Anthem for Doomed Youth'.

> What passing-bells for these who die as cattle?
> – Only the monstrous anger of the guns.
> Only the stuttering rifles' rapid rattle
> Can patter out their hasty orisons.
> No mockeries now for them; no prayers; nor bells,
> Nor any voice of mourning save the choirs, –
> The shrill, demented choirs of wailing shells;
> And bugles calling for them from sad shires.
>
> What candles may be held to speed them all?
> Not in the hands of boys, but in their eyes
> Shall shine the holy glimmers of goodbyes.
> The pallor of girls' brows shall be their pall;
> Their flowers the tenderness of patient minds,
> And each slow dusk a drawing-down of blinds.

The grave pathos and extreme beauty of sound in some of these lines are at first likely to keep uneasy thoughts at bay. But then doubts begin to creep in. No matter how reluctantly, I find myself agreeing with Jon Silkin that it is less than satisfactory for the bugles to be calling for the soldiers from the sad shires. For it was precisely those shires that were likely to have sent them out to fight. I do not mean by this that all the men came from the land but that, as we have seen, it was this vision of England that the men were supposed to be fighting for. The bugles were therefore less likely to be calling for the men to come back than calling for them to go and do their duty, and get killed. The bugles constitute a mockery of real sadness. (You could try to read the line ironically but that would not feel at all right.) Owen, however, turns away from any hard inspection of what those sad shires constitute, and settles for the pathos of the sestet. And here, suddenly, the men are dignified in death, and any question of the rightness of response of those 'patient minds' is left aside.

Silkin's objection against this, that Owen too easily moves towards pity and compassion has, I think, undeniable justice. 'The poetry is in the pity' Owen famously wrote in the intended preface to the collection of his poems which was not published until after his death. Yes, but pity can degenerate into something close to condescension, as it seems to me to do in those poems where Owen pretends to speak through the mouths of ordinary line soldiers and ends up with the sort of ventriloquism that we saw was common enough in Edwardian poetry, and where a writing down can easily become a writing off.

> 'But poor young Jim, 'e's livin' an' 'e's not;
> 'E reckoned 'e'd five chances, an' 'e 'ad;
> 'E's wounded, killed, and pris'ner, all the lot,
> The bloody lot all rolled in one. Jim's mad' ('The Chances').

These last lines are the best in the poem, and yet their apparently colloquial toughness seems to me weakened and compromised by the Kiplingesque echoes. I know that it is difficult to speak critically of poems that were being written under the conditions that Owen had to endure; and had he lived it is fairly certain that he would have tightened lines, and cancelled phrases which testify, if anything can, to the almost impossible difficulties of finding a language adequate to his experience (e.g. 'Batter of guns and shatter of flying muscles,/ Carnage incomparable, and human squander' – 'Mental Cases'). Would he, though, have got rid of those Keatsian coy intensifiers that you can also regularly find in his work? 'Now, he is old; his back will never brace;/He's lost his colour very far from here' ('Disabled'). Such flaws seem to me more endemic and are, I think, part and parcel of that pathos which goes with slack rhythms and syntactic inversions.

The point is, I think that pity is an emotion that is often fatal to poetry. It allows for a kind of melancholy or sweet sadness that deflects attention away from the hard questions. As Silkin says:

> the (southern) English tendency is to elevate compassion into a religiose sentiment, and thus remove it from the earth, making innocuous any enquiry as to the state of the victim and the cause of his suffering that a more earth-bound and singular tenderness might have made. It is at once politically expedient and morally less taxing as a mode.[2]

Harsh words, but properly so, I think.

'Pity would be no more/If we did not make somebody poor', Blake sardonically remarked. Most of Owen's poems are preoccupied with the pity rather than the making of poverty (that is, the making of soldiers). At the end of 'Insensibility' he curses those who have by choice made themselves immune

> To pity and whatever moans in man
> Before the last sea and the hapless stars;
> Whatever mourns when many leave these shores;
> Whatever shares
> The eternal reciprocity of tears.

Well, yes, but to adapt Dr Johnson, pity is the last refuge of the scoundrel. Anyone can claim to feel it, as Sassoon pointed out in 'Base Details' ('You'd see me with my puffy petulant face,/Guzzling and gulping in the best hotel,/Reading the Roll of Honour. "Poor young chap,"/I'd say – "I used to know his father well".').

No, that is not true pity. Nevertheless the bugles calling from sad shires imply an eternal reciprocity of tears that blocks off harder lines of enquiry – which in the end have to do with questions about what it is to be English. For underlying most of Owen's work is, I think, a desperate desire to retain a belief in that Englishness out of which his poems come and to which they repeatedly return.

This is why the best as well as the worst of them are characterized by compassion. Take for example, that perfect little poem 'Futility'.

> Move him into the sun, –
> Gently its touch awoke him once,
> At home, whispering of fields unsown,
> Always it woke him, even in France,
> Until this morning and this snow.
> If anything might rouse him now
> The kind old sun will know.
>
> Think how it wakes the seeds, –
> Woke, once, the clays of a cold star.
> Are limbs, so dear-achieved, are sides,
> Full-nerved – still warm, – too hard to stir?
> Was it for this the clay grew tall?
> – O what made fatuous sunbeams toil
> To break earth's sleep at all?

I think this is a very fine elegy, words and cadences so controlled that it is as though they drop into pools of silence, the movement and hesitancies perfectly judged in their expression of grieving incredulity. You might want to find fault with the phrase 'kind old sun', but in fact I think it belongs in the poem. For what Owen is writing about is the sense of betrayal: England fostered the man and now he is dead. No kindness can bring him back to life. But the point is this: that the poem might be about any young man dead before his time;

there is nothing in 'Futility' to let us know that the youth was killed in battle. It is as though Owen has to suppress the worst knowledge in order to get the poem written. Yet it is implied in the poem's last lines, which have about them a vibrancy of bitter despair even though that despair is never directly addressed.

Of course Owen knew that those who died in battle typically did so without dignity. He carried about with him photographs of the horribly maimed and butchered and, whenever he was home on leave and conversation had become fatuously complacent about the glorious sacrifice, he would produce the photographs. Yet this side of him does not often get into the poetry. It appears, momentarily, in 'Asleep', which focuses on a soldier killed by, I suppose, shrapnel:

> There was a quaking
> Of the aborted heart within him leaping . . .
> Then chest and sleepy arms once more fell slack.
> And soon the slow, stray blood came creeping
> From the intrusive lead, like ants on track.

'The aborted heart.' That cuts deep. And when you think that the dead man is quite likely to attract ants, the horror of that image of the 'creeping blood' becomes obvious. This is especially true because the line is a syllable short, so that the movement of the blood works through the line's dragged incompleteness, the need there is to place stress on so many key words; 'And soón the slów, stráy blóod came creéping'. Getting three heavy stresses together as Owen here does is technically very difficult and shows with what unremitting attention he is managing his effect. Yet the poem ends with a dying fall: 'He sleeps. He sleeps less tremulous, less cold,/Than we who must awake, and waking, say, Alas!' The pity throbs through the alexandrine. But in 'Easter, 1916' Yeats rejected the consolation of death as sleep. 'No, no, not sleep but death.' And 'Alas'. Is that *all* that can be said?

'Dulce Et Decorum Est' shows that there were occasions when Owen could say more. It is significant that commentators should feel it to be among his less successful poems. For this is a poem of precise anger.

> If in some smothering dreams you too could pace
> Behind the wagon that we flung him in,
> And watch the white eyes writhing in his face,
> His hanging face, like a devil's, sick of sin;
> If you could hear, at every jolt, the blood
> Come gargling from the froth-corrupted lungs,

> Obscene as cancer, bitter as the cud
> Of vile, incurable sores on innocent tongues –
> My friend, you would not tell with such high zest
> To children ardent for some desperate glory,
> The old Lie: Dulce et decorum est
> Pro patria mori.

If you could pace . . . watch . . . hear. But the strength of these lines comes from the way Owen's language, in its Keatsian exactness, brings us as close as poetry can ever do to the experience itself. We all *do* pace, watch, hear. The stresses are remorselessly insistent:

> If yóu could heár, at evéry jólt, the blóod
> Come gárgling from the fróth-corrúpted lúngs.

The fact that 'at every jolt' is fenced round with commas makes for an insistence we can't avoid recognizing; the pause after 'hear' gives what follows extra impact and it's reinforced by the heavy stresses on *ev*ery jolt; and when we come round the line-ending, 'Come gárgling' has the effect of a spondee, a terrible actuality being attested to. It is this which makes the verse paragraph unwind towards the climax on the word 'Lie', where the voice crashes down on the capitalized word. There are other poems where Owen writes with an equal precision, if with less anger: 'The Sentry', 'Smile, Smile, Smile' and 'Exposure', seem to me the best of them.

When he writes like this Owen may seem very like his friend, Siegfried Sassoon. In fact, although Sassoon's help and encouragement proved invaluable to him, Owen is by far the better poet. Years ago, D. J. Enright remarked that Sassoon's satires nearly always hit their target, but that the target was usually a sitting duck. It is fair comment. What propels Sassoon into the most memorable of his war poems is that very English feeling of outraged decency. He loathed all the things it was proper to loathe: the callous incompetence of generals, the warmongering hysteria of those who did not have to fight, the hypocritical patriotism of the home front. In a clutch of poems he spoke out against these things, and he did so in ways that may be called verse journalism. His language is invariably reach-me-down, his rhythms slack or gruffly approximate. Just occasionally the journalism goes up a notch or two, as at the end of 'Lamentations', where, after some clumsy lines describing a soldier whom war has driven mad, Sassoon concludes, 'In my belief/Such men have lost all patriotic feeling'. This laconic statement gets its edge from the fact that during the Great War only officers could be classified as liable to 'neurosis' or breakdown. Any signs of mental instability among rankers were treated as attempts at malingering. In his book *No Man's Land* Eric Leed provides horrifying evidence of the ways in which army doctors responded to the suffering of men who had gone mad at the front. Veterans of years of trench warfare would be put through 'tests' (shut into total blackness, bombarded with noise) until one way or the other they broke – which usually meant being found fit for duty. Others were shot for cowardice in the face of the enemy. It is the very laconicism of Sassoon's line which allows you to sense the bestiality of the war.

More often though, Sassoon uses the clichés of journalism to make his entirely honourable protests. 'To Any Dead Officer' ends:

> Good-bye, old lad! Remember me to God,
> And tell him that our politicians swear
> They won't give in till Prussian Rule's been trod
> Under the heel of England . . . Are you there? . . .
> Yes . . . and the war won't end for at least two years;
> But we've got stacks of men . . . I'm blind with tears,
> Staring into the dark. Cheero!
> I wish they'd killed you in a decent show.

There, it seems to me, you have both the virtues and the limitations of decency. Good that Sassoon uses the politicians' clichés in order to underline the mindless brutality of their words. But: 'Cheero!/I wish they'd killed you in a decent show.' Really? What would such a show be like? Isn't this the public-school boy speaking out on behalf of precisely those military 'virtues' that had helped to bring the war about? What can Sassoon want – the banqueting of foes? It is when you read these lines, stripped of the presumed irony that is sometimes wrongly attributed to them, that you sense the force of Hugh MacDiarmid's criticism of Sassoon. In 1936, when *Sherston's Progress* was completed, MacDiarmid wrote a verse review of this devious autobiography of Sassoon's.

> Despite the undeniable honesty, the little literary gift,
> What is *Sherston's Progress* but an exposure
> Of the eternal Englishman
> Incapable of rising above himself,
> And traditional values winning out
> Over an attempted independence of mind.

Severe, you may say. But I think MacDiarmid is right. For even more than Owen, Sassoon was implicated in a dream of England – of being a fox-hunting man – that made it finally impossible for him to get beyond the limits of decency.

II

It is for this reason, I think, that Isaac Rosenberg emerges as a valuable alternative to both Owen and Sassoon. I do not think that Rosenberg is any more technically gifted than Owen, but he seems to me to have had, or to have shown, an independence of mind that Owen lacked. This may have had something to do with the fact that as a line soldier he did not have to feel committed to that sometimes Olympian pity which Owen showed for his soldiers, nor to the outraged decency of Sassoon. I think that it also had a great deal to do with the fact that Rosenberg was a Jew. His response to the 'great adventure' is deeply sardonic. He is never fooled by appeals to those 'verities' and sad shires for which others believed or persuaded themselves to believe they were fighting.

I do not wish to overrate his achievement and I am not very interested in Rosenberg the poet-painter. Some commentators have seen in 'Louse Hunting' a verbal equivalent of those expressionist canvases which Rosenberg's teacher at art school, David Bomberg, was tackling while Rosenberg was a student. Perhaps, but other poets could have written 'Louse Hunting'. Who else, though, could have written 'Break of Day in the Trenches'?

> The darkness crumbles away –
> It is the same old druid Time as ever.
> Only a live thing leaps my hand –
> A queer sardonic rat –
> As I pull the parapet's poppy
> To stick behind my ear.
> Droll rat, they would shoot you if they knew
> Your cosmopolitan sympathies.
> Now you have touched this English hand
> You will do the same to a German –

It is a kind of free-verse notation, with only one line conforming to that staple iambic pentameter which Owen and Sassoon so regularly use. Yet in context 'It is the same old druid Time as ever' is anything but consolatory. The line breathes a world-weary, darkly comic spirit. Don't think there's anything special about this war, this horror, it says; we've seen it all before. I suggest, though I do it with some hesitancy, that this is a Jewish sensibility, in which 'They' become gentiles who think the world made for them and their especial virtues. Not so, the poem says. In fact, the droll rat seems to 'grin innocently as you pass/Strong eyes, fine limbs, haughty athletes/Less chanced than you for life'. The tone of 'Break of Day' is one of resigned, wry fatalism. Rosenberg pulls a poppy and puts it behind his ear. It is a symbol of life which is at the same time a reminder that death, when it comes, will probably be in the form of a blood-red bullet wound. This is the 'chance' of war, and you could not imagine Rosenberg believing in a decent show or thinking that the war might have had some grand design, some purpose that would finally make all come right.

I must not give the impression that Rosenberg is indifferent to the deaths of others. 'Dead Man's Dump' is a poem that could only have been written by someone who knew and responded at a very deep level to the horrors front-line soldiers had to suffer, and for all its imperfections – an occasional clumsiness of phrase and more than occasional uncertainty of rhythm – it is clearly an important poem. It is also quite without consolation. The deaths of the men it responds to make no sense.

> A man's brains splattered on
> A stretcher-bearer's face;
> His shook shoulders slipped their load,
> But when they bent to look again
> The drowning soul was sunk too deep
> For human tenderness.

Owen used that word 'drowning' vividly in 'Dulce et Decorum est', but here it is surely far more terrifying. This is a final blanking out, the utter negation of a life. 'Thanks to the human heart by which we live,/Thanks to its tenderness, its joys and fears,/To me the meanest flower that blows can give/Thoughts that do often lie too deep for tears.' I do not know whether Rosenberg may have had Wordsworth's conclusion to the 'Immortality Ode' somewhere at the back of his mind when he came to write these lines in 'Dead Man's Dump'. It is possible. At all events what he responds to is a depth beneath any that Wordsworth, Christian and humanist that he was, would have dared to acknowledge.

It is so with some earlier lines in the same poem:

What fierce imagining their dark souls lit?
Earth! have they gone into you!
Somewhere they must have gone,
And flung on your hard back
Is their soul's sack
Emptied of God-ancestralled essences.
Who hurled them out? Who hurled?

The fierce, compacted rhythms of these lines comes from an urgency of questioning made the more appalling because you realize that there can be no answer. Which means that there can be no consolation.

III

When Eleanor Farjeon asked Edward Thomas why he was prepared to fight in the Great War he bent down, picked up a fistful of earth, and held it out to her. I do not see in that gesture anything of the mystical notion of *la patrie*. On the contrary: it is abashed, defiant, wry. Thomas was always trying to grasp the significance of experiences which one way or another eluded him although in doing so they signalled a kind of withheld power and undeniable if unattainable reality. 'I cannot bite the day to the core,' he said at the end of 'The Glory', and that sense of wanting to possess experience and failing to do so is present in most of his poetry. Yet the failure is of course by no means absolute. Indeed Thomas's work is remarkable for its feeling of absent presences: of intimations glimpsed, nearly held, tracked almost to their sources. He 'brooded long', Alun Lewis said, in a phrase which exactly catches the dark, ruminative quality of Thomas's voice; and most of his poetry is built out of brooding, or it results from a momentary intuition that can come only to someone whose essentially solitary nature makes him unusually receptive to the interaction of mind – which often means memory – and outer stimulus.

This is the case, for example, with the much-anthologized, entirely unique 'Old Man', with its inimitable ending. (How inimitable may be seen from the number of more recent poets who have tried, and failed, to capture the movement of lines which are the slow, patient, exquisitely honest movement of a mind brooding long.)

As for myself,
Where first I met the bitter scent is lost.
I, too, often shrivel the grey shreds,
Sniff them and think and sniff again and try
Once more to think what it is I am remembering,
Always in vain. I cannot like the scent,
Yet I would rather give up others more sweet,
With no meaning, than this bitter one.

I have mislaid the key. I sniff the spray
And think of nothing; I see and I hear nothing;
Yet seem, too, to be listening, lying in wait
For what I should, yet never can, remember:
No garden appears, no path, no hoar-green bush
Of Lad's-Love, or Old Man, no child beside,
Neither father nor mother, nor any playmate;
Only an avenue, dark, nameless, without end.

It was Robert Frost who famously pointed out to Thomas that he had always been a poet even though Thomas had for so long denied his own abilities. Perhaps he did so not out of mere perversity, as has often been said, but because he could not believe that the strong, quizzically flexible cadences of his utterance were proper for poetry. And certainly you will not find Thomas's kind of voice among the Edwardian poets, look where you will. So much the worse for them, of course. For as you attend to the movement of Thomas's lines you immediately see why he is so important and why Frost, who knew that poetry must always echo 'sentence-sound', recognized his friend's value.

Í, tóo, often shrível the gréy shréds,
Sníff them and thínk and sníff agáin and trý
Once móre to thínk what it ís I am remémberíng,
Álways in váin.

Which is as far as may be from the inept use of the iambic pentameter that at precisely this time Ezra Pound was justly compaining about. 'The first heave was to get rid of [it]', he said. Would he have been so insistent if he had known these lines of Thomas? I doubt it. It is not merely the way Thomas throws stress away from metric regularity in the interests of catching or enacting the movement of his brooding thoughts; it is also the way he uses line endings and run-ons, so that you get the authentic kick from 'Once more', his way of remarking the persistence of his efforts to 'think what it is I am remembering', followed by the half-mocking despair of the phrase that greets you as you come round that line ending: 'Always in vain'.

'Only an avenue, dark, nameless, without end.' Thomas was an inveterate walker, and many of his poems are about paths through woods – the path perilous which may allow for dark thoughts of death and oblivion. (Thomas was haunted by thoughts of death.) Or they are paths that lead into the secret heart of England, which you follow and which suddenly bring you to a place which seems to hoard a secret meaning you cannot entirely know. This, I think, is part of the meaning of that magical poem, 'Adlestrop'.

> Yes. I remember Adlestrop –
> The name, because one afternoon
> Of heat the express-train drew up there
> Unwontedly. It was late June.
>
> The steam hissed. Someone cleared his throat.
> No one left and no one came
> On the bare platform. What I saw
> Was Adlestrop – only the name
>
> And willows, willow-herb, and grass,
> And meadowsweet, and haycocks dry,
> No whit less still and lonely fair
> Than the high cloudlets in the sky.
>
> And for that minute a blackbird sang
> Close by, and round him, mistier,
> Farther and farther, all the birds
> Of Oxfordshire and Gloucestershire.

Thomas of course loved names. They had an almost talismanic power for him, as the poems to his daughters and sons show ('If I should ever by chance grow rich/I'll buy Codham, Cockridden, and Childerditch,/Roses, Pyrgo, and Lapwater,/And let them all to my elder daughter.') Such names are redolent of a stored history and in 'Adlestrop' the history is glimpsed within that 'minute' when the blackbird's song seems to come out of the very heart of England and awake a harmony of birdsong, provide a vision of a kind of paradisal nature.

But the glimpse and the minute are all that are offered. In his excellent account of Edward Thomas, Stan Smith speaks of him as the 'superfluous man', anxiously journeying in search of an identity he will never find, one that will let him live at peace with himself and/or because of a discovered place of belonging. It is certainly true that Thomas's wandering is quite unlike that of Wordsworth or Clare. Different as those two poets were, both by temperament and in social position, they had a sense of belonging that can hardly be attributed to Thomas. (In Clare's case it was denied him with, as we have seen, tragic consequences.)

Thomas never belonged, I think. Hence his constant shifts of house. For someone who aspired to 'rootedness' he was extremely restless, although I think this inevitable. Hence also that sense, so uniquely powerful in his work, of the sudden but transitory apprehension of a secret heart of things. In this he may be compared to the George Gissing of the *Private Papers of Henry Ryecroft*, with its powerful evocations of different spots of England, each of which seems to carry within it an identity centuries deep. This will explain, I think, why Thomas so lavishly and otherwise inexplicably over-praised the publication of Doughty's unreadable *The Dawn of Britain*. And there are moments in his poetry when he has the same unfocused nostalgia for the concept of Britain – even the word – that you find in Kipling. In a seductive poem, 'Haymaking', he watches men about to begin their labour in the fields:

> The men leaned on their rakes, about to begin,
> But still. And all were silent. All was old,
> This morning time, with a great age untold,
> Older than Clare and Cobbett, Morland and Crome,
> Than, at the field's far edge, the farmer's home,
> A white house crouched at the foot of a great tree.

I can see the attraction of these lines but I also detect considerable dangers in them. For this 'reading' of history somehow deflects attention away from actualities that Clare and Cobbett had to attend to, even if Crome and Morland (a very sentimental painter, by the way), did not. I mean quite simply that the social relations involved in labour, the exploitation, hardship, struggle, defeat and renewed struggle – these are absent from Thomas's account. 'The great age untold' isn't a unified heart of England in the way that Thomas wants to believe, and wants to persuade us.

That is why he needs to see by glimpses. Doing so allows him to guess at harmonies that a more settled view would disrupt. Take, for example, the lovely little poem 'Tall Nettles'.

> Tall nettles cover up, as they have done
> These many springs, the rusty harrow, the plough
> Long worn out, and the roller made of stone:

Only the elm butt tops the nettles now.

This corner of the farmyard I like most:
As well as any bloom upon a flower
I like the dust on the nettles, never lost
Except to prove the sweetness of a shower.

Edna Longley has remarked that Thomas was a master of the short lyric and she rightly draws attention to the key use here of the word 'prove'. Thomas, I would add, makes several of these lyrics out of moments of discreet ecstasy, as in 'Sowing' or 'Digging' or 'Thaw'. But the point about 'Tall Nettles' is that this corner of the farmyard stores a secret history, hidden by the nettles, but recoverable as a testimony to an England of shires, farms, age-old values associated with working the land, and known only to initiates who glimpse it in their journeyings, as Thomas does in 'I Never Saw That Land Before', which ends

I neither expected anything
Nor yet remembered: but some goal
I touched then; and if I could sing
What would not even whisper my soul
As I went on my journeying,

I should use, as the trees and birds did,
A language not to be betrayed;
And what was hid should still be hid
Excepting from those like me made
Who answer when such whispers bid.

'Some goal/I touched then.' That seems to me to typify much of Thomas's poetry, and its discretion and value certainly depend on his finding for the most part a language not to be betrayed. It is a language charged with an almost numinous quality of responsiveness and you cannot separate it from those hesitant, searching, qualifying and occasionally emphatic rhythms and cadences by means of which Thomas renovates English verse.

The key poem to all this is, I suppose, 'Lob'. Because it has been so excellently discussed by both Stan Smith and Edna Longley I shall keep my comments as brief as possible.[3] You might say that Thomas's Lob is the equivalent of Jefferies's Hodge or Kipling's Hobden. But this would be less than fair. For Thomas is at once more discreet and more in possession of his subject than they are. Lob is at first no more than a glimpsed figure who says to the young Thomas: 'Nobody can't stop 'ee. It's/A footpath, right enough.' He is a free man, a kind of tutelary spirit of the countryside, in short a numen, whom Thomas also invokes in 'May the Twenty-Third', when

> Old Jack Noman appeared again,
> Jaunty and old, crooked and tall,
> And stopped and grinned at me over the wall,
> With a cowslip bunch in his button-hole
> And one in his cap.

However, there is something forced and sentimental about this poem, something which, if it reminds us of Hardy's vision of Giles Winterbourne as 'Autumn's very brother', also reminds us that Hardy rejects this kind of facile anthropologizing by returning Giles to the specific social relations and economic process by means of which he is securely placed within an unfolding history. Old Jack Noman is, by contrast, an ahistorical emanation, at once gratuitous and forlornly literary. Thomas does better when he writes of Farmer Hayward in 'Women He Liked', for here the poem ends on a note of dark, laconic irony which calls into question the unguarded, annealing continuities on offer in other poems:

> Many years since, Bob Hayward died, and now
> None passes there because the mist and the rain
> Out of the elms have turned the lane to slough
> And gloom, the name alone survives, Bob's Lane.

Here, it is worth noting that the elms – the reassuringly familiar feature of a known landscape – create a miasmal gloom that cuts off any avenue into the past. 'Bob's Lane' 'survives', but as a name without meaning, without connections; and that this should be so ought to warn us against reading 'Lob' as an uncomplicated endorsement of continuity. .

Who was the man who said 'Nobody can't stop 'ee'? The poet asks various people and is not told. Indeed, he has the strong impression that a secret is being withheld from him. But then one man, 'A squire's son', does tell him – something.

> He sounds like one I saw when I was a child.
> I could almost swear to him. The man was wild
> And wandered. His home was where he was free.
> Everybody has met one such man as he . . .
> He is English as this gate, these flowers, this mire.
> And when at eight years old Lob-lie-by-the-fire

> Came in my books this was the man I saw,
> He has been in England as long as dove and daw,
> Calling the wild cherry tree the merry tree,
> The rose campion Bridget-in-her-bravery . . .

And then the poem astonishingly opens up a history of English names of flowers, of places, of legend and tale, all of them associated with Lob the free man who, whatever his name

> Lob-lie-by-the-fire, Jack Cade,
> Jack Smith, Jack Moor, poor Jack of every trade,
> Young Jack, or old Jack, or Jack What-d'ye-call,
> Jack-in-the-hedge, or Robin-run-by-the-wall,
> Robin Hood, Ragged Robin, Lazy Bob,
> One of the lords of No Man's Land, good Lob, –
> Although he was seen dying at Waterloo,
> Hastings, Agincourt, and Sedgemoor too, –
> Lives yet.

And as the teller of this extraordinary tale finishes and turns away Thomas has 'one glimpse of his back', and it is enough to prove the man 'of old Jack's blood'.

'Lob' is a remarkable poem, Thomas's most impassioned avowal of the continuity of an English tradition that is here more than glimpsed, because it is attested through the loving naming of names, the stitching together of lore and legend, that guarantees its survival.

But only through the enabling powers of language. For Lob is not certainly to be identified in any other way. The poem allows merely that his putative values have passed to the squire's son; and we have then to reflect that squirearchical values of the sort defended by Alfred Austin are very dubious ones through which to hope for a continuation of a past Thomas cared for. This may explain why, in 'Haymaking', he collapses historical actualities into a kind of seamless account of history or tries to blend elements that won't really go together.

There is another point. 'Young Jack' would soon be leaving Wiltshire for France. Beneath much of Thomas's poetry runs, I think, an unstated fear that the war may change everything. It is true that not many of his poems actually make mention of war; but it seems to me that most of them are affected by it. ('Adlestrop' was written in 1915.) That passionate, even aching desire for securing a held vision of continuity, of a heart of England, takes much of its power from a deep-seated apprehension of its going. At the end of 'This Is No Case Of Petty Right or Wrong', Thomas says

> But with the best and meanest Englishmen
> I am one in crying, God save England, lest
> We lose what never slaves and cattle blessed.
> The ages made her that made us from dust:
> She is all we know and live by, and we trust
> She is good and must endure, loving her so:
> And as we love herselves we hate her foe.

Perhaps the best way of reading that is as a rather shamefaced admission that in crying 'God save England' Thomas sees himself as no better than the worst (meanest) and no worse than the best: they are all caught up in the patriotism of the hour. But what is it that Thomas says 'must endure'? Presumably the secret heart of England that we have seen so many of his poems glimpsing or momentarily penetrating. And yet:

The flowers left thick at nightfall in the wood
This Eastertide call into mind the men,
Now far from home, who, with their sweethearts, should
Have gathered them and will do never again. ('In Memoriam, (Easter 1915)')

This tiny lyric evokes England as an untended garden, a lost paradise. The final line looks as though it is going to offer its consolation of a future when all will once more be well. But 'and will do' leads not to 'once again' but the final, utterly bleak 'never again'.

Or consider 'Fifty Faggots'. They were once 'underwood of hazel and ash'. Now they make a thicket and 'Next Spring/a blackbird or a robin will nest there,/Accustomed to them, thinking they will remain/Whatever is for ever to a bird'. But the dream of continuity is betrayed by time. Change, unknowable, dark, ominous, provides the poem's undertow.

> Before they are done
> The war will have ended, many other things
> Have ended, maybe, that I can no more
> Foresee or more control than robin and wren.

The hesitancies of movement are, of course, typical, but the sense of an ending in 'many other things' is acute, no matter how much it is qualified by the 'maybe', marked off by commas as a way of checking the slide towards black pessimism.

The finest of all Thomas's ponderings of change is, of course, in the famous 'As the Team's Head-Brass'. Everyone who has commented on this poem has rightly noted its points of comparison with Hardy's

'In Time of "The Breaking of Nations" '; but the differences are as
important. For Hardy's is a vision of continuity: the team of
ploughing horses and the lovers will outlast the annals of war. This is
not true of Thomas's poem.

> As the team's head-brass flashed out on the turn
> The lovers disappeared into the wood.
> I sat among the boughs of the fallen elm
> That strewed an angle of the fallow . . .

The stresses in that first line are unusually dramatic. I would read the
line 'Aś the team's heád-brass flaśhed oút on the túrn' although I can
see that you could as well put the first stress on 'teám's'. But the
reason I favour a stress on 'As' is because it links the flash of the
head-brass with the lovers' disappearance; and I have a shrewd
feeling that Thomas associates this flash with the flash of a gun. (For
it is clear from the poem that by now Thomas is in uniform.) The
wood then becomes a refuge for the lovers from the horrors of war,
or can be so associated in his mind. But he sits on a fallen elm. The
elm, I have already remarked, seems to me to be an unofficial symbol
of (southern) England at this period. Of course, it was everywhere,
but it clearly commands an important place in Thomas's sense of
landscape and its here being fallen is surely significant? The
ploughman tells him it was felled by a blizzard, and that on exactly
the same night one of his mates was killed in France. The felling of a
tree and of a man are thus ominously linked by a blizzard which, in
the violent way it makes a breach in nature, tells of destruction.

The poet says to the ploughman

> 'Everything
> Would have been different. For it would have been
> Another world.' 'Ay, and a better, though
> If we could see all all might seem good.' Then
> The lovers came out of the wood again:
> The horses started and for the last time
> I watched the clods crumble and topple over
> After the ploughshare and the stumbling team.

The lovers emerge from the wood on cue as the ploughman
speaks of all seeming good. Do they suggest resilience, survival? Or
has the wood proved at best a temporary refuge? Or are they
disappearing into the past along with the ploughman and his team?
For we can hardly avoid the sense of finality in that phrase 'for the

last time', nor the 'stumbling team', with its suggestion of lost certainty and strength. It can remind us that 'May The Twenty-Third' ends with Thomas avowing gladness for a past moment and yet saying that 'The elm seed lay in the road like hops,/That fine day, May the twenty-third,/The day Jack Noman disappeared'. It's as though Jack Noman has walked out of history.

In this context, it is worth mentioning 'Gone, Gone Again'. At first this lyric seems to be about the season's turning: But then

> And now again,
> In the harvest rain,
> The Blenheim oranges
> Fall grubby from the trees
>
> As when I was young –
> And when the lost one was here –
> And when the war began
> To turn young men to dung.

The shock of that last line does not merely spring from the fact that we had perhaps expected another line beginning 'And when'. It is also that it suddenly, and with a kind of brutal weariness, sees nature as a process of despoilation, of change as decay and loss. And so the old house, which enters the poem, is 'Outmoded, dignified,/Dark and untenanted,/With grass growing instead//Of the footsteps of life'. This is the house at the heart of England, which I spoke of in the previous chapter, but no longer seen as a symbol of survival, of continuity, but as a finished way of life. True, Thomas ends the poem by sinking into a self-pitying identification with the house; but the true charge seems to me to lie with the sense of an ending. Or, to put it differently, what 'Gone, Gone Again' testifies to is that feeling of destroyed continuities which is also implicit in other poems I have touched on and which may explain why elsewhere Thomas so urgently evoked a secret heart of England, as though by doing so he could discover or retain an assurance that the fistful of earth he held up to Eleanor Farjeon wasn't simply a handful of dust.

IV

Some time early in the 1930s Edward Thomas's widow, Helen, visited Ivor Gurney at Dartford Asylum, where he was to spend the rest of his short, tragic life. She discovered that he refused ever to go into the asylum's grounds because 'it was not his idea of the country at all – the fields, woods, water-meadows and footpaths he loved so well – and he would have nothing to do with that travesty of something sacred to him'.[4] That word 'sacred' is not lightly invoked. Although in the excellent introduction to his great edition of *The Collected Poems of Ivor Gurney* P. J. Kavanagh rightly remarks that Gurney is not a 'local' poet – with all the limiting meanings that the word holds, there can be no doubt that Gurney saw, felt and *knew* himself to belong to a particular place. In 'Crickly Hill', written from wartime France where Gurney fought with the Gloucesters, he begs 'You hills of home, woodlands, white roads and inns/That star and line our darling land, still keep/Memory of us . . .'. And the Wordsworthian sense of transactional relationship with place is always there. That is why he refused to go for walks in the grounds of his asylum. Dartford simply wasn't his place.

Gurney came from the Cotswolds and his poems show how deeply he possesses and feels himself to be possessed by that area of England:

> Sand has the ants, clay ferny weeds for play
> But what shall please the wind now the trees are away
> War took on Witcombe steep?
> It breathes there, and wonders at old night roarings;
> October time at all lights, and the new clearings
> For memory are like to weep.
> It was right for the beeches to stand over Witcombe reaches,
> Until the wind roared and softened and died to sleep. ('Possessions')

The implication of this and of several other, related poems cuts even deeper than 'Binsey Poplars'. The sense of loss is more exactly defined in terms of place and relationship to place; and of course the loss isn't the result of the depredations of time or of human carelessness. To say that 'Possessions', like 'As the Team's Head-Brass', links the felling of trees to war is to make an obvious point. More important is the fact that both Thomas and Gurney present the breach in nature as possibly final. And what makes this especially poignant in Gurney's case is his recognition that because of his incarceration he will never be able to become the sustaining historian of his particular area of England.

In the preface to the *Lyrical Ballads* Wordsworth had spoken of the poet as one who, 'in spite of things silently gone out of mind and things violently destroyed . . . binds together by passion and knowledge the vast empire of human society . . .'. The neo-enlightenment optimism of this remark is scaled down in the opening of 'Michael' to the statement that Wordsworth will tell his story 'with yet fonder feeling, for the sake/Of youthful poets, who among these hills/Shall be my second self, when I am gone'. Gurney has no such belief in possible continuity. In 'Moments', one of the many heart-wrenching poems he wrote out of his madness, and which acknowledges a sense of being divorced from place in a manner similar to 'The Flitting', he notes that 'high autumn goes beyond my pen/And snow lies inexprest in the deep lanes'. He is saying that there is nobody now to redeem his particular England, to express it, to give it meaning through utterance.

In a great burst of creativity that occurred between 1919 and 1922, Gurney found a means of expression adequate to his needs. The transformation from minor poet to major is quite extraordinary. Certainly his two published volumes of wartime poetry suggest nothing of what is to come. *Severn and Somme* (1917) and *War's Embers* (1919) are good of their kind, but the kind is recognizably Georgian.

> Only the wanderer
>   Knows England's graces,
> Or can anew see clear
>   Familiar faces.
>
> And who loves joy as he
>   That dwells in shadows?
> Do not forget me quite,
>   O Severn meadows.

What separates this 'Song' of his first volume from others very like it is Gurney's delicate sense of rhythm, which is very much a musical sense. (It comes off best when sung to Finzi's setting.) And the well-known 'To His Love' from *War's Embers* is perhaps equally to be distinguished by Gurney's dramatic-musical sense of how to pace a line and how to deploy enjambement:

> You would not know him now . . .
>   But still he died
> Nobly, so cover him over
>   With violets of pride
>   Purple from Severn side.
>
> Cover him, cover him soon!
>   And with thick-set

> Masses of memoried flowers –
> Hide that red wet
> Thing I must somehow forget.

This sense of musical form had undoubtedly been fostered during Gurney's time at the Royal College of Music, where he came under the influence of Vaughan Williams, and was bowled over by Williams's 'Fantasia on a Theme of Thomas Tallis'. The Elizabethan madrigalists and composers are, I think, behind most of what is best in these early poems. (Gurney may have learned about Tallis from Williams, but Byrd was his own discovery, as two late poems tell us.) But to break out of the conventions that, no matter how well he used them, limited him, Gurney needed something else. That he found it and that it freed him to become a major poet we can see from a poem called 'The Silent One'.

> Who died on the wires, and hung there, one of two –
> Who for his hours of life had chattered through
> Infinite lovely chatter of Bucks accent:
> Yet faced unbroken wires; stepped over, and went
> A noble fool, faithful to his stripes – and ended.
> But I weak, hungry, and willing only for the chance
> Of line – to fight in the line, lay down under unbroken
> Wires, and saw the flashes and kept unshaken,
> Till the politest voice – a finicking accent, said:
> 'Do you think you might crawl through there: there's a hole.'
> Darkness, shot at: I smiled, as politely replied –
> 'I'm afraid not, Sir.' There was no hole no way to be seen
> Nothing but chance of death, after tearing of clothes.
> Kept flat, and watched the darkness, hearing bullets whizzing –
> And thought of music – and swore deep heart's deep oaths
> (Polite to God) and retreated and came on again,
> Again retreated – and a second time faced the screen.

It is possible to overpraise this extraordinary piece of writing. Certainly it gives off an air of such casualness that we might at first think it to be a notebook jotting waiting to be worked up into a poem. Yet this is deceptive. True, the rhyming is intermittent, the syntax sometimes abruptly notational ('Darkness, shot at'), the punctuation apparently uncertain and heavily dependent on parenthesis or dash. But this is perhaps part of the poem's meaning. The experience it records can't be 'shaped' by conventional means. And after all it isn't *that* casual. Those many dashes, for example, introduce comic or brutal qualifications of statements in a manner that catches the absurd, terrifying contradictions of this moment of war. And although the 'finicking accent' seems to be asking a question, the absence of a question-mark makes it plain that under the politely voiced request an order is being given. So that Gurney's polite 'I'm afraid not, Sir', is a drily witty use of that same clipped, English manner. And the richly comic '(Polite to God)' depends for much of its effect on being placed at the beginning of a run-on line.

'The Silent One' is, in fact, an example of Gurney's anti-heroic, wry humour, which abounds in these poems, as for example in 'Of Grandcourt', where he rejects the chance to volunteer for the front line. ('Stars looked as well from second as from first line holes.') But the horror is also there, no matter how laconically or matter-of-factly voiced. In fact, the opening five lines of 'The Silent One' seem to me to engage, honestly, painfully, truthfully, all those contradictory feelings about war that are inevitable and yet suppressed from most war poetry. The shock opening line yields to that phrase 'hours of life', which both suggests its brevity and its being packed with 'chatter'. And if we think the word suggests triviality we are made to amend our thoughts by 'Infinite lovely chatter', where 'infinite' qualifies both 'lovely' and 'chatter'; and then *that* is qualified by the run-on shock of 'A noble fool', which is itself qualified by the calm certainty of 'stepped over', which is then qualified by 'faithful to his stripes'. (Should he have been faithless?). And then comes the final, blank, almost dismissive – 'and ended'.

'The Silent One' is a complex of feeling and responses, and its expression of these becomes possible because of the way Gurney has turned away from Georgian notions of poetic decorum. Although most of the lines can be read in terms of five stresses they are in no sense iambic pentameter. And the loosening of syntax and rhyme that goes with this loosening of rhythm enables Gurney to find a voice that can engage fully with the contradictions and complexities of his experience. There is no doubt that for this new freedom he owed a large debt to Walt Whitman.

Whitman had been in the air for some time. Swinburne admired him, and the Sheffield-based utopian socialist and homosexual Edward Carpenter had imitated him, especially in his long and, sadly, rather tedious poem, *Towards Democracy*. Gurney may have come to know about him through Vaughan Williams, whose 'Sea Symphony' incorporates some of Whitman's lines, but this cannot be known for sure and does not very much matter. What does is that

Whitman proved so liberating an experience for him. (Very much as he seems to have proved for D. H. Lawrence's poetry.) It is not that Whitman helped Gurney to sound un-English. It is rather that, by helping him to break away from the conventions of Georgian poetry in which he had been pinned, Whitman allowed Gurney to find his own, very English voice, one that would be free of the effete musicality and soft melancholy that disfigures all but the best work of de la Mare and Housman, and which is everywhere to be seen in the more minor figures, such as Harold Monro, Laurence Binyon, John Drinkwater, and others who figure largely in Edward Marsh's anthologies of *Georgian Poetry*. Whitman, we can say, allowed Gurney to voice concerns that must otherwise have stayed 'inexprest'.

Gurney's discovery of certain Elizabethan and Jacobean poets and dramatists, especially Ben Jonson and George Chapman, was equally liberating. His praise of Chapman sounds very like a description of his own verse: 'The football rush of him, and that country knowledge,/That pluck driving through work, endless that wearying courage,/Still unwearying.' By the time he was writing these lines Gurney was into a period of manic creativity, of long night walks, of hectic monologues delivered to understandably weary family and friends; and it would end with his being committed. But before that happened much had to be said. Indeed, it almost feels as though he knew that it couldn't go on and that he had therefore to set down all he could before the snow and much else besides would become 'inexprest'.

No doubt much of this feared impermanence had to do with his mental state. But I do not think we can easily dissociate it from Gurney's general fear – touched on or brooded over in different poems – that his England is coming to an end. The war, so it must feel, is not so much the cause of a final breach with the past as the definitive expression of that breach. And so 'Cotswold, my two thousand year home' has to be captured for poetry before it disappears from history. Even cloudscapes, therefore, have to be recorded: 'one's eyes rest looking to far Cotswold away/Under cloud ceilings whorled and most largely fashioned/With seventeenth-century curves of the tombstone way' ('Friendly are Meadows'). The clouds are familiarly and lovingly described in a manner that links them to the Cotswold churchyards of grey tombs and gravestones that Gurney knew well, both from his youth and his ceaseless walking through the countryside. It is an harmonious landscape,

'A slow gradual symphony of worthiness, fulfilledness.' And, as the description of the clouds implies, it is most intimately known.

This is partly a matter of how Gurney sees his area of England. In a terrible poem of his madness, 'What Evil Coil', he says that he 'cannot move to sight, whose bread is sight'. The extraordinary syntax of that first phrase, which has about it a physical immediacy quite different from anything that could come from 'being moved by a sight', tells us a great deal about the intensity of Gurney's relationship to his two thousand year home. It explains why, in what is almost a manifesto poem, 'The Escape', he should say that 'nor is anything done/Wiselier than the moving or breaking to sight/Of a thing hidden under by custom – revealed,/Fulfilled, used (sound-fashioned) any way out to delight'. You could imagine Wallace Stevens or William Carlos Williams giving assent to this, for this is surely Gurney saying that the poet – any man – must become an ignorant man again. But fulfilled? That, I think, goes well beyond their aesthetic of the innocent eye. For this implies a history: what is revealed to Gurney is not merely something that exists in space but in and through time.

Wherever you look in Gurney's poetry you find that his intimate, loving awareness of Gloucestershire is inextricably bound up with his sense of its history, and in this he is very different from Thomas. For as we have seen, the full meaning of history is always being somehow withheld from Thomas. He glimpses it, but no sooner has he done so than it is withdrawn. For Gurney, on the other hand, the landscape is a kind of palimpsest, in which a complex past can be made out.

> One comes across the strangest things in walks:
> Fragments of Abbey tithe-barns fixed in modern
> And Dutch-sort houses where the water baulks
> Weired up, and brick kilns broken among fern,
> Old troughs, great stone cisterns bishops might have blessed
> Ceremonially, and worthy mounting-stones . . .
>   and a manor's bones
> Spied in the frame of some wisteria'd house
> And mill-falls and sedge pools and Saxon faces;
> Stream-sources happened upon in unlikely places,
> And Roman-looking hills of small degree . . . ('Cotswold Ways')

The title is something of a pun. For if it implies roads and paths, it also implies habits and customs, especially those to do with work.

This is not merely a peopled landscape, it is one that can be scrutinized for the evidence it yields of ways in which successive generations have used the land and, more particularly, water, which is weired up, held in troughs, cisterns, or becomes a mill-fall. It is, in short, a landscape redeemed from the merely picturesque by evidence of work, and that evidence is everywhere. 'The Dearness of Common Things', as one poem is called, includes 'Woodaxes, blades, helves. . . . Wool, rope, cloth, old pipes/Gone warped in service.' A poem called, simply, 'Kilns' – and who else would have made a poem out of such a subject? – speaks of

> Farmhouse cottage, loved of generations of men,
> Fronting day as equal, or in dusk shining dim;
> Of the Dane-folk curious of the sticky worthy stuff . . .
> And the helping of fathers build well of the new brick . . .

'Kilns' is a celebration of brick-making, and of those who did the making. Work, in fact, is important for Gurney. Hence the wonderful 'Felling a Tree', which begins with him expressing his delight in 'The surge of spirit that goes with using an axe', becomes a comically exuberant description of his work, now clumsy, now getting it right, turns towards a doubt as to the rightness of what he is doing – is this making a breach in nature similar to that which took the trees from Whitcombe Steep? – and finally celebrates the sacramental relationship between tree-feller and the tree that 'for long had watched Wales glow strong,/Seen Severn and farm, and Brecon, Black Mountain times without reckon./And tomorrow would be fuel for the bright kitchen – for brown tea, against cold night'.

An even finer poem, 'The Lock-Keeper', studies with rapt attention the man at various tasks:

> You might see him at morning by the lock-gates,
> Or busy in the warehouse on a multitude
> Of boat fittings, net fittings; copper, iron, wood,
> Then later digging, furious, electric
> Under the apple boughs, with a short stick,
> Burnt black long ages, of pipe between set teeth,
> His eyes gone flaming on the work beneath –

'The Lock Keeper' may seem to be like Gurney's 'Lob' or Hobden the Hedger. And in a sense he is. For he, too, is a keeper of the country's secrets, and he seems to contain within himself a history of place and imply a continuity. He had, Gurney tells us, 'Wisdom of every various season or light' and 'There was nothing he did not know; there was nothing, nothing.' Yet there is a difference, I think. Gurney says of the lock-keeper that he had 'A net of craft of eye, heart, kenning, and hand'. It seems to me that the pun of kenning/cunning is meant to create a homology. Gurney's 'archetypal' Englishman, although he never speaks, is implicitly given a manner of speech that is even more complex and at the same time more local than Lob or Hobden. For Gurney wants to draw into his poetry the fact of Roman and Danish settlements and of their effect on his two thousand years' home. Hence the 'Roman-looking hills' of 'Cotswold Ways', hence the repeated mentions of Dane and Saxon; hence, too, the poem, 'The Bare Line of the Hill', which begins

> The bare line of the hill
> Shows Roman and
> A sense of Rome hangs still
> Over the land

and which ends

> The regal and austere
> Mantle of Rome is thrown
>
> As of old – about the walls
> Of hills and the farm – the fields.
> Scabious guards the steeps,
> Trefoil the slopes yield.

Housman's Uricon lies firmly buried. Gurney's sense of the Roman is alive, not simply in the apprehension of how the landscape has been shaped by 'that old power', but in the names of the flowers. 'Scabious' is the original Latin; 'trefoil' is the Anglo-Saxon version of the Latin *trifolium*.

It is this deep-rooted, familiar knowledge of how much of his inheritance has been shaped by, for example, Roman and Dane, that explains Gurney's eclectic-seeming language. Not for him the Anglo-Saxonries of William Barnes or of the 1890s. I think of the subdued kennings he introduces into poems, as when he speaks of a 'clutch-frost', or calls the sun 'fire-swinger', and of how they will help to explain why he says of his lock-keeper that he has a 'craft of kenning'. What Gurney is after is not merely a deeply committed recording of his particular area of England but a language that will embody his awareness of its past and possible extension into the

present. Latin words, Nordic kennings, Elizabethan locutions: these
are all likely to appear in the poems, as though Gurney is the conduit
through which a much-ravelled language flows down to the
twentieth century.

This sometimes leads to rather odd conclusions. In 'By Severn',
Gurney says that 'If England, her spirit lives anywhere/It is by
Severn', which is perhaps taking local piety too far, although he
adds:

> If for the drab atmospheres and managed lighting
> In London town, Oriana's playwrights had
> Wainlode her theatre and then coppice-clad
> Hill for her ground of sauntering and idle waiting,
> Why, then I think, our chiefest glory of pride
> (The Elizabethans of Thames, south and northern side)
> Would nothing of its meeding be denied,
> And her sons' praises from England's mouth again be outcried.

It is obviously forcing matters to try to locate the heart of England in
one particular place, for if the vision is to be at all persuasive it must
be elusive; here, there and everywhere. Nevertheless, Gurney's poem
has this much to recommend it: that he can make mention of an
actual hill, 'Wainlode', with the reverberations its name summons
up, and that he can dare to use a word such as 'meeding'. Besides, the
uncoiling rhythms of these flexible lines suggest a man able to think
generously and expansively, and to retain a kind of amplitude of
response to the thoughts that engage him.

This cannot have been easy. More than any other poet of his
generation Gurney seems to me to have had the sense that the
continuities he evoked or wished to take for granted were under
immediate threat, or had been wiped out. This occasionally leads to
the merely peevish, as in his protests over 'bungalow culture'. (In, for
example, 'Changes' and 'The Bargain'.) More deeply the war clearly
presented itself to him as a very real disaster, and not for merely
personal reasons. His single-handed attempt to create a poetic
medium, through words and rhythms, that will be rich enough to
carry the burden of history is therefore extraordinarily impressive.
For what Gurney is surely trying to do is to free the language – *his*
language – from the orthodoxies that are evident in most Edwardian
and Georgian poetry and, whether he knew it or not, in most of the
poetry of the Great War. Gurney does not share such orthodoxies
any more than he shares an official 'vision' of England, of the kind I

have been attempting to analyse over these past two chapters. Instead, his pieties are local, as Clare's and Hardy's before him were. Indeed, he rarely speaks of 'England' and when he does, as in 'By Severn', he is obviously sceptical of the likely success of its being realized through the means customarily employed by those poets I have been previously engaged with.

And this leads to a further, all-important point. At its best and most typical, Gurney's passionate identification with his area of England and with voices that will serve it is not only unofficial, it is subversive. 'I'm afraid not, Sir.' This is the voice of a man who will resist the coercive claims of 'decency' and who uses irony as a way of keeping clear of commitments that can only make him 'English' in a way that captures him, denies him his own identity. It is not a compliant voice. Far from it. We have met this voice before, in the poetry of Clare. We shall meet it again, although saying different things and in different ways, in the poetry of W. H. Auden.

Further reading

There is a vast literature about the Great War. Perhaps the most lucid introductory guide is that by A. J. P. Taylor, although Arthur Marwick's *The Deluge* is also to be recommended. Paul Fussell's *The Great War and Modern Memory* is a seminal work on the writers and much else besides; and there are more restricted studies of the poets by Bernard Bergonzi (*Heroes' Twilight*) and Jon Silkin (*The Poetry of the First World War*). Wilfred Owen's *Collected Poems* are published by Oxford, edited by Jon Stallworthy. Oxford also publish *The Collected Poems of Edward Thomas*, edited by R. George Thomas, and *Ivor Gurney*, edited by P. J. Kavanagh. Isaac Rosenberg's *Collected Poems* are published by Chatto and Windus. Of the many anthologies of poetry of the Great War the most contentious is probably Silkin's, the most helpful Maurice Hussey's. D. J. Enright's essay on Owen and Sassoon may be found in Volume 7 of the Penguin *History of English Literature*. For an account of and criticism of Sassoon's autobiographies, see my essay in *Moderns and Contemporaries*, 1985.

- 5 -

W. B. Yeats:
The Responsibilities of the Poet

In his fine poem 'MCMXIV', which looks back to the outbreak of the Great War, Philip Larkin notes how, with its declaration, an innocent world 'Changed itself to past without a word'. Edwardian and Georgian England had never been 'innocent', of course. But Larkin's point is that the war opened up a huge, unbridgeable gap between Then and Now. And it is undoubtedly true that those soldiers who went blithely to war and who survived until November 1918 were tempted to look back to pre-war England as a lost paradise. Some of them were poets. Not many, because as we have seen, Owen, Rosenberg and Thomas were all dead by the time the war came to its end. Of those who survived, two in particular deserve to be mentioned.

Edmund Blunden, whose *Undertones of War* (1928) is deservedly regarded as one of the finest memoirs to have come out of those dreadful years, has sometimes been linked to the Georgian movement in poetry. There is some justification for this. In many ways Blunden is a pastoral poet and his chosen verse forms rarely break with the conventions that other Georgian poets worked in, contentedly enough it would seem. Yet Blunden has strengths that set him apart from such poets as Harold Monro, John Drinkwater and Brooke. In addition, he had to endure the experience of war itself, and this forms the subject-matter, overt or implied, of a great deal of his poetry. Although Blunden is a pastoral poet, the horrors of his years in France are never far away from his mind.

For Blunden, war is a terrible breach in nature, or in his expectations of the natural, good life. It is a characteristic effect of his poetry to apparently focus steadily on a natural scene and then gradually reveal that this is a landscape of memory, unavailable to him in the present, or that its features are invaded by the appalling actualities that war has exposed him to. Unlike Owen and Sassoon or Rosenberg, however, Blunden does not try to find a language adequate to these actualities. On the contrary, he maintains a level tone and a repertoire of pastoral images that eloquently imply the inability of language to cope with his experiences of war. In 'Death of Childhood Beliefs' he writes about an earlier, innocent self, and ways in which he came to discard outworn superstitions and credulities. Then comes the following stanza:

> Drummers jumping from the tombs
>   Banged and thumped all through the town,
> Past shut shops and silent rooms
>   While the flaming spires fell down; –
> Now but dreary thunder booms.

It takes a minute or two before you realize that these drummers are not simply part of a child's nightmare or bible-induced vision of apocalypse. This is the war. The drummers are artillery men and that extraordinary line 'While the flaming spires fell down' records with the flat inevitability of a children's tale what was actually happening in the French countryside.

Or take the example of 'Rural Economy'. Here, Blunden writes about a farmed landscape that looks odd because 'There was winter in these woods,/And still it was July'.

> In sight, life's farms sent forth their gear,
>   Here rakes and ploughs lay still,
> Yet, save some curious clods, all here
>   Was raked and ploughed with a will.
> The sower was a ploughman too,
> And iron seeds broadcast he threw.

Leave aside the weakness of 'life's farms' – a very Georgian locution – and what we have here seems to me deeply impressive. Blunden turns to good effect the clichés about gunfire that rakes and shells that plough. Are the curious clods the bodies of dead soldiers? I do not know, but I think it probable, and the phrase chills because of its level quizzicality, its air of slightly detached, almost puzzled innocence. (This tone is very close to that employed by the American poet, Louis Simpson, when he writes his marvellous poems about young American soldiers in France during the Second World War, a world away from what they knew and trying to accommodate their experiences to a familiar language and knowledge.)

This tone seems to be part of an overall strategy that Blunden desperately needed. It was a way of staying sane, and you feel that at any moment it may crack wide open, like the ice in what is perhaps his most famous poem, 'The Midnight Skaters', where he imagines death at watch 'within those secret waters'.

> Then on, blood shouts, on, on,
> Twirl, wheel and whip above him,
> Dance on this ball-floor thin and wan,
> Use him as though you love him;
> Court him, elude him, reel and pass,
> And let him hate you through the glass.

Just how deeply Blunden needed that tone, and needed also the tight stanza forms he customarily used, is clear from the occasions he tried other methods, for example the blank verse of 'The Still Hour'. What we have in this poem is a long, loosely connected series of reveries about childhood images and voices which slowly blend into the sounds of voices in Flanders, of 'ridges battered into chaos/Whence one deep moaning, one deep moaning came'. Nobody would wish to deny the intense horror of the experiences Blunden is trying to focus on here, but the fact is that, lacking metrical shapeliness and the carefully controlled level voice that he uses so well in the poems to which I have drawn attention – and there are others – 'The Still Hour' lapses into prosaic slackness.

That is not a charge you could think of bringing against Edgell Rickword. Like Blunden, Rickword managed to survive the war – although at the cost of serious injuries to his eyes and lungs – and he wrote a number of tense, bitter poems about his experiences on the Western Front. They were included in a volume published in 1921, *Behind the Eyes*. Rickword's tone is very different from Blunden's: it is sharper, more sardonic, more knowing. But like Blunden he keeps it under tight control, and the tightness owes much to his technical grasp of rhyme and metre. Rickword is in fact a very suave technician, as you can see from 'I Knew A Man' or 'Winter Warfare', which ingeniously imagines how

> Colonel Cold strode up the line
> (tabs of rime and spurs of ice):
> stiffened all that met his glare:
> horses, men and lice.

The world of winter, the world of war: they interpenetrate each other, seize each other's language, between them usurp all that's knowable.

Rickword also differs from Blunden in that where Blunden is self-consciously indebted to a very native tradition of English poetry, although a surprisingly eclectic one (Shelley as well as Hardy), Rickword is altogether more aware of new developments. He was an intense admirer of Donne and he also took a great deal from the French symbolists and poets of the decadence. These influences come together in *Invocation to Angels*, the volume he published in 1928, and which contains his finest work. Some of these poems are elegantly tart and/or sensuous love poems (as for example 'Intimacy', 'Beyond Good and Evil', 'Obsession', 'Chronique Scandaleuse', 'Necropolis') which, while they owe something to Baudelaire, never fall into mere pastiche. But there are also a number of poems which record or evoke a taut disgust with the cultural and social goings-on of post-war England, and in this too Rickword is very different from Blunden, who either would or could not bring himself to confront or comment on the events of the 1920s.

In 'Luxury' Rickword writes:

> The churches' sun-dried clay crumbles at last,
> the courts of Justice wither like a stink,
> and honourable statues melt as fast
> as greasy garbage down a kitchen sink.

The nearly bland equilibrium of these lines prevents them from being merely a tapping of the poison of cynicism and hatred. Nevertheless, hatred is never far away from these poems and it does much to explain why, after Rickword had finished as a poet, he turned to politics and became a member of the Communist Party.

It may also explain why he has been, as I think, puzzlingly and improperly neglected as a poet, even though tribute is correctly paid to his editorship during the 1920s of *The Calendar of Modern Letters*. It is easy enough to write him off as a poet who abandoned his own talent for the unrewarding life of a party hack. It is also very unfair. Rickword had finished as a poet before he took up politics, and it will not do to argue that his political convictions destroyed his talent as a poet.

But there is another reason why his reputation has suffered. For if he was alert to much of the nastiness of post-war England, a nastiness recorded and inadvertently revealed, for example, in Evelyn Waugh's diaries,[1] he only belatedly began to show it in his poetry, and by then other, more powerful voices had made themselves heard. Besides, Rickword's marxist reading of history hardly gets into his poetry, whereas it is a feature of the major poetry of the 1920s that it offers different and differently persuasive readings of history or, to be more exact, of how to account for the disasters that have overtaken Europe.

For a number of reasons that poetry was not written by English poets. How could it have been? So many who might have produced it were dead. Of those left alive, Robert Graves, whose war poetry is slight and unimportant, wrote *Goodbye to All That* and left England (there will however be more to say about him in a later chapter); Blunden does not seem to have been interested in historical questions beyond a 'then' and 'now'; and as we have already seen, for Gurney history is change is catastrophe, as, for example, in 'The Bargain'.

> Waltheof's field will become a rubbish heap.
> Villas will stand there and look polite; with folk polite
> Where sedges stood for the wind's play and poet-delight,
> But Severn will be sorry and it can never be right.

There is a good deal of criticism of what might be called 'villa culture' in Edwardian England. (Forster provides something of a counter-attack in *A Room With a View*.) But the sense of England becoming a waste tip for the detritus of a culture turns into a cliché of the 1920s.

The best English poets of the early years of the twentieth century did not see England in these terms. But as I have suggested, both Thomas and Gurney deeply feared that they were living at the end of . . . well, of a culture, a civilization. They are too tactful to use the words, but the muffled apprehensions nevertheless amount to saying as much. It is an apprehension shared by a greater poet than either, W. B. Yeats, to whom I must now turn. Before I do so, though, I need to draw attention to what may well look to be a gap in my account of English poetry in the 1920s. What of women poets? The question needs to be raised, for two reasons. First, the poets killed in the war were of course men, so that it might be thought that there was a vacuum into which women poets could rush. Secondly, before, during and after the war, women's movements and pressures had been the product of and further encouraged the raising of women's consciousness to an extent that it would seem reasonable to suppose might emerge in poetry as well as prose. During the war period women had worked beside men, often in jobs that had previously been classified – or thought of – as exclusively male, they had gone as VADs to the war front, had protested against the war, had in various ways discovered a new confidence and a range of experiences out of which a poetry of some significance might have come.

For reasons I can only guess at, this did not happen. The anti-war poetry of such poets as Vera Brittain or Eleanor Farjeon seems to me no better than the stuff of Jessie Pope. As for the women poets who began to write or to gain recognition during the 1920s – Elizabeth Daryush, Ruth Pitter, Anna Wickham and, above all, Sylvia Townsend Warner – their work feels limited in both scope and form; and with the exception of the last-named they have little purchase on social or political issues. Not only this: what they *do* write about is in so half-hearted a manner that I am left with the strong feeling that they doubted their right to be poets. If you try to compare their work with that of Marianne Moore or Elizabeth Bishop, for example, you see how great a gap there is between the English poets and their great American counterparts. I suspect that the poets I have named, as well as others who appear in contemporary anthologies, lacked a confident sense of a keen, critical audience. They therefore exemplify in its most extreme form a danger that their male counterparts were also exposed to: of not expecting to be taken seriously and therefore of not being sure how seriously they should take themselves. For the kind of flutings that passed for critical comment in the journals and newspapers of the time (and which were so savaged by Rickword in the *Calendar of Modern Letters*) do not amount to a proper critical reaction. Moreover, I think it virtually certain that English poets of the 1920s, male and female alike, had no sense of a kind of constituency they could test themselves against. The contrast with Yeats is deeply instructive.

II

The main outlines of Yeats's development as a poet can be quickly sketched in. He was born in 1865, grew up in an artistic household, was as he himself said 'intensely religious', and grew to hate the scientific positivism that dominated contemporary thought. He also hated most contemporary art and its naturalistic concern with the drab actualities of life. His own early poetry owes a good deal to Rossetti and is a poetry of dream and reverie, of murmured incantations. It is a poetry meant to be overheard, and in subject matter and cadence deliberately turns away from the dailiness of things. Yeats reaches the perfection of this mode in a volume called *The Wind Among the Reeds* (1899), and most commentators, including myself, think that if he had died then he would be remembered as a minor poet of charm and skill, and very much a part of the *fin-de-siècle*: of the Rhymers' Club, the *Yellow Book*, as one of those poets like Ernest Dowson and Lionel Johnson who lived and died for the perfection of an art they knew could never make them popular, since England was the country of the philistines, of Ruskin's attack on Whistler, of the trial of Oscar Wilde. Yeats writes about this in that section of his *Autobiographies* called 'the Tragic Generation'.

Four people helped to lift him out of the limitations of this view of art as disciplined retreat. A little should be said about each of them because they were much involved in the process whereby Yeats became a great poet. This is not of course to say that they determined or shaped his development. He did those things. It is, however, to say that without them he would have found it that much more difficult to come to think creatively about and to confront those large issues – social, political, cultural – where he speaks, not with the authority, but with the open candour of a great public poet. Poetry for Yeats becomes a crucial act of intervention in Irish affairs, it is a means towards declaring, and an offered example of, Irish consciousness. And to say this is to make plain how greatly he differs from twentieth-century English poets, in scale, ambition, responsibility. But to understand how exactly this comes to be means saying something about these four important friends.

The first was John O'Leary, whom Yeats met in 1885. O'Leary was an Irish patriot who had suffered for the cause and yet who insisted that there were some things a man must not do to save his nation. One of them was to write bad propaganda or nationalistic verse. It was O'Leary more than anyone who began to shape Yeats's thoughts about Ireland, about the need to achieve freedom, about the need for a distinctive and proud Irish culture, and about the kind of nation that would result from and sustain such culture. By the 1890s Yeats was developing his 'Celtic twilight' visions of an Irish society composed of a peasantry and gentry bound together by common virtues and interests.

Four years after his first meeting with John O'Leary Yeats was introduced to Maud Gonne. She was the kind of patriot O'Leary had warned Yeats against, all uncompromising fervour. She was also beautiful. Yeats fell in love with her, suffered for his love which was not returned, and out of his unhappiness made a number of great poems.

As he developed a theory of history, so Yeats came to regard Maud Gonne as a type of destructive beauty, a Helen created by the pressures of the historical moment in which she lives, destroying her own complete perfection in the interest of an abstract cause – for he seems never to have believed that Maud fully understood her own vision of Ireland – and causing great unhappiness to others. (Which by and large means himself.) Once Yeats had fashioned his own vision of the 'good' Ireland, he never much altered it, although he certainly came to change his mind about how it could be realized. The 'natural' bonding of peasantry and gentry is, of course, a Ruskinian piece of medievalizing and even in Ireland – a land of much peasantry and a (largely imposed) gentry – it looks like a piece of myth-making. The myth included a role for women. They should 'labour to be beautiful', Yeats has one woman say in 'Adam's Curse', and although such beauty may mean social grace or fullness of being, it can also come close to reflecting a male prejudice in favour of women holding their tongues and letting themselves be loved. Certainly, Yeats never wavered in his hatred of women's involvement in radical politics. (And of course it could only be in radical politics that women chose to be the equal of men.) Years after his meeting with Maud Gonne, when he came to write his elegy for Eva Gore-Booth and Con Markiewicz, Yeats spoke of Eva's involvement in working-class politics in Manchester:

> I know not what the younger dreams –
> Some vague Utopia – and she seems,
> When withered old and skeleton-gaunt,
> An image of such politics.

But we must all grow old and die. These lines would be hateful if it were not for the saving stress on 'seems' which leaves the way open for a different view of her life. It is not, however, a view that the poem encourages. Yeats is sure that the lives of the sisters have been wrecked by their involvement in political matters. But history may be to blame. 'The light of evening, Lissadell', the poem begins; and such light shining on the country house is surely symbolic of the end of an era? When, later in the poem, Yeats addresses the girls directly, he tells them that 'The innocent and the beautiful/Have no enemy but time'. And there again his reading of history leads him to view the sisters as victims of the historical moment.

In developing this reading of history, in which cycles of civilization succeed each other on a two-thousand-year pattern, and in which one type passes into its anti-type, Yeats had been helped by his friendship with Arthur Symons. For it was Symons who introduced Yeats to the French symbolists (Symons in fact wrote an important study of the movement, which he dedicated to Yeats); and Yeats's discovery of the symbolists' work matters for two reasons. First, it sharpened and perhaps even shaped his conviction that the artist of his time must choose 'perfection of the life or of the work'. That is to say, Yeats saw the symbolists as possessing a dedication to their art which was in haughty defiance of a society they knew would never understand or care for them. Living at the fag-end of (English) civilization meant that the gap between the dreaming artist and the objective world of casual or outer lives was unbridgeably wide. Out of this was to come Yeats's sense of responsibility to his art which would be placed at the service of his vision of the ideal Irish society, where no such gap would exist. Secondly, symbolism implied a 'reading' or understanding of the world in ways that could not be defeated by the rationalism of positivistic science. For a symbolist ideally discovers deep truths underlying the casual phenomena of the everyday world. Yeats became passionately interested in the work of Shelley and Blake, two great systematizers; and with the help of A. E. Ellis he produced an edition of Blake's poems which offers an interpretation of their underlying meanings.

'Underlying' is the key word. As a religious man, Yeats needed a 'systematic' interpretation of history, one that made purposive sense. That is why he joined the Order of the Golden Dawn, became a freemason, and chose to read historical events and just about everything else besides as part of a great pattern. In *All Religions Are One*, Blake had said that 'The Religions of all Nations are derived from each Nation's different reception of the Poetic Genius, which is everywhere call'd the Spirit of Prophecy'. This is very close to Yeats's view of the matter. For him, all truths are stored in *Spiritus Mundi*, the mind of the world, and they are transmitted as various signs and symbols which the adepts of each nation must decipher so as to fit them into an overall pattern. The connections between this and the late-nineteenth-century interest in comparative religion and anthropology are clear enough.

Finally, there is Lady Gregory. Yeats met this formidable woman during the 1890s. Conor Cruise O'Brien has said that Yeats started the Irish literary renaissance in 1893 (spurred by O'Leary's ideals), and that 'Lady Gregory got in on the ground floor in 1894, with Yeats's encouragement, and she remained an acknowledged and conspicuous part of it from then on'. Yeats, he adds, 'loved to celebrate this in verse and prose'. This is undoubtedly correct, but Yeats seems to have needed Lady Gregory as much as she needed him. Which may be no more than to say that theirs was a marriage of true minds, and certainly their friendship was a very remarkable one. In the first place, her interest in collecting folk-song helped Yeats to focus his concern for a 'rooted' literature and language. There is nothing faddish about Lady Gregory's work, if only because in Ireland there was a great, largely untapped literature waiting to be brought up; and obviously such a literature would be of immeasurable benefit in defining a national culture. When he wrote his elegy for Lady Gregory's son, Robert, who was killed in action in the Great War, Yeats said:

> We dreamed that a great painter had been born
> To cold Clare rock and Galway rock and thorn,
> To that stern colour and that delicate line
> That are our secret discipline,
> In which the gazing heart doubles her might.

Some commentators have taken this as a reference to the kinds of visionary landscape paintings that Yeats was certainly interested in, helping to explain his admiration for Blake's followers, Calvert and Palmer. But 'secret discipline' does not refer to this kind of pre-symbolist art. Yeats is saying that art of true worth must be rooted in place. Thus Gregory's art was rooted in the intimately known landscapes of Counties Clare and Galway, whose colour and line impose a discipline on the attentive artist. Similarly, in 'The Municipal Gallery Revisited', Yeats writes:

> John Synge, I and Augusta Gregory, thought
> All that we did, all that we said or sang
> Must come from contact with the soil, from that
> Contact everything Antaeus-like grew strong.

Yeats's concern for 'rootedness' owes a great deal to his meeting with Lady Gregory.

So, too, does his concern with the Irish theatre. Although it is not possible here to discuss in detail the importance of the Abbey Theatre in Yeats's life, this much at least needs to be said: that his meeting with Lady Gregory was crucial in making Yeats turn towards realizing a dream that Ireland should have its own drama. To quote O'Brien again, Lady Gregory's 'strong and supple adaptation of the speech of Irish country folk – Kiltartan – became the liturgical language of the Abbey Theatre, Dublin'. With money from Annie Horniman, Yeats and Lady Gregory founded and wrote for the Abbey Theatre, and encouraged work from other Irish writers. Hence, of course, John Synge's involvement. It was Synge's writing about the Aran islanders and above all his great play *The Playboy of the Western World* which both confirmed Yeats in his belief that Irish drama was a huge force in the renaissance of Irish culture, and convinced him that the ideal Ireland must be that of the gentry and peasantry. For when the play was first staged there were riots at the Abbey. The *Playboy* was supposed to be a slur on the Irish and especially on Irish womanhood. Middle-class philistinism and hysterical nationalism opposed the true vision of great art.

It is perhaps not surprising that in view of these difficulties at the Abbey, Yeats should come to write of his weariness over 'Theatre business, management of men'. Yet his involvement with it undoubtedly had much to do with the change of style that becomes so marked a feature of his poetry in the first decades of the twentieth century. For now his poetry turns to face an audience. His rhythms become springier, tougher, more colloquial, and his diction becomes at its best an extraordinarily adroit blend of eloquence and matter-of-factness. You can see how he manages this new language in 'The Fascination of What's Difficult'.

> The fascination of what's difficult
> Has dried the sap out of my veins, and rent
> Spontaneous joy and natural content
> Out of my heart.

This language, packed with verbs, almost Drydenic in its public manner, is very different from the languorous, hushed tones of the earlier poetry. (It was from the vantage point of this hammered style that Yeats began to re-write the earlier work and so 're-make' himself.)[2]

Yeats's involvement with the Abbey, frustrating and time-consuming though it was, increased his sense of responsibility towards the fashioning of an Irish culture fit for the emergent national consciousness. And out of this comes the volume of 1914, called significantly enough *Responsibilities*. Although Yeats may have had lodged somewhere at the back of his mind the fact that in 1911 Maud Gonne had published an article in the *Irish Review* on the need for school canteens and had called her article 'Responsibility', this is not of great significance; his own title is far more than a riposte to the world of practical politics, as we can see from the volume's two epigraphs, both of which may be taken to be Yeats's own work. 'In dreams begins responsibility', runs one, and the other 'How am I fallen from myself, for a long time now I have not seen the Prince of Chang in my dreams.' (Yeats attributes this to 'Khoung-Fou-Tseu'.) Both epigraphs speak of the need to take responsibility for dreams: of Ireland, of Irish culture, and of love and friendship as images of human attainment. *Responsibilities* deals with all these dreams, and it does so in poems whose great technical variety denotes a further responsibility: of the poet to the craft of verse making. The volume is a kind of masterwork or *meisterstück*, in the sense that it self-consciously sets out to demonstrate its author's skills as a craftsman, and undoubtedly succeeds in so doing. You cannot read through *Responsibilities* without recognizing, and feeling humbled by, its extraordinary prowess. Yeats's responsibility to the task of making poetry is fully attested to. He has been loyal to those poets of his early days whom he speaks for in the opening poems of the volume and whom he praises because, for all their failings, they 'never made a poorer song/That [they] might have a heavier purse,/Nor gave loud service to a cause/That [they] might have a troop of friends.'

And it is here that we come to the crux of the matter. For Yeats is radically different from nearly all English poets of the twentieth century, simply because they lack his complex sense of responsibility. You cannot hope to be fully responsible to your art unless you know – or at least take into consideration – what art is for. For Yeats, poetry serves the profoundly critical and creative purpose of being both for and about a nation's culture. It is an intervention in the history of that culture, meant to contribute to it in crucial ways, to testify to its vitality, to modify the stance of others, to engage in what is seen as a living process. But if you live at what you conceive to be the end of a culture – and that is what the sense of being at the end of a tradition amounts to – you can have no such energy of purpose. The best English poets we have considered so far – Hardy, Thomas and Gurney – consider that they are at the end of the line. Their sense of the past includes a sense of its absolute uncoupling from the future. Whether they are correct is not my concern. Their conviction is. Their best poetry comes out of a last, desperate, deeply rooted wish to testify to the worth of what they are convinced is about to disappear. It is possible to say that there is nothing new in this, that it is in fact a strategy that had been employed by poets so otherwise different from each other as Pope and Wordsworth. But the difference is this: that none of these later poets has any sense of a fit audience, be it ever so few, to whom they can address their work, so that their producing poetry of worth is a triumph against the odds which they feel to be stacked against them. Pope had his circle, Wordsworth had his. But Hardy, Thomas and Gurney feel themselves to be living out on the end of an event. You may, if you like, argue that their sense of an ending is properly to be seen in terms of the end of particular class formations or of the role of the déraciné poet in an increasingly complex society; or you may say that all three of them are victims of the historical process which they lack the terms (or will) to understand. There is truth in all these contentions. But the fact remains that whatever the cause or the explanation, you come face to face with the inescapable truth that the best English poets during the period so far covered in this book cannot feel themselves responsible to the kinds of large social issues that engage Yeats.

And if you turn to the more minor poets you are faced with still more instructive matter. For what you then find is a creation of a 'seamless' past whose present 'health' is offered in terms that reveal the absurdity of the whole enterprise, and in a language which is so dead as certainly to imply the entire death of a culture. Thus, while Yeats was discovering how to incorporate Irish idiom – words, phrases and rhythms – into his poetry, Robert Bridges, who became Poet Laureate in 1913, in that same year accepted the presidency of the Society for Pure English, which for all its claims not to interfere in 'living developments' typified the kind of cultural appropriation of the language which spells death to a would-be living literature. Bridges' first poem as Laureate appeared in *The Times* on Christmas Eve, 1913:

> Now blessed be the tow'rs
>   that crown England so fair
> That stand up strong in prayer
>   unto God for our souls:
> Blessed be their founders
>   (said I) an' our country folk
> Who are ringing for Christ
>   in the belfries to night . . .

There, yet again, in 'pure English' – that is, a language drained of any vitality – is the dreary, ridiculous pretence that England is a collection of rural communities, bonded together in Anglican accord. What kind of responsibility is this? To whom? Certainly not to the 'country folk' themselves, who would, of course, never read *The Times*. Nor to the language and nor, therefore, to the larger responsibilities of poetry, to a living culture.

Consider, by contrast, a clutch of poems which are included in *Responsibilities*, and which between them make up a statement about Ireland and Irish politics in 1912–13: 'To A Wealthy Man', 'September 1913', 'To a Friend Whose Work Has Come to Nothing', 'Paudeen' and 'To A Shade'. Since they are grouped together in a manner that's intended to reinforce their meanings we need to provide a little in the way of context for them. In her commendable study, *Yeats, Ireland and Fascism*, Elizabeth Cullingford shows how bitterly frustrated Yeats became over certain happenings during that year. In the first place there was the fiasco of the proposed Dublin Gallery of Modern Art. Hugh Lane, a picture dealer of taste with a large and valuable private collection of French paintings, offered it to the city on condition that a gallery be built to house it. In January 1913 the Municipal Council agreed to put up £22,000 if the public would donate the rest. Yeats wrote 'To A Wealthy Man' – initially called 'The Gift' – and published it in the *Irish Times* on 8 January. His attack on 'Paudeen', on all those who would not give money because they lived by prudential values, was answered by William Martin Murphy, a rich businessman who owned the *Evening Herald* and *Irish Independent*. Murphy was supported by Arthur Griffith, whose extreme nationalism led him to attack the plans for the Gallery (*a*) because Dublin couldn't afford it and (*b*) because the proposed architect, Edwin Lutyens, was English. Following on this came the Dublin Lock-Out, when James Larkin tried to unionize Murphy's Dublin United Tramway Company and 'Murphy retaliated by sacking anyone who joined'. What happened next was certainly extremely squalid.

> Philanthropists contrived a scheme to send workers' starving children to temporary fosterage in England. The project was condemned by the Archbishop of Dublin as likely to damage the children's faith. A cynical observer might have have concluded that the Archbishop was less worried about infidelity than insubordination: if the children were fed the workers could hold out longer. The Dublin clergy, zealous of the children's souls though careless of their bodies, encouraged the mob to prevent

their departure. A Catholic middle-class backlash took place and the police allowed rioters to besiege railway stations and ports.[3]

Cullingford has no trouble in showing that Yeats behaved impeccably in all this, and the great letter he wrote to the *Irish Worker*, attacking the corruption of the police and hypocrisy of the clergy, certainly calls into question Conor Cruise O'Brien's claim that he was for most of his life a fascist. (It also makes for a vivid contrast with the kind of poem which Bridges was sending *The Times*.) These twin matters will explain the rhetorical anger of 'Paudeen', 'To A Friend' and, more importantly, 'To A Shade', where Yeats speaks about Lane's frustrations to the ghost of Parnell: 'Your enemy, an old foul mouth, had set/The pack upon him.' The cant that had destroyed Parnell is now working to destroy Lane and to prevent the realization of a culturally enlightened – 'sweet' – Ireland.

It is this ability to intervene in current, critical issues which makes Yeats's poetry so different from and more valuable than contemporary English poetry. To say this is by no means to endorse all his positions. In what follows I shall offer reservations against some of his stances and I am even more critical of others. But this is possible – even necessary – just because Yeats's poetry occupies public space, as it were. This means that although much of it springs from deeply held or long-pondered convictions, it can come into being as a way of writing to the moment: it is occasional in the sense that a particular event requires Yeats to comment, and the comment is tested by and puts to the test the values, certainties, commitments, that he has fashioned out of his developing sense of responsibilities. Given this it is inevitable that Yeats is vulnerable to the charge of 'getting it wrong' or of 'misunderstanding'; or of an improper certainty. But this is what being his kind of poet necessarily entails. Yeats both takes away from poetry its Arnoldian 'infallibility' and at the same time gives it a centrality which Arnold's way of thinking about the poet and poetry could never achieve. These comments bear particularly on the poems I am here considering.

According to Cullingford, Yeats thought that 'the great man is genuinely the servant of his people, although he alone determines the form his service will take. For Nietzsche the "noble" man has rights but no obligations: for Yeats rights entail duties.' Perhaps, but what I find in 'To A Wealthy Man' is a rancorous contempt, even hatred, that cannot be fully explained or justified by the events of 1912/13. The events become somehow displaced by Yeats's determination to compare Lane with great Italian Renaissance princes:

> What cared Duke Ercole, that bid
> His mummers to the market-place,
> What th'onion-sellers thought or did
> So that his Plautus set the pace
> For the Italian comedies?
> And Guidobaldo, when he made
> That grammar school of courtesies
> Where wit and beauty learned their trade
> Upon Urbino's windy hill,
> Had sent no runners to and fro
> That he might learn the shepherds' will.

It would be absurd to deny the panache of these lines. If you except Tennyson's lovely, late poem to Edward FitzGerald you have to go back to Marvell before you will find the tetrameter better handled. Yet this panache comes near to, and occasionally topples into, posture. It is the posture of a snobbish ranter. 'Onion-sellers', 'shepherds'; aren't they the equivalent of that peasantry which Yeats is usually so keen to invoke as integral to his dream of an Ireland united in politics as well as culture?

There is an analogous problem about 'September 1913'. Here, Yeats's contempt for the prudential values of those who oppose him – Murphy and his ilk – leads him to contrast contemporary Ireland with a past rich with heroes whose 'wasteful virtues' brought each of them a martyr's death.

> Was it for this the wild geese spread
> The grey wing upon every tide;
> For this that all that blood was shed,
> For this Edward Fitzgerald died,
> And Robert Emmet and Wolfe Tone,
> All that delirium of the brave?
> Romantic Ireland's dead and gone,
> It's with O'Leary in the grave.

It is difficult to read these lines without thinking that Yeats is recommending the blood sacrifice which had famously been at the heart of his play *Cathleen ni Houlihan*, set in 1798, the year of the uprising in which both Fitzgerald and Wolfe Tone died. When the play was performed at the Abbey in 1902 Cathleen, the spirit of Ireland, was played by Maud Gonne, and at one key moment in the play the herione is made to say 'They that have red cheeks will have pale cheeks for my sake, and for all that, think they are well paid.'

The words were greeted with ecstatic applause, as was the play's ending. A young man enters to announce the French have landed at Killala, come to help the rising. Has he seen an old woman – i.e. Cathleen – going down the path, he is asked. No, he answers, 'but I saw a young girl, and she had the walk of a queen'.[4]

Two years after the staging of *Cathleen ni Houlihan*, Yeats gave a lecture on Robert Emmet to an American audience, in the course of which he imagined Emmet going to his death

> full of a kind of ecstasy of self-sacrifice. . . . And out of his grave his ideal has risen incorruptible. His martyrdom has changed the whole temper of the Irish nation. . . . In Ireland we sing the men who fell nobly and thereby made an idea mighty. When Ireland is triumphant and free, there will be yet something in the character of the people, something lofty and strange, which shall have been put there by her years of suffering and by the memory of her martyrs. Her martyrs have married her forever to the ideal.

'September 1913' is written out of an angry despair, a voiced belief that memory of the martyrs no longer holds good. Yeats cherished memory. In the dedicatory verses to *Responsibilities* he spoke of one of his 'fathers' who was 'A hundred-year-old memory to the poor'; and his intense concern for the sanctity of such memory means that he lashes out against those who have 'come to sense' and who merely 'fumble in the greasy till' rather than murmur name upon name: of Wolfe Tone, Fitzgerald, Emmet, O'Leary. The phrase 'murmur name upon name', however, appears in 'Easter 1916', and that poem is about the extraordinary moment where the power of memory has shown itself in the most devastating way possible. For the new martyrs have indeed 'risen incorruptible'. Yeats is brought to face the full implications of that memory which in 'September 1913' he had wholly celebrated, which undoubtedly is essential to a nation's sense of its identity, but which may turn out to be curse as much as blessing. It is not so much the attack on those who add 'the prayer to the shivering prayer' that concerns me about 'September 1913'. Rather, it is the endorsement of the dream of 'Romantic Ireland'. For such a dream may carry with it a responsibility to accept the blood sacrifice, for oneself and for others. Can such a responsibility be justified?[5]

III

The short answer is, no. This is what 'The Second Coming' is about. The blood-dimmed tide that has been loosed on the world is not merely sweeping over Russia and mainland Europe; it is threatening to engulf Ireland. Seeing this, Yeats comes to understand the full implications of what memory may mean, of what the ecstasy of self-sacrifice may entail; and these things cause him to redefine his sense of responsibilities. He does not become any less of an Irish patriot. But the events of 1916 and the following years reveal the full horrors of entering history. It is a subject that preoccupies him in a number of great poems, including 'Easter 1916', 'Meditations in Time of Civil War', 'Leda and the Swan' and, more problematically, 'In Memory of Eva Gore-Booth and Con Markiewicz'.

'Easter 1916' has often been compared to Marvell's Horatian Ode, and the comparison is just. Both poems try to keep a difficult balance while exploring and weighing the terrible complexities of recent events; neither is merely evasive or rhetorical, although because they resist the chance to make final judgements both have been seen – perhaps unfairly – as evasive. As is well known, the events of Easter 1916 took Yeats entirely by surprise. He had not known what was in the offing and he makes that much clear in the poem's opening section, whose typically anapaestic trimeter line implies the trivia of a Dublin existence where all are thought to wear 'motley'. Only at the end of the section do the anapaests disappear, with the hammer-blow of 'All changed, changed utterly', which, while it can be read as a pure iambic line has, in its forced, shocked utterance the feel of a molossus ('All chánged, chánged útterly'). Yeats names and honours those who resigned their part in the casual comedy, but it is the problematic nature of their heroism that most concerns him. Their strong certainty of purpose both rebukes the casual flux of human affairs lived for the moment and gives those same affairs an allure that is new in his poetry. The paltriness of fumbling in a greasy till is, as it were, transmuted by events into instinctive acceptance of the living moment. Or rather, what Yeats had seen as living by prudential values becomes redefined: the commonness of life is now seen in terms that make it natural, unselfconscious, glad with movement:

> A shadow of cloud on the stream
> Changes minute by minute;
> A horse-hoof slides on the brim,

> And a horse plashes within it;
> The long-legged moor-hens dive,
> And hens to moor-cocks call;
> Minute by minute they live:
> The stone's in the midst of all.

And then follows the grieving recognition that 'Too long a sacrifice/ Can make a stone of the heart'. In 'September 1913' Yeats had celebrated the 'wasteful virtues' of Emmet and the others who had 'weighed so lightly what they gave'. But now?

In his marvellous autobiography, *An Only Child*, Frank O'Connor writes of the time during the Civil War in Ireland when he fought on the Republican side. Taken prisoner by the Free Staters he spent much of his time reading Goethe's *Faust*. He also came to be increasingly suspicious of the notions of heroism and martyrdom that sustained the fighters on both sides. One line from *Faust* so impressed him that he wrote it out and pinned it over his bed. 'Grey is your theory, dear friend, and green is the golden tree of life.' O'Connor had become sickened by the mystique of 'dying for the cause'. He tells of his revulsion at the song made up to celebrate the death of one young soldier whom O'Connor had seen, minutes before his execution, sobbing and screaming in abject terror at what was to happen to him. According to the song the soldier went to his death gladly. O'Connor protested at the horror of it all. 'And did Pearse not want to die?' he was asked. 'No,' he replied, 'He awoke too late.'

Perhaps. Perhaps not. Yeats did not think so, but he did come to share O'Connor's fear of what sacrificial death might mean. In 'The Rose Tree', one of a group of poems written out of the Easter uprising, Yeats has Pearse and Connolly discuss how the Irish rose may bloom once more:

> 'But where can we draw water,'
> Said Pearse to Connolly,
> 'When all the wells are parched away?
> O plain as plain can be
> There's nothing but our own red blood
> Can make a right Rose Tree.'

The blood sacrifice is beyond reason. Or rather it is an expression of commitment immune to all feeling: so at least Yeats believed, and it explains why he places Con Markiewicz at the head of those whose sacrifice he celebrates and, at the same time, questions. As woman she is most cruelly the victim of the historical moment at which she chooses to act. The original sweetness of her voice has become shrill in argument. Her mind has become a 'bitter, an abstract thing' (the phrase comes from 'On A Political Prisoner'). Like Maud Gonne, Con Markiewicz has destroyed herself for the cause. That, at least, is Yeats's view of the matter.

'O when may it suffice?', Yeats asks in the last section of 'Easter 1916', and answers, 'That is heaven's part'. I grant that to say this may seem evasive, but I do not think it is. What the phrase implicitly acknowledges is that once you have let violence loose you can't choose when to lock it up again. From the shocked awareness of this truth Yeats turns to the traditional role of poetry as consolation. The poet must

> murmur name upon name
> As a mother names her child
> When sleep at last has come
> On limbs that had run wild.
> What is it but nightfall?

But the murmured cadences of those lines are cut off by the insistent 'No, no, not night but death.' The poet may not retreat from the actualities of what happened into the false consolations of lyricism. Yet these consolations seem to return with the litany of names:

> MacDonagh and MacBride
> And Connolly and Pearse
> Now and in time to be,
> Wherever green is worn,
> Are changed, changed utterly:
> A terrible beauty is born.

I have argued with more than one friend who thinks that these final lines are merely rhetorical and so constitute an evasion of responsibilities. Yeats, they say, is letting 'poetry' win over hard thought. I can see the force of the argument but I cannot accept it. What else can he do? He has already explored the terrible beauty of the martyrs' act, of their being metamorphosed into stony certainty of purpose. To honour their achievement is not to underestimate its cost. Indeed, it seems to me that it is the cost which most engages him. Hence the importance of the poem's appearing in the same volume as 'The Second Coming' and 'A Prayer for my Daughter', poems which brood on the terrors of history. Again, the contrast with English poets is instructive. There is only one English poet who even begins to approach Yeats's passionately intelligent concern with what he sees as the 'mere anarchy' being loosed upon the twentieth-century world, and that is Auden.

Michael Robartes and the Dancer was published in 1921. By then Ireland had become, in Yeats's own phrase, 'a whirlpool of hate', and worse was to follow with the outbreak of the Civil War. In a letter of the time Yeats commented gloomily, 'Perhaps there is nothing so dangerous to a modern state, when politics take the place of theology, as a bunch of martyrs. A bunch of martyrs (1916) were the bomb and we are living in the explosion.' In 1923 he wrote 'Meditations in Time of Civil War', and in the sixth section of that poem he speaks in anguish of how

> We had fed the heart on fantasies,
> The heart's grown brutal from the fare;
> More substance in our enmities
> Than in our love. . . .

'We' honestly admits to the shared dream of an heroic past – *Cathleen ni Houlihan*, 'September 1913' – whose realization in the present has become terrifying.

The same year he composed his great sonnet 'Leda and the Swan'. This poem has been the subject of a great deal of commentary, not all of it to the point; but its central meaning is clear enough. Yeats is writing here about the violence of entering history, and about how all, even the most innocent, are caught up in it. The rape of Leda becomes, in his imagination, an instance of the ways in which violence is both intoxicating and terrible. Moreover, as in 'Easter 1916' so here: once you let violence loose you cannot decide when to lock it up again; its consequences are further violence, unpredictable, appalling, cataclysmic. From the rape of Leda came Helen and Clytemnestra, Castor and Pollux.

> Being so caught up,
> So mastered by the brute blood of the air,
> Did she put on his knowledge with his power,
> Before the indifferent beak could let her drop?

That brilliant pun on 'Being so caught up' makes it inevitable, I think that the answer to the question in these lines is 'yes'.

And this explains why in 'Easter 1916' Yeats sees Con Markiewicz as caught up by the events of her time and why in the elegy he composed for her and her sister he should see the girls as 'dear shadows' who only in death come to 'know it all,/All the folly of a fight/With a common wrong or right'. But here we do come to a critical question. For all the tenderness with which Yeats here speaks of the girls, and for all the magnanimity he elsewhere displays towards Maud Gonne, the fact remains that he never swerves from his view of their 'folly', he never thinks of them as other than victims, he never considers the possible justification of their 'fight'. Why not? The answer has to be that he is committed to a dream of Irish culture which W. H. Auden contemptuously called 'the parish of rich women', and which, although it certainly amounts to more than that, is nevertheless not entirely or easily defensible. (Auden's phrase is more accurate about Yeats's image of Lady Gregory, and the Gore-Booth sisters, than it is about the women themselves.)

IV

Yeats of course was too intelligent not to realize just how vulnerable was his dream of Anglo-Irish culture. In the first section of 'Meditations in Time of Civil War' he writes magnificently about the failure of the country-house tradition in Ireland. It is not merely that 'Maybe the great grandson of that house/For all its bronze and marble 's but a mouse', where the angry splutter of the second line admits to a lost vitality of purpose. More radically, Yeats knows that violence and bitterness are inextricably present in the creation of the country-house tradition. For after all, the Anglo-Irish ascendancy got their houses by usurping the land. They ascended on the backs of others. Deep at the heart of the literature of the country house is and must be a sense of possible guilt. That is why Ben Jonson is so keen to insist that Penshurst is a model of social relations ('Thou art built with no man's ruin, no man's groan'); and it is why Jane Austen should wish to introduce Elizabeth Bennet and Fanny Price, among others, to the country house. Their marrying the heirs of such property will bring a much-needed flow of new blood as well as symbolizing those harmonious relationships which image social peace.[6]

The Anglo-Irish poet faces even more acute problems when he comes to celebrate the country-house tradition. The taking of the land is not merely an act of appropriation by one class over another; it is imperialistic, the domination of one nation over another. Yet such houses, 'where all's accustomed, ceremonious', symbolize Yeats's cultural, social and political ideal for Ireland. The ideal is most perfectly realized in Lady Gregory's house, Coole Park, and in two poems Yeats sets out his sense of its significance. As is well known, he had himself bought an old, broken-down tower on the edge of her estate. It became both the artist's tower, image of a lonely search for truth, and the indication of how he placed his art at the service of the landed gentry, or more particularly, of Lady Gregory.

Perhaps the first important poem to make use of the tower is 'In Memory of Major Robert Gregory', and we need to note that Yeats writes this poem not merely to celebrate Gregory's life and mourn his death, but to affirm his commitment to values that are, so it seems, to become time's victims. For Gregory's death is, after all, one of millions that contribute to the 'blood-dimmed tide'. This does not necessarily mean that 'Our Sidney and our perfect man' has died prematurely. Yeats implies that Gregory knew his work to be finished in one brief flaring of creative intensity and that he therefore chose death rather than wasting into unprofitable old age. (At the time of writing the poem Yeats, in common with others, had been led to assume that Gregory had killed himself. Only later was it discovered that he had been accidentally shot down.) In 'An Irish Airman Foresees His Death' Yeats presents Gregory in the act of balancing all, seeing himself poised between 'this life, this death'. In the Elegy, Gregory is more mysteriously presented as Renaissance man born out of time: 'What made us dream that he could comb grey hair?' But this is alluded to rather than paraded as fact, for the simple reason that Yeats needs to proceed tactfully. To celebrate an act of suicide is not easy; but on the other hand, it will hardly do to suggest that Gregory behaved irresponsibly. The solution Yeats fashions is to imply that the values by which Gregory lived or with which he associated are edging towards extinction. Hence the importance of the tower, which Gregory helped to decorate. It is an image of a way of life – service to high art, to the country-house ideal – whose day is nearly done.

> Now that we're almost settled in our house
> I'll name the friends that cannot sup with us
> Beside a fire of turf in th'ancient Tower,
> And having talked to some late hour
> Climb up the narrow winding stair to bed:

> Discoverers of forgotten truth
> Or mere companions of my youth,
> All, all are in my thoughts tonight being dead.

The country-house ideal takes for granted sociability, and the token for such sociability is eating. But in Yeats's house friends 'cannot sup with us'. The sense of living on into the fag-end of a tradition is implicit, it seems to me, in that deliberate antiquated 'th' tower'. In other words, the tower is self-consciously maintained as a symbol of a disappearing world. (In 'Meditations in Time of Civil War' Yeats says that he has taken Thor Ballylee 'that after me/My bodily heirs may find,/To exalt a lonely mind/Befitting emblems of adversity'). At the end of the Elegy, the poet's attention is called to the 'bitter . . . wind/That shakes the shutter'; and this is the apocalyptic 'roof-levelling wind' of 'A Prayer for My Daughter'.[7] It is Shelley's wind of revolutionary change blowing in from the Atlantic, but bringing for Yeats the deadly energy of democratic vistas.

It is in this context that we need to consider the two poems in which Yeats celebrates Lady Gregory and her house. The first of these, 'Coole Park, 1929' is an extremely beautiful poem, both decorous and passionate in its affirmation of the values which Yeats associates with his great friend; and the amplitude of its cadences finely tells of his and fellow-writers' gratitude for all that she meant to them:

> They came like swallows and like swallows went,
> And yet a woman's powerful character
> Could keep a swallow to its first intent;
> And half a dozen in formation there,
> That seemed to whirl upon a compass-point,
> Found certainty upon the dreaming air,
> The intellectual sweetness of those lines
> That cut through time or cross it withershins.

But as that last line indicates, the house's accomplishments succeed almost in defiance of time; and time will have its way. The last stanza makes this abundantly clear:

> Here, traveller, scholar, poet, take your stand
> When all these rooms and passages are gone,
> When nettles wave upon a shapeless mound
> And saplings root among the broken stone. . . .

This is not empty fear. During the 1920s many great houses in Ireland were burnt down, others were abandoned; still others were falling into decay. Coole Park itself was no longer in Lady Gregory's ownership, although she continued to live there. But some years after her death in 1932 the house was pulled down.

It is Yeats's near certainty of the house's fate that makes him want to celebrate what it stands for. He is its elegist, and he returns to the role in 'Coole Park and Ballylee, 1931'. But here I am not so persuaded that all is as it should be. I baulk when I come to the insistent claim that Lady Gregory is 'a last inheritor/Where none has reigned that lacked a name and fame/Or out of folly into folly came'. What, *none*? And anyway, although the phrase 'name and fame' may at first seem strikingly sonorous, isn't it rhetorical tat at best, and at worst shrilly snobbish? The same seems to me true of the moment where Yeats asks us to believe that 'gardens rich in memory glorified/Marriages, alliances and families,/And every bride's ambition satisfied'. Reading that, I recall Mr Dombey reflecting that 'a matrimonial alliance [with himself] *must*, in the nature of things, be gratifying and honourable to any woman of common sense. . . . That Mrs Dombey must have been happy. That she couldn't help it.' And what are we to make of the poem's conclusion?

> We were the last romantics – chose for theme
> Traditional sanctity and loveliness;
> Whatever's written in what poets name
> The book of the people; whatever most can bless
> The mind of man or elevate a rhyme;
> But all is changed, that high horse riderless,
> Though mounted in that saddle Homer rode
> Where the swan drifts upon a darkening flood.

I grant that the last line has a certain majesty in its dying fall, but the theme of 'traditional sanctity and loveliness' which has on other occasions been treated with some scepticism (as in 'Ancestral Houses'), is here made part of an uninflected threnody for past glories. Much the same thing happens in 'The Municipal Gallery Revisited', where Yeats announces of Lady Gregory, Synge and himself, that 'We three alone in modern times had brought/Everything down to that sole test again,/Dream of the noble and the beggar man'. You might say that Yeats is to be defended because he is speaking out of a proper deference to Lady Gregory's social standing. But when does such deference become servility? And yet even this isn't the point. For what Yeats ignores in these poems is Lady Gregory's own critical awareness of the culpability of the tradition in which he now uncritically places her. You have only to read her *Journals* of the 1920s to see how far he has mythicized her, just as he mythicized Hugh Lane, and in doing so has made a simplified and sentimentalized image out of someone who was far more complex than he wants to admit, since to do so would upset his own dream of the country-house ideal.

My own view is that Yeats, a man of passionate intensity, increasingly convinced himself that what he read into local and world affairs spelled death, not only for his ideal, but for any worthwhile dream of Ireland.

This is why, I think, he turned to Byzantium, as a refuge of art and artifice against the cruelties and inadequacies of life. In 'Sailing to Byzantium' he speaks of wishing to leave a country where 'Caught in that sensual music all neglect/Monuments of unageing intellect'. The country is not Ireland, perhaps, and yet in a way it is. For the monuments of unageing intellect – Coole Park, Thor Ballylee? – are clearly of no appeal to young Ireland, or so Yeats has come to feel. The country might of course stand more generally for the post-war world. In his very interesting essay, 'Barbarism and Decadence', Renato Poggioli suggests that decadence in Yeats's poem is represented by the 'modern and changing West', and that Yeats willingly exchanges it for the 'eternal East'.[8] The decadence Poggioli has in mind is 'the sickness of youth'. Certainly, the cultivated cynicism of the 1920s amounts to a kind of decadence. But the passionate tone of 'Sailing to Byzantium' suggests Yeats's need to save himself. The poem concerns more his desire to make his soul than the country he has left behind, but at the end he is returned to the flux of history, to 'What is past or passing or to come.'

This, I think, is where Yeats's responsibilities always lead him, and it is not perhaps to be wondered at that on occasions he should seem to be petulant or arrogant or shrilly venomous when speaking of them or on behalf of those to whom he feels most responsible. Yeats can be extremely, tediously snobbish. He can also be offensively harsh. But his intemperate manners and speech arise out of the inevitable vulnerabilities of a poet who sees himself enacting or speaking for large responsibilities. As such, he is a potent force in a way that no English poet of the twentieth century can match, although one of them comes near to it and another, T. S. Eliot, tries to speak responsibly on behalf of English culture. Whether he succeeds in doing this is what I must next consider.

Before I do so, however, I must meet at least one among many possible objections to what I have said. It is that to contrast Yeats favourably with English poets is unfair to the extent that they have to engage with the pressures of a history which has broken into pieces any single confident identification of 'Englishness', whereas Yeats's 'Ireland', forged in the heat of potentialities, has not been subjected to such pressures. But this will not do. Quite apart from the fact that it was those very pressures which made possible a sense of national identity, there is Yeats's engagement with the history – including the contemporary history – of Ireland, an engagement remarkable because it refuses to simplify to the point of obliterating rival versions, rival visions. Far from it: his intensities acknowledge, gain their very strength from, the acknowledgement of contradictory forces. This way of being a poet is very different from the one advocated by Matthew Arnold, who thought it the poet's duty to banish from his mind all feelings of contradiction, and irritation, and impatience. For Arnold, the poet should be an undivided, unitary self, projecting an ideal of cultural wholeness. It is an ideal which Eliot seems to have wished to emulate.

Further reading
There is of course a mass of writing about Yeats. Apart from the books mentioned in this chapter I have profited from Donald Torchiana's *Yeats and Georgian Ireland* and some of the essays in Seamus Heaney's *Preoccupations*. Richard Ellmann's *Yeats: Man and Masks* and *Yeats: The Identity of the Poet* are not without interest, and Frank Kermode's *Romantic Image* and Graham Hough's *The Last Romantics* have proved influential and sometimes persuasive. There are also good discussions of individual poems in Dudley Young's *Out of Ireland*, 1975; and in *Saving Civilization*, 1984, Lucy McDiarmid tries to place Yeats in the context of the political and cultural conservatism of the 1920s and 1930s. Daniel Coffey's *Agony at Easter* is a good study of the Easter uprising and I much admire J. G. Farrell's novel, *Troubles*, which is about a later period, when the struggle for independence was at its height. There is a biography of Maud Gonne by Samuel Leverson and a recent study of Lady Gregory by Mary Lou Kohfeldt, *Lady Gregory: The Woman Behind the Irish Renaissance*, to add to Elizabeth Coxhead's earlier biography, of 1961.

As to texts: Yeats's *Collected Poems* are published by Macmillan, as is the Variorum edition of his poems and the *Autobiographies*.

- 6 -

T. S. Eliot: Becoming 'English'

I

F. R. Leavis's famous *New Bearings in English Poetry*, 1932, did a great deal to canonize T. S. Eliot as the most important and influential poet and critic in modern English poetry.[1] To put Leavis's claim as tersely as possible: Eliot's poetry was diagnostic of the ills of modern civilization and therefore truly creative in plying the steel to all affected parts; as for his criticism, it provided a crucial and definitive reappraisal of the tradition of English poetry. As a result of the essays gathered together in *The Sacred Wood* (1920), and of others that appeared during the subsequent decade, it was possible to see the true strength of English poetry as lying in certain Elizabethan and Jacobean poets and the line they handed on to their successors. That line had, however, become lost somewhere in the seventeenth century, when a dissociation of sensibility set in; and although it came to light again in the poetry of Pope it had been entirely lost by the end of the eighteenth century. As a result, the Romantic and Victorian poets represent a prolonged decay of the once-living tradition. Blake is rash, Byron has an uninteresting mind, Shelley is woolly-headed, Tennyson is all vapid sonority and Browning's poetry is of no interest to 'an adult sensitive mind'. What is needed is a return to a poetry of 'urbanity', 'poise' and 'civilized values'.

I will admit that there is an element of the parodic in this and that Eliot did not make as much use of certain terms as Leavis and the Scrutineers. Nevertheless, they were following where he led, and if you look at it from one point of view – theirs – he is recommending, indeed requiring, a re-connecting of poetry to an abandoned tradition where poets felt their thoughts and where there was an endless series of exquisite adjustments between the individual imagination and the community which it reciprocally fed and was nourished by. If you look at it from a different point of view, you notice that Eliot has a very deep dislike of political radicalism. Milton is got rid of with the same apparent finality as is his great admirer, Shelley. (It is significant that Leavis is also conservative in his social and political thinking, and that he shares Eliot's attitudes to Milton and Shelley.)

You could of course say that Eliot was doing what any serious poet does: creating the taste by which he is to be enjoyed. In his essay on Baudelaire, he remarked that the poet is one 'who not merely restores a tradition which has been in abeyance, but one who in his poetry re-twines as many straying strands of the tradition as possible'. It became usual to say that in many of his key essays Eliot restored the tradition that had been in abeyance and that in his poetry he re-twined many of its strands.

There is, however, something very odd about all this. For Eliot was an American, and although he became a British citizen in 1927 we might still wonder just how deeply and intimately he could know, feel, and embody that tradition about which he speaks, with which he claims to identify, and which as it happens is only one tradition, to be identified with royalism, Anglo-Catholicism, and with the politics of authority. Besides, the tradition in which Eliot is interested seems on occasions less specifically English than European, including as it does Dante and a number of French poets. In his great essay, 'Cavafy and Eliot – A Comparison', George Seferis writes:

> Sprung from a line of puritans, [Eliot] sets out from America, at that time still provincial in matters of literature, to discover the workshops of the old world. For him tradition is not a matter of inheritance; if you want it, you must work hard to acquire it. An Englishman would not feel like this. But Eliot came from a rootless place, a place without a past.

Behind Seferis's remark lurks an unstated question: just how much *can* Eliot know of that tradition which he claims to restore and whose strands he seeks to re-twine? When Henry James wrote his marvellous essay on Hawthorne, he found himself criticizing *The Marble Faun*, much of which is set in Rome, on the grounds that Hawthorne tried 'to project himself into an atmosphere in which he has not a transmitted and inherited property'. Apply these words to Eliot and they pose an obvious problem. What is it that he can be said to know of the tradition whose guardian he takes himself to be?

One way of beginning to focus on this problem is by looking at *The Sacred Wood*'s most famous essay, 'Tradition and the Individual

Talent', and especially its most famous remark: 'Poetry is not a turning loose of emotion, but an escape from emotion; it is not the expression of personality, but an escape from personality. But, of course, only those who have personality and emotions know what it means to want to escape from these things.' In recent years the remark has been much quoted by those who see it as unguardedly confessional and who wish to read into Eliot's poetry – they would say 'read from it' – hidden facts or problems of a very personal nature. And they have been able to use the facsimile edition of the manuscripts of *The Waste Land*, which publishes many passages Eliot cancelled, often at Pound's suggestion, in order to further their arguments about the poem's 'secret' meaning. It would be silly to deny that the remark does have a personal application, but I am less interested in any hints it may offer as to Eliot's psychological or sexual condition than in the fact that it alerts us to the problem of his being American. For we can surely interpret Eliot's words as meaning that the difficulty for an *American* poet is that all he has to go on or appeal to is personality and emotions, simply because he lacks a tradition from which to start; and he must therefore come to Europe to find that tradition and be enabled to escape from the 'turning loose' of emotion which is all that the American poets of Eliot's and earlier generations could appeal to. The remark is, I am suggesting, deeply anti-Whitman.

If I am right about this, we can say that Eliot adopts the same position as Henry James, whom he greatly admired. And I have no doubt that he would have agreed with the views James expresses in his famous letter to W. D. Howells:

> I sympathize even less with your protest against the idea that it
> takes an old civilization to set a novelist in motion. . . . It is on
> manners, customs, usages, habits, forms, upon all things
> matured and established, that a novelist lives – they are the very
> stuff his work is made of; and in saying that in the absence of
> those 'dreary and worn-out paraphernalia' which I enumerate as
> being wanting in American society, 'we have simply the whole
> of human life left', you beg (to my sense) the question.

Ezra Pound would also have agreed with James's remarks. Indeed Pound, who was Eliot's compatriot and friend, and who took temporary root in London before Eliot, was even more ardent than James in his determination to find in Europe 'all things matured and established'. But it seems to me that in the end this led him to create a *musée imaginaire*, a tremendous gallimaufry of names and titles which never composes itself into any sort of order or recognizable tradition. Pound is a kind of super-tourist: voraciously intelligent, perceptive, curious; but with the inevitable limitations that being such a tourist imposes.

In 1920, the year that Eliot produced *The Sacred Wood*, Pound left London and England, spitting out his disgust at the misguided heroism of those who had died in the Great War:

> For an old bitch gone in the teeth,
> For a botched civilization . . .
>
> For two gross of broken statues,
> For a few thousand battered books.

Of these lines from 'Hugh Selwyn Mauberley', Michael Hamburger excellently remarks that 'Pound's antiquarian and literary view of Europe is apparent. . . . Most of the men who died in the war were not even aware of the "broken statues" and "battered books".' If you reduce 'civilization' to the terms Pound thinks appropriate it shows merely that you are speaking as a tourist. You can know a culture, a tradition, only in terms of visible artefacts. But that is not how it is at all. In his *The Truth of Poetry*, Hamburger makes what I think is the definitive judgement on 'Mauberley', when he says that 'Mauberley shares his creator's aesthetic preoccupations to such an extent that [the poem] cannot be regarded as representative of anything but those very specialized preoccupations'.[3] This is not to deny the poem's brilliance, nor would Hamburger wish to deny it. You cannot blink away Pound's great skills as a maker of verse, nor his extraordinary ability to step inside cultural moments and, through exact parody, provide both criticism of and judgement on – for example – the decadence. But no matter what the poem's worth it is certainly not the considered and apt judgement on England that some of Pound's most impassioned and uncritical admirers take it as being. The fact is that Pound's totalitarian view of what constitutes culture cuts him off from any real understanding of how a culture comes into being and is sustained. It is at least possible that the same, or something very like it, is true of Eliot.

In his essay on Baudelaire, Eliot remarks that Baudelaire's 'ability to go beneath appearances to the recurrently pervading elements in life was the result of the peculiar dogged strength with which he felt the torturing impact of the great modern city upon the lonely individual'. If we leave aside so minor a poet as James Thomson

('B.V.') and his 'The City of Dreadful Night', we can say that Eliot is probably the first English-speaking poet to write about the modern city, and although what he says about Baudelaire might be applied to Dickens, it applied much more accurately to Eliot himself. Dickens undoubtedly recognizes the potential horrors of the city – its ways of atomizing society and creating conditions of quite new loneliness – but at the same time recognizes those counter-impulses that make community within the city entirely possible. And this points up an essential difference between the two. For Dickens's way of seeing the city is a good deal more complex than Eliot's, and I think that this has less to do with the time at which he wrote (London certainly wasn't any more dreadful in the early years of the twentieth century than it had been in the middle of the nineteenth), than with the fact that he knew it more intimately. The reason is that he was English. Eliot's sharp, melancholic sense of being an outsider is clearly strengthened by his reading of the French symbolists, but I do not think that the tone of 'The Love Song of J. Alfred Prufrock' can be explained by that alone. However, before I touch on this I want to make mention of 'Portrait of a Lady'.

As the poem's title indicates, it is a kind of Jamesian exercise, about a 'civilized' relationship between an ageing woman and a young man, in which she does all the talking, while he observes her, cool, detached, wittily reflective; and capable – just – of a sense of the sad loneliness that comes through her posturings. Both speaker and observer are essentially isolated individuals. Yet neither Baudelaire nor even James is the presiding genius behind the poem. It is another French poet, Laforgue.

Laforgue clearly exercised an extraordinary hold on Eliot's imagination.

> You will see me any morning in the park
> Reading the comics and the sporting page.
> Particularly I remark
> An English countess goes upon the stage.
> A Greek was murdered at a Polish dance,
> Another bank defaulter has confessed.
> I keep my countenance,
> I remain self-possessed
> Except when a street piano, mechanical and tired
> Reiterates some worn-out common song
> With the smell of hyacinths across the garden
> Recalling things that other people have desired.
> Are these ideas right or wrong?

This precise mode of utterance – 'particularly I remark' – suggests someone whose feelings are carefully held in check. Underneath it may lurk a wish for contact, for the vulnerabilities of love. But this cannot be acceded to, because in its bourgeois commonness – the smell of hyacinths across the garden, the love-song ground out by the street piano – it collapses the good taste by which this man, with great effort and at great cost, sustains his life. And so 'I remain self-possessed'. Except that he doesn't. The primness, the almost clownish melancholia – these features undoubtedly derive from Laforgue, both the poet and the man, who, according to Gustave Kahn, always looked

> fort correctes, de hauts gibus, des cravates sobres, des vestons anglais, des pardessus clergymans, et de par les nécessités, un parapluie immuablement placé sous le bras.

This is quoted in Arthur Symons's *Symbolist Movement in Literature*, which we know that Eliot read, in which case he would have noted Symons's description of Laforgue's style:

> Verse and prose are alike a kind of travesty, making subtle use of colloquialism, slang, neologism, technical terms, for their allusive, their factitious, their reflected meanings, with which one can play, very seriously. The verse is alert, troubled, swaying, deliberately uncertain, hating rhetoric so piously that it prefers, and finds its piquancy in, the ridiculously obvious.

A 'ridiculously obvious' remark in which Laforgue took especial delight was one that released suggestions, quietly but devastatingly, of a lost or uncertain identity. 'Suis-je moi? Tout est si compliqué!/ Où-serais-je à présent, pour tel coche manqué?' Much of his poetry is concerned with the sense of life as made up of missed opportunities, of coaches not entered, roads not taken, moments – as it seems – not dared.

So in its way is Corbière's poetry. Michael Hamburger remarks of Corbière's poems that they are 'exercises in truthfulness, a truthfulness seemingly confined to the self-confessions of a man whose recurrent complaint is that he has no self, of a lover who has no beloved'. You could clearly apply these words to 'The Love Song of J. Alfred Prufrock'. Nevertheless, the tone of Eliot's poem seems to me much closer to Laforgue than to Corbière. 'Fastidious whimpering' Hart Crane called this tone, which is brilliant but unfair. For the poem is a good deal more guarded than Crane is prepared to admit.

Even its epigraph implies that the speaker, while prepared to speak, isn't prepared to give everything away, or that he is more conscious of his effects than Crane will allow. He is forced into the role of habitual voyeur, eavesdropping, eyeing, but himself fearful of being watched, his self-consciousness that of the outsider who feels he never can belong, will never be accepted. 'And I have known the eyes already, known them all – /The eyes that fix you in a formulated phrase,/And when I am formulated, sprawling on a pin.' Inside the near-comic precision of this mimsyish speech is a terrified self-knowledge of himself as someone apart, who will never begin to speak out.

II

Prufrock and Other Observations was published in 1917. *Poems* (1919) marks a considerable shift, although one that is less surprising when we realize that most of the key poems in the earlier volume had been written some years before their publication in book form. ('Prufrock', for example, was finished as early as 1910–11.) The quatrain satires of *Poems* are, however, different from what has gone before not merely in the tight formality of their mode but in a quality of disgust that feels new, or at least newly charged. You could argue that it had been implicit in 'Portrait of a Lady', but there the desire to avoid entanglement with another human being had been not only the poem's subject but the occasion for exposing the man's self-centred fears of being 'known'. You could also say that the satires voice a disgust at immediate post-war society which connects with poems of Edgell Rickword, at whose work I glanced in the previous chapter. But again there is a difference. Rickword's satire is directed against the materialism of a society whose rapaciousness is often best imaged in gluttonous, fetid sexuality. Eliot's satires are likely to be directed against sexuality itself.

> The sleek Brazilian jaguar
> Does not in its arboreal gloom
> Distil so rank a feline smell
> As Grishkin in a drawing-room.
>
> ('Whispers of Immortality')

'Feline smell' is very close to 'female smell'; and 'the good old female smell' was a phrase Pound cut from a draft of *The Waste Land*. In 'Sweeney Among the Nightingales' we have a scene that could almost be out of Grosz or Beckmann:

> The person in the Spanish cape
> Tries to sit on Sweeney's knees
>
> Slips and pulls the table cloth
> Overturns a coffee-cup,
> Reorganized upon the floor
> She yawns and draws a stocking up.

But yet again there is a difference. The German expressionists are involved in a self-lacerating, pitiless study of a society of which they are a part. Eliot's fastidious language – the drawling sneer on 'Reorganized' is a good example – is intended to distance him from what he describes; and 'person' tells us how de-humanized he finds the people he is writing about. Sexual encounters in these poems are occasions of horror, they invite loathing. Being an outsider is now clearly an advantage.

To this loathing must be added another, that of Jews. It comes out in 'Sweeney Among the Nightingales', it is at the heart of so disfigured a poem as 'Burbank with a Baedeker: Bleistein with a Cigar' and it invades the finest poem of the volume, 'Gerontion'. This aspect should not be over-emphasized, however, because it is not central to the poem. (Whereas 'Burbank with a Baedeker' is, for all its allusive cleverness, anti-Semitic and nasty.) At its best 'Gerontion' is a most subtle poem that engages with images of decadence, religious, social, cultural and, perhaps above all, sexual. Christ the tiger comes into a world of 'depraved May, dogwood and chestnut, flowering judas,/To be eaten, to be divided, to be drunk/ Among whispers . . .'. We know that the reference is to *The Education of Henry Adams* (1918), where Adams speaks of the rich beauty of the Maryland spring, 'sensual, animal, elemental'. But now the juvescence of the year is not to be welcomed in pagan or Christian full-heartedness, but by

> Mr Silvero
> With caressing hands, at Limoges
> Who walked all night in the next room;
> By Hakagawa, bowing among the Titians;
> By Madame de Tornquist, in the dark room
> Shifting the candles; Fraülein von Kulp
> Who turned in the hall, one hand on the door.

As far as I know it was Eliot who invented this device of introducing names pregnant with cultural and social implications. (The device that Scott Fitzgerald brilliantly stole for his lists of those who attended Gatsby's parties.) Memory is fragmentary, incoherent. The speaker cannot explain the significance of the names or of what their owners are actually doing. And yet, seemingly enigmatic though they may be, these epiphanic, silent moments – for no one speaks – tell us of declensions, possible depravities: is Silvero a faith-healer, is he caressing himself, money, another body; does he walk all night out of suppressed agitation, is he an insomniac, is he keeping someone company? We cannot know, but all the possibilities point to something disturbing, as they do in the case of the man bowing in mock deference to a culture he does not understand, or in humble pride of ownership; as they do in the case of the medium shifting candles ('shiftily' is not far off there – what is she wanting to hide?); and as they do in the case of Fraülein von Kulp, moving silently away, turning before her escape, or before entering a room of assignation.

If memory will not cohere, neither will history, with its 'many cunning passages, contrived corridors'. As has more than once been pointed out, Eliot is here importantly punning on the corridor that was imposed between Germany and Poland at Versailles. Such contrivance is far from coherence, and 'Unnatural vices/Are fathered by our heroism. Virtues/Are forced upon us by our impudent crimes'. This is both a fine, rhetorical balancing of unforeseeable reversals, a far more generous account of the inexplicable disasters of the Great War than Pound managed in those lines from 'Mauberley' to which I have drawn attention, and, it must be said, more deeply probing than anything you can find in the post-war poetry of English-born writers. 'Gerontion' is a remarkable achievement because of Eliot's ability to bring before us a consciousness of life as hedonistic casualness, which can only 'multiply variety/In a wilderness of mirrors'. The echo is from Jonson's *Alchemist*, where Sir Epicure Mammon dreams his voluptuary dream of a hall of mirrors 'Cut in more subtle angles, to disperse/And multiply the figures, as I walk/Naked between my succubae'. But in 'Gerontion' the mirrors become a nightmare of egotistic containment: wherever you turn you see yourself. This is the most exquisite torment for those fearful of being seen. The ultimate horror of such egotism lies in the unavoidable promise of entire extinction:

> What will the spider do,
> Suspend its operations, will the weevil
> Delay? De Bailhache, Fresca, Mrs Cammel, whirled

Beyond the circuit of the shuddering Bear
In fractured atoms. Gull against the wind, in the windy straits
Of Belle Isle, or running on the Horn,
White feathers in the snow . . .

Eliot is here echoing George Chapman who, at the end of his play
Bussy D'Ambois has Bussy warn the Heavens that he is coming and
speaks of 'those that suffer/Beneath the chariot of the snowy
Bear . . .'. Chapman himself is drawing on that classical tradition
which asserted that sinners were punished by being sent spinning out
into space, to be lost for ever. Yet it seems to me that the ending of
Eliot's poem is not merely about individuals who suffer when the
kissing had to stop. The names somehow suggest a larger ending;
perhaps that of Europe itself. This point bears directly on his most
famous and most discussed poem, *The Waste Land*. It also brings us
to the heart of the Eliot problem.

III

In the essay to which I have already referred, George Seferis says of
Eliot:

> He feels strongly how paper-thin, how groundless, how unreal
> and anarchic is, in fact, the order offered by the mechanical
> society of today, his inheritance of material good. He is aware of
> the drying up of the sources of inspiration. He has given himself
> up, both by inclination and in accord with the tenets of his own
> tradition, to the examination of conscience; he audits and he
> evaluates. Life, for him, is not pleasure; indeed, for Eliot
> pleasure has something in it of sarcasm; it gives the impression
> of a bruised fruit, a wound in a tender body. For him the
> element which makes mankind alive is the struggle between
> good and evil. He sees a world that is losing its principle of
> existence, that is dying out just because this struggle is sinking
> down into apathetic vulgarity. From this feeling comes the
> symbol of 'the waste land,' and those going to and fro there, in
> the words of Dante, *fece per viltà il gran rifiuto* – they are the
> people who have never lived, because they denied both good and
> evil.

Seferis is writing after Eliot's conversion to Anglo-Catholicism, but
what he says undoubtedly accounts for much of the strength of

feeling in *The Waste Land*. It also explains why F. R. Leavis so ardently championed the poem. For him, Eliot's achievement lay in his tracing the root cause of the malaise of post-war society to its loss of vitality and specifically of sexual vitality.[4] The sexual disgust of the satires and the intimations of entropic breakdown in 'Gerontion' now find their objective correlative in the casual, meaningless coupling of, for example, the pub women in 'A Game of Chess', and of the city typist and clerk in 'The Fire Sermon'.

Or do they? I am not the only person to feel that the sly fastidiousness of Eliot's writing in such passages is in fact, nasty, prurient, voyeurish. As James Simmons says in his polemical broadside, 'No Land is Waste, Dr Eliot', 'That man's not hollow, he's a mate of mine'. But companionship is not a quality you can ever associate with Eliot's poetry. Prufrock had been terrified of being looked at. Tiresias, safely invisible, is free to stare at others. He watches as the typist

> lays out food in tins.
> Out of the window perilously spread
> Her drying combinations touched by the sun's last rays,
> On the divan are piled (at night her bed)
> Stockings, slippers, camisoles, and stays. . . .
> He, the young man carbuncular, arrives,
> A small house agent's clerk, with one bold stare,
> One of the low on whom assurance sits
> As a silk hat on a Bradford millionaire.

Nothing will reconcile me to these lines. For what we are given seems to me far less the fastidious disapproval of a loveless relationship than the diseased, prying speculations of a warped mind. (Even the sun becomes a kind of fetishist.) And the fascinated revulsion is so marked – why 'carbuncular' for example? – that you come to feel that perhaps the true subject is not the couple themselves but the person who is spying on them. Yet although Eliot identified Tiresias as 'the most important personage in the poem', he also said that he was 'a mere spectator and not indeed a character'. And if that is so, we have surely to accept that the disgust so evident in the passage is a betrayal, rather than a proper expression, of what Eliot himself feels. Many of the poem's cancelled passages strengthen this point: they are even more unguarded in their venomous hatred. The original opening, for example, was a drunken monologue by a man out on the town, close in detail to some of Evelyn Waugh's diaries of the

1920s. No doubt the 'bright young things' of that decade were as unlovable as such people usually are, but it is a far leap from that, very local, perception to a general indictment of post-war society.

One of the problems which faces anyone trying to come to terms with *The Waste Land* is the difficulty of knowing exactly where Eliot stands with regard to the 'evidence' on offer. Just how diagnostic is it supposed to be? Are different scenes and images the fragments which can be shaken kaleidoscopically into a pattern, or are they grains of dust whose secret history will never be fully revealed? It is of course possible to argue that Pound's editorial genius and preoccupations give the poem the appearance of greater shape and coherence than Eliot originally intended. Eliot, you might say, gave Pound a mass of impressions and out of them Pound fashioned another version of 'Hugh Selwyn Mauberley'. But I do not find this very convincing. 'He do the Police in Different Voices' had been one of Eliot's proposed titles for his poem, and the quotation from *Our Mutual Friend* takes me to the core of what I dislike about *The Waste Land*. In Dickens's novel the words are spoken by Betty Higden, who is recommending the talents of Sloppy, the young, brain-damaged boy she lovingly protects, and whose invisible skill as a ventriloquist causes her great pleasure. In a way that Eliot did not intend, *The Waste Land* sometimes seems to me to degenerate into a species of not very skilled ventriloquism, as for example, when the pub-women of 'A Game of Chess' are supposed to be speaking.

In 'Poetry in Wartime' (1942), Eliot remarked of Dante that 'his love of Florence is revealed, not by the recital of her martial glories, but by his vehement lament over her corruption'. There have been attempts to apply these words to *The Waste Land* but they are surely doomed to failure, because although London is unceasingly present in Eliot's poem we are asked to believe that we see the city not through Eliot's eyes but through those of different pairs, of which Tiresias's are the most important. We are also supposed to register it through a range of voices. And the problem with this kind of presentation, a problem which extends to Eliot's use of classical allusion, of parody, echo, direct quotation, is that we can never be sure whether we are listening to a witness giving evidence or to a judge summing up. In short, we know where Dante stands in regard to Florence, but we do not know where Eliot stands in regard to London.[5]

Only we *do*. For although Tiresias may be the presiding presence, the fact of the matter is that it is Eliot who gives him his words, his vantage points, his judgements. Tiresias is his master's voice. As with the other 'characters' in the poem he, too, is a ventriloquist's doll. And it is here that the problem for the attentive reader of the poem becomes irresolvable. For Tiresias's voice is surely meant to utter the 'fragments' out of which we compose or at least part-assemble a sense of the valid past, of the tradition which offers itself as vital opposition to the contemporary waste land. The Grail legend, the fisher-king motif: what are these but attempts to suggest the shadowy possibilities of a recovered wholeness, political, social and cultural? At all events, it seems as though they are meant to suggest more than a *musée imaginaire*. And yet, because we don't know how or with what seriousness to take Tiresias, it is precisely what they do suggest. In *Saving Civilization*, Lucy McDiarmid writes:

> *The Waste Land*'s fifth section puts . . . more starkly the
> antagonism between civilization and community, because its
> revelation of love occurs in the jungle, the place outside of
> civilization; before and after London Bridge, Ganga existed. The
> time implied by the references to the Upanishads is mythic time,
> when Gods talked to men and demons. The setting is non-Western,
> prior, in recorded history, to 'Jerusalem Athens Alexandria/
> Vienna London'. . . . Here God revealed in the voice of the thunder
> utters three imperatives: give, sympathize, control. The
> association of give, sympathize, and control with the jungle
> implicitly allies civilization with the vanity, selfishness, and
> indulgence embodied in the denizens of the city.[6]

McDiarmid is almost certainly right in arguing that Eliot opposes 'community' and 'civilization', but she does not seem to realize the implications of this. In the first place, 'civilization' is, as I have argued, merely a gaggle of inauthentic voices, of couplings and separations which tell us more of the observer than of those he is observing. In the second place, 'community' as McDiarmid defines it, and as it is refracted through Tiresias's entirely problematic vision, feels forlornly remote from any achievable reality. This may of course be the point, but it is at least possible to say that if Eliot creates these oppositions it is because he has no very secure sense of either. He is still the outsider.

On the other hand, there are moments in the poem where voices seem, like those at the end of 'Prufrock', to invade the solipsistic world where each man fixes his eyes before his feet. I think, for example, of *'ces voix d'enfants, chantant dans la coupole!'* where

Verlaine's line flashes momentarily into the world of popular song, reminding us of the possibility of lifting the curse from the waste land. Then it is gone again. It is as fleeting as 'the awful daring of a moment's surrender/Which an age of prudence can never retract'. These lines are spoken in reply to the question 'what have we given?' 'My friend', the questioned one – Eliot? – replies, 'blood shaking my heart'. . . . And you wonder, who is the friend? Is it 'the third who walks always beside you'? Or is it 'you'? And who is that? I do not think we can offer confident answers to these questions. What matters is that for almost the first time in his poetry Eliot allows for the semi-intimate accents in which two people may speak communicatively to each other. It goes away, this manner, and is replaced by the dread-haunted 'each in his prison/Thinking of the key'. Nevertheless, it, or something like it, returns:

> *Damyata*: The boat responded
> Gaily, to the hand expert with sail and oar
> The sea was calm, your heart would have responded
> Gaily, when invited, beating obedient
> To controlling hands

These lines gather up a theme that has appeared elsewhere in the poem, in the references to Tristram and Isolde, Elizabeth and Essex. But the love relationship is spoken of in the conditional tense: it has no present life. It is another community, like the community of fishermen and voices of the children, which is ungraspable. And anyway, 'Hieronymo's mad againe'. The final fragment, shored against ruin, speaks of yet one more exile from community. Kyd's hero, driven mad by the death of his son, arranges for the death of the murderers. But they are the token of how little he can trust the people among whom he lives. The desire for relationship is intense. The chances of achieving it seem infinitely remote.

IV

In 1927 Eliot was received into the Anglo-Catholic church. At the same time he affirmed his commitment to monarchism. He had deliberately chosen to enter a particular kind of English culture, one that would align him with Dryden and Johnson and, for that matter, with Matthew Arnold. He had become part of a community of self-appointed spokespersons for England.

The most considered poetic statement to emerge out of his religious conversion is *Ash Wednesday*. It is a poem about the pulverizing of the ego, and it concludes with the prayer 'Suffer me not to be separated//And let my cry come unto thee'. I take it that Eliot wishes to knit up as much as possible in the poem's concluding lines. Speaking of the poetry of this period of Eliot's life, Hugh Kenner says that it 'is related less intimately now to the speaking voice than to renovated decorum of the impersonal English language'. I am not at all sure what 'the impersonal English language' is supposed to be, but it sounds suspiciously like Arnold's dream of a language 'innocent' of all class, regional or dialect inflections, and equally 'innocent' of political or social implications. There is no such language, although certain grammarians and conservatively minded custodians of culture have tried to make us believe it exists, and it is entirely possible that Eliot may have shared their belief. On the other hand, the cadences of *Ash Wednesday* are far more personal than those of the earlier work, so that the tensions between appetency and negation are realized through rhythms taut with contradictory longings:

> And the lost heart stiffens and rejoices
> In the lost lilac and the lost sea voices
> And the weak spirit quickens to rebel
> For the bent golden-rod and the lost sea smell
> Quickens to recover
> The cry of quail and the whirling plover . . .

It has, however, to be said of these beautiful lines that the pain of renunciation is focused on the natural rather than the human world; and I suspect that Eliot would have found it more difficult to imagine the pain of renunciation of the human – or, shall we say, the earthly. At all events, in 'Marina' the earthly is dismissed by 'a wind/A breath of pine, and the woodsong fog'.

Still, I would not wish this remark to stand as implying a disabling criticism of 'Marina', which seems to me far and away the best poem of this immediate period. As both its title and epigraph imply, it is about an awakening. Seneca's Hercules, who in his madness had killed his wife and children, wakes to horror; Pericles's daughter, Marina, is miraculously restored to her father in a scene which Eliot thought one of the greatest moments in all literature and which obviously had an especially deep meaning for him. The poem begins with someone literally coming to his senses: smell, hearing, sight, begin to awake and freshen. But this awaking moves beyond appetency by means of deeper intimations: of 'Whispers and small laughter between leaves and hurrying feet/Under sleep, where all the waters meet'. Once more we encounter the 'voix d'enfants' which rise, inexplicably, as tokens of community, or from deep-buried apprehensions of inseparableness: of sounds that imply love and the recovery of radical innocence. In the Grail legend, a chorus of children sings at the foot-washing ceremony which precedes the restoration of the wounded fisher-king and the lifting of the curse from the waste land. For Eliot, the major effect or 'sign' of the curse is isolation, 'each in his prison', afraid of love, of communication. Lifting the curse makes possible and goes with the acknowledgement of responsibilities for past actions, for making a life: 'I made this, I have forgotten/And remember./The rigging weak and the canvas rotten/Between one June and another September./Made this un-knowing, half conscious, unknown, my own'. The rhymes tell of a new firmness of purpose, as does the emphatic 'I remember' and the last line, whose hesitations are finally dispelled by the intensely self-conscious 'my own', which confronts the fact of a life made out of a huddle of patchwork improvisations – as most lives are.

The poem ends with a near reprise of its opening. But there are differences:

> What seas what shores what granite islands towards my timbers
> And woodthrush calling through the fog
> My daughter.

The scent of pine has now become 'my timbers', the woodthrush which had sung now 'calls'. Yet these developments towards self-knowledge and responsibility are, I think, less important than the fact that where the opening section had ended with the necessarily somewhat awkward and formal 'O my daughter', now the phrase 'My daughter', implying as it does a silence before speech, a gap where a word had been, prepares for a greater intimacy of relationship: of loving kinship that breathes through the words as a prayer of gratitude.

It is of course *The Four Quartets* that comprise Eliot's most exhaustive exploration of consciousness. I do not intend to offer a detailed commentary on them, since we already have quite enough published discussion of the *Quartets*.[7] My concern is merely to draw attention to some of the ways in which Eliot teases out his apprehensions of consciousness, of England and, perhaps, of being English.

Henri Bergson, one of Eliot's early masters, argued that a person's knowledge of the world was bound to be limited by the selective activity of his perception. But at certain unpredictable moments of liberation we become aware of an unsuspected widening of our field of perception. These moments are rare. Our practical outlook on the world means that our sense of the past in particular is incomplete. It is this sense that the moments of liberation bring alive. Bergson's thesis may perhaps seem close to Hans Meyerhoff's argument that in the modern world a sense of the past becomes thought of as dangerous to present energies. Time becomes seen as commodity, and the past, because it is the past, is regarded as 'dead and useless'. In contrast to the ancient and medieval outlook, 'time in the modern world has become more and more an instrument serving no other function than to produce goods for consumption and profit'.[8] However, there is a crucial difference between the two. For whereas Meyerhoff is alert to the social and political dangers of loss of memory, Bergson's concern is more insidious, mystical and, I suspect, related to a notion of *la patrie*. He is saying that we can recover a dream of a unified culture, or can do so at moments of inner liberation. This is, I think, of worrying relevance to the *Four Quartets*.

The *Quartets* circle round some of the ways we live in time, they provide flashes of awareness of 'timeless' moments; and these moments of heightened or liberated consciousness are often linked to 'Now and in England'. *Burnt Norton* starts from a visit Eliot paid in 1935 to an uninhabited mansion, on the site of a former house which had been burnt down some 200 years previously. It is a place of ghosts, where

> Footfalls echo in the memory
> Down the passage which we did not take
> Towards the door we never opened
> Into the rose-garden.

The sense of a past that we both recognize and cannot recall – the sense of *déjà vu* – leads to the wonderful passage about entering 'our first world'.

> There they were, dignified, invisible,
> Moving without pressure, over the dead leaves,
> In the autumn heat, through the vibrant air,
> And the bird called, in response to
> The unheard music hidden in the shrubbery,

> And the unseen eyebeam crossed, for the roses
> Had the look of flowers that are looked at.

The unemphatic, rapt gravity of these lines, in which there can be no room for rhetorical flourish, and from which the last strain of Laforgueian irony has been rinsed away, gives them a truthfulness that seems to be unchallengeable. Whether 'they' are Adam and Eve, parents, the ancestral owners of the house – this matters less than the sure perception of a garden thronged with presences, and especially of 'the leaves ... full of children,/Hidden excitedly, containing laughter'. And there, yet again, are 'les voix d'enfants'. They will return at the end of the poem, when:

> Sudden in a shaft of sunlight
> Even while the dust moves
> There rises the hidden laughter
> Of children in the foliage
> Quick now, here, now, always –
> Ridiculous the waste sad time
> Stretching before and after.

The persistence of children's voices throughout Eliot's later poetry suggests, I think, how deep was his distress over the corruptions of adulthood. And although this can no doubt be accounted for, at least in part, by tensions within Eliot's psyche, it surely has something to do with his being American? For much in American life and literature offers childhood as the paradise from which adolescents are expelled into the fallen world of maturity. Ironically enough, this is in part derived from that very Romanticism for which Eliot always expressed distaste.

Eliot's affirmation of the glimpsed liberated consciousness, caught in the paradox of 'Quick now, here, now, always', is arrived at by way of a key moment in section II

> To be conscious is not to be in time
> But only in time can the moment in the rose-garden,
> The moment in the arbour where the rain beat,
> The moment in the draughty church at smokefall
> Be remembered; involved with the past and future.
> Only through time time is conquered.

We have of course come across such moments before. Eliot's poetry is indeed largely a poetry of moments, of apprehensions or epiphanies, to be accepted or rejected. What is new is the idea of history as bound up in these moments or, to use Eliot's own Miltonic pun, 'involved'. Memory defeats the tyrannies of time but its most important function is to suggest a possible timelessness for when we are most truly conscious. And these timeless moments are offered, not merely as a way out of the prison of appetency, but as a way into a view of an annealed culture, of 'England'. The 'draughty church at smokefall' is linked to rose-garden and arbour as evidence of a culture known through Anglo-Catholicism, royalism, and the tradition of the country house which has so often been made to stand for the 'ideal' of English culture. Eliot has finally arrived at a firm apprehension of community. It is of course a familiar one, and a reason for this is that it is a recognizably literary one. Moreover, it is one that Eliot himself had helped to renovate, in the critical essays which did so much to (re)define a particular and very exclusive English tradition. And this ought, I think, to make us pause. Is Eliot's vision really a valid apprehension of the past or a rehearsal of orthodoxies which are part of the dominant cultural patterns of English life, where continuities are 'felt' or 'intuited' in so far as they support an essentially conservative, reactionary politics?

Eliot places great stress on the creation of timeless moments, because he needs to suggest that they will somehow compose a vision of continuities achieved 'out of time'. Such a vision is Platonic, Arnoldian, and is meant to achieve its consummation in *Little Gidding*, the last of the quartets. Little Gidding is a church which had been burned by Cromwell's troops and subsequently restored. Now, in 1942, it is again threatened by the fires of war. Yet 'Here, the intersection of the timeless moment/Is England and nowhere. Never and always'. 'England' is offered as an ideal, a wished-for cultural unity, very different from the bitterness of faction and class-interests that make its actual history and which explain how the church came to be burned in the first place. In the third section, Eliot says: 'This is the use of memory:/For liberation – not less of love but expanding/Of love beyond desire, and so liberation/From the future as well as the past'. It is of course impossibly difficult to lift lines out of the sinuous unfolding of his argumentative meditation without being unfair, but at the risk of misrepresenting him I suggest that what Eliot offers here, while it is undoubtedly meant to be assuaging, is both coercive and unavailing. His pondering of the vast, contra-dictory forces that led to the English civil war – 'Of a king at nightfall,/Of three men, and more on the scaffold' – produces the following:

> We cannot revive old factions
> We cannot restore old policies
> Or follow an antique drum.
> These men, and those who opposed them
> And those whom they opposed
> Accept the constitution of silence
> And are folded in a single party.

I recognize how deft is this use of the language of politics to suggest that in death – which will include the death of factions, of their divisive continuities – there is an enabling image of reconciliation, of annealing. The problem is that in the end Eliot's 'single party' will be Anglo-Catholic, monarchist, authoritarian. To put it bluntly, reconciliation has to be on his terms.

> A people without history
> Is not redeemed from time, for history is a pattern
> Of timeless moments. So, while the light fails
> On a winter's afternoon, in a secluded chapel
> History is now and England.

These lines evoke a seamless, cultural unity. But for such a unity to depend on the Bergson-like availability of moments of liberated consciousness is to say that it is an ideal which is not only unreachable (even if it were desirable), but that it depends on Eliot's *choosing* to see 'History is now and England' in a particular way. He can make the choice because, for all those acts of allegiance he proclaimed in 1927, he is not intrinsically part of the complex culture and history he writes about, and so cannot fully understand or be aware of tensions created by the complexities of the past as they affect the present. His view of England is that of the aesthete, and it produces a *musée imaginaire*. I can see why this would appeal to many critics and commentators, especially those in the academic world. For it is closely aligned to the politics implicit in the shaping of the English canon of literature and the way it is discussed. That is why, *pace* F. R. Leavis and others, it is impossible to imagine Eliot as offering new bearings in English poetry, and why his followers – critics and poet-critics such as Christopher Ricks and Geoffrey Hill – give the impression that they are feeding cadaverously on a cadaver. Eliot's early dismissal of the Romantics must have been particularly welcome to those who found, let us say, the politics of Shelley impossibly uncomfortable. From now on Shelley could be downgraded as an inefficient lyricist. If you wanted lyricism then that of the seventeenth century – all poise, wit and civility (and of course resistance to radical forces) – would provide the model. But who defines civility? The answer seems to be, those who speak on behalf of Anglo-Catholicism, monarchism, political authoritarianism. It is a reflection that leads me to my next chapter.

Further reading
As with Yeats, so with Eliot: there is a vast output of books about him. Apart from those mentioned in the chapter, I strongly recommend Piers Gray's *T. S. Eliot's Intellectual and Poetical Development* (1982). Hugh Kenner's *The Pound Era* is a more contentious though suggestive work. Although Helen Gardner stays within the bounds of orthodox literary criticism her writing on Eliot is undoubtedly useful. I think particularly of her books on the *Art of T. S. Eliot* and *The Composition of Four Quartets*. There is an excellent discussion of Eliot in Stan Smith's *Inviolable Voice: Modern English Poets and History*. Valerie Eliot's facsimile *The Waste Land* is an invaluable piece of work. Eliot's *Complete Poems* are published by Faber. Richard Ellmann's *Eminent Domain*, which includes essays on Yeats, Eliot and Auden, is also worth consulting.

- 7 -

W. H. Auden: The Enemy Within

In *The Strings are False* Louis MacNeice recalls a summer afternoon in 1927 when, as an Oxford undergraduate, he had been lolling in a canoe, drifting along the Isis as it ran through lush, green water meadows beside a railway embankment. A noise from the embankment made MacNeice look up. A string of empty coal waggons came into view, clanking their way from nowhere to nowhere. It was the perfect image of 'the placid dotage of a great industrial nation'.

This epiphanic moment is a sort of dystopic reverse of Edward Thomas's vision of Adlestrop. The effect of the Great War on young writers included, we might say, a draining away of those myths that had sustained, no matter how despairingly, earlier generations. The heart of England is now empty or without purposive activity. In a brilliant though perhaps slightly unscrupulous essay on MacNeice, Derek Mahon identifies him as a kind of tourist, without allegiances but with a keen eye and ear for all that he registers as he passes from one place to the next. 'Of what sensitive person is the same not true?' Mahon asks.[1] It is certainly true of Mahon, whose poetry rigorously excludes political and social considerations. Whether it is so true of MacNeice I doubt. On the other hand, the view from the canoe is offered as one of quizzical, laconic detachment. You might see in it the heartless self-containment of an ex-public-schoolboy whose life was safely insulated against the decline that threatened others, and which they certainly weren't prepared to take as 'placid', if only because from their more vulnerable and engaged vantage point the post-war malaise took away their work, their food, their self-respect. After all, the year before had been the year of the General Strike.

In so far as the children of the rich and favoured registered the fact of the strike they mostly saw it as the opportunity for raggish behaviour: driving buses and trains to help the government defeat the workers. MacNeice's pose is one that doesn't allow him to take sides. (By 1936, however, he was coming to speak of political matters, was 'on the left'; and to that extent Mahon's thesis won't do.) Many of his Oxford contemporaries seem equally to have chosen the aesthetic stance – action was for the hearties. W. H. Auden, however, worked for the strikers.

I notice from the biographies and memoirs about him that most of Auden's commentators don't seem able to make up their minds about this. Perhaps because they would find such action inconceivable in themselves they suggest that Auden wasn't really being serious, that he was slumming, that he enjoyed the chance to be outrageous. I think they confuse manner and matter. Probably Auden did present his activities as though they were something of a joke. To do so would both free him to continue and provide him with the kind of disguise he needed or felt himself to need if he was to operate as a kind of enemy within. I don't doubt that Auden wanted to shock. I do doubt whether that was *all* he wanted to do. Very early on he seems to have decided that the society he was a part of (i.e. public school) was nasty in just about every way. And the public school ethos had not only had much to do with promoting the Great War as a glorious adventure; it was, in 1926, making sure that the new enemy – the workers – would be brought to heel. In a memoir of Auden, John Betjeman said that when they were at Oxford together he realized that Auden was a new type of undergraduate: 'aware of slum conditions in Birmingham and mining towns and docks'. The flippant casualness of that remark – its cadences are very close to turning into a line from one of Betjeman's own poems – shouldn't disguise the fact that Betjeman was right to see Auden as different, as indeed an enemy within. (And his deeds of 1926 make it clear that he was one.)

There is something of the dandy about the young Auden. Not in the manner of dress, of course; nor yet in the way of that behaviour which identifies the Children of the Sun – Brian Howard, Harold Acton and their set, who, as Auden said, 'made new glosses on the noun Amor'.[2] But Auden *is* a dandy in the sense that he has a hard concern for his own ideas; and in the sense that he has a certain arrogant, but I think entirely proper, readiness to offend respectability. To take one example. Critics find it hard to believe that Auden meant it when he said that the walk along the canal by the gasworks and municipal rubbish dump was the most beautiful in Oxford, and they record with blank wonder his enjoyment of industrial scenery, of 'the view from Birmingham to Wolverhampton'. This latter is perhaps more swiftly dealt with. Auden had wanted to be an engineer, and throughout his life he proclaimed his love for the machinery of industrialism, for 'saddle-tank loks, beam-engines/and over-shot waterwheels' ('A Lullaby'). But he was also contemptuous of the kind of poetry which went in for oohing and aahing in front of a landscape. As he remarked in the wonderful 'Letter to Lord Byron', 'To me art's subject is the human clay,/And landscape but the background to a torso'. I think the reason for this is that he knew that love of landscape is often accompanied by the kind of detestation of human activity that first surfaces in the eighteenth century as the cult of the Picturesque and which, through various mutations, has remained one of the abiding vices of the English. Auden read landscape in terms of enclosure, exclusivity, unearned wealth, of 'hunting vermin with the Quorn'; the fact that at school and university he would have met many sons of those who were proud to own the land no doubt intensified his sense of being the enemy within. So that when he makes use of landscape it's as allegory or symbol. Auden is never merely descriptive.

Nor does he surrender to the myth of Oxford as the sweet city of dreaming spires. Auden's Oxford was mostly a place of metaphysical distress, of 'kindness to ten persons'. Or, if that seems too strident, it can at least be said that his preference for the walk along by the gasworks makes perfectly good sense when you think of the processes of class-separation, of insulated snobbishness and complacent incuriousness that are endemic in collegiate Oxford. I suspect Auden's third-class degree was that Oxford's revenge on his witty indifference to it.

What I am attempting to describe are some of the ways by which Auden could come to learn strategies for survival as an enemy within a society he had good reason to think of with loathing. (Just as his contemporaries Blunt, Burgess, Philby, would learn them, although time and again they must have breathed sighs of incredulous relief at the stupidity of an establishment that could not or would not understand when the enemy broke cover.) Auden's manner could be flippant, but this was an element in his strategy, and I disagree absolutely with Graham Hough when he claims that Auden's typical attitude is that 'of the left-wing schoolmaster, personally pledged to destroy the system, but emotionally and institutionally tied to its values'.[3] Auden was not tied, and he hated the system.

I need at this point to add an extra element to what I have so far been saying. Auden was homosexual at a time when homosexual acts were still a crime against society. The practising homosexual had therefore to act with cunning, and this is something that Auden writes about in his early poems. Take, for example, 'The Secret Agent'. In his indispensable *Reader's Guide to W. H. Auden*, John Fuller notes that the last line of this blank-verse sonnet, 'Parting easily who were never joined', is taken from the Old English poem, 'Wulf and Eadwacer', which is 'the monologue of a captive woman to her outlawed lover. . . . Thus the situation is one of unconsummated love. The spy represents the individual's emotional urge to make contact with another human being. . . . "They" who ignore his wires, and eventually shoot him, represent the conscious will, the Censor, which represents the individual's emotional desires.'[4] This is convincing, whether we see 'They' as forces within the spy himself – his ego, perhaps – or as social conventions. In a sense it hardly matters which we emphasize, for the repressive ego is aware of the need to conform to society's prejudices or norms. The pleasure-seeking Id must be contained – but at great cost to the individual, of course. And to say this is to make plain that although Auden had read and been fascinated by Freud, he was far from accepting Freud's pessimistic account of civilization and its discontents. He did, however, accept that given the pressures to conform in the kind of society in which he grew up the possibilities of life leaking vaguely away were only too real. Thus the ironically titled 'A Free One' speaks of an apparently successful person – successful in a worldly sense, that is – whose repressed desires mean that he is always 'poised between shocking falls, on razor edge', taut with the fear of surrendering to 'the varied action of the blood'. And in the Blakeian poem which begins 'Now the leaves are falling fast', Auden writes: 'Whispering neighbours, left and right,/Pluck us from the real delight;/And the active hands must freeze/Lonely on the separate knees'. The active hands aren't necessarily desiring homosexual contact, but the whispering neighbours undoubtedly stand for the repressive forces of 'normality' which forbid the expressing of sexual energy, so that such energy can do nothing but 'run away in the dark'.

Auden's position might seem on the basis of what I have so far said to be that of the Romantic individualist. It isn't, though, for as we shall see he is opposed to the kind of liberalism that seeks deliverance through personal love. For Auden this is mere egotism. On the other hand he is strongly contemptuous of 'they' – of that incurious uniformity of behaviour and prejudice which perpetuates the unjust society; and no matter how much he changed as he grew older he seems never to have wavered in his dislike of this. In his typically allusive and suggestive study, *The Enchafèd Flood*, about the 'Romantic Iconography of the Sea', he has a deft analysis of the behaviour of the Ancient Mariner's fellow shipmates and of how their failure to be other than a crowd means they must share the one fate. ('With heavy thump, a lifeless lump,/They dropped down one by one.') And Auden links them with the 'They' of Edward Lear's limericks, that vague but threatening force which speaks with one voice, disapproving, censorious, bullying.

To oppose such a voice needs cunning, whether that cunning takes the form of playing the fool or of other kinds of irony. 'Our hopes were still set on the spies' career/Prizing the glasses and the old felt-hat', Auden wrote of himself and Isherwood, and it's clear that he enjoyed playing games of camouflage and duplicity. Understanding this helps to explain the almost feverish dazzle of *Paid on Both Sides*.

There is no point in attempting a detailed account of this extraordinary and in many ways confusingly obscure early work (John Fuller's unravelling of many of its most difficult passages seems to me definitive); but several features deserve attention. Auden is on record as saying that 'at school I lived in a Fascist state', and the ethos of the public school hangs heavily over his charade.[5] In particular, the emphasis on physical fitness and 'healthy', 'manful' sports can be linked to the world of the O.T.C. and training up youths to kill. Auden's generation was haunted by guilty feelings about the Great War, and the feud between the Nowers and Shaws, which is in a sense the running theme of *Paid on Both Sides*, allows Auden the chance to lay bare the public-school ghastliness that championed the war and its years of killing. At one point a Spy is brought in, to be tried by a jury, 'wearing school caps'. Father Christmas asks whether there is any evidence against the Spy, and in a reply that is no reply but a gaggle of absurd and all-too recognizable clichés, John Nower says:

> Yes. I know we have and are making terrific sacrifices, but we cannot give in. We cannot betray the dead. As we pass their graves can we be deaf to the simple eloquence of their inscriptions, those who in the glory of their early manhood gave up their lives for us? No, we must fight to the finish.

Auden brilliantly and viciously blends the tones of headmaster, school chaplain and political leader here. The Spy probably stands for the same sort of forces or energy as the Secret Agent. He is the Id, sexual energy, which threatens public-school decorum – the micro-cosmic society Auden knew best – and so must be shot. (In *The Orators*, the voice that makes 'The Address for a Prize-Day' says that haters of life include those who 'when the saving thought came shot it for a spy'.)

In *Paid on Both Sides* the spy is shot by John Nower, but it is Nower's mother, Joan, who is the dominant force here, threatening the spy and, it seems, forcing John to act a man's part and kill. Mothers come out of the charade particularly badly. Joan Nower makes an early call to arms: 'Unforgetting is not to-day's forgetting/ For yesterday, not bedrid scorning,/But a new begetting/An un-forgiving morning'. She plans that the feud shall continue for ever. Towards the end, John tries to end the ritual blood-letting by marrying Anne Shaw, and her mother has him killed. The feud is to continue.

What is Auden up to here? Some commentators feel that a good deal of the anti-mother emphasis comes from the Lawrence of *Sons and Lovers* and *Fantasia of the Unconscious*, both of which Auden undoubtedly much admired, just as he thought of Lawrence as a 'healer'. But because the Mother-figures represent dangerous, tyran-nical forces that present themselves in terms of love, loyalty and honour, I think we have to see these terms as social, as much as if not more than psychological. Nor are they merely to do with preserving the social status quo, although that is part of it. Running at a deep level through *Paid on Both Sides* is a uniquely cunning attack on the kind of matriarchal position that had much to do with preparing men for the Great War and urging them into it. This isn't simply a matter of the White Feather Clubs or the poster campaigns. It is more to do with that element in upper-class and aristocratic Edwardian life, where women bred up soldier sons who could most fully justify their mothers' lives by becoming dead heroes. You have only to look at the photographs of poor, trapped Julian Grenfell, whose mother Lady Desborough arranged for *The Times* to publish his obituary together with his poem 'Into Battle', in order to feel that his true obituary is the closing chorus of *Paid on Both Sides*.

> Though he believe it, no man is strong.
> He thinks to be called the fortunate,
> To bring home a wife, to live long.
>
> But he is defeated; let the son
> Sell the farm lest the mountain fall:
> His mother and her mother won.

Auden's rejection of heroism is as sane and bracing as it is anarchic; and it finds memorable expression in the very fine poem, 'Here on the cropped grass of the narrow ridge', where the 'bones of war' are made to say that

> Unable to endure ourselves, we sought relief
> In the insouciance of the soldier, the heroic sexual pose
> Playing at fathers to impress the little ladies.[6]

This seems to me a typically audacious thrust at an inner history of Edwardian England. 'Unable to endure ourselves' may be looking back to something like Brooke's famous wish to turn from a world grown old and cold and dreary, but the more brilliant insight comes with the notion that the soldiers' heroic sexual pose was adopted as a way of becoming their mothers' lovers. (For 'Playing at fathers' surely implies an oedipal drive, which will of course never be realized: playing at the role they become its victims, unable to break free, to form separate identities.) Auden here seems to me touching on a deep, difficult matter that to my knowledge nobody else has wanted to look at – although in some remarkable pages of his war novel, *The Pretty Lady*, Arnold Bennett comes close to it.[7]

II

Auden's dislike of the world his generation had inherited is well known, because he so often voiced it. In a review of Bertrand Russell's *Education and the Social Order* – it appeared in the *New Statesman* in October 1932 – he concluded: 'The failure of modern education lies not in its attention to individual needs, nor to methods, nor even to the moral ideas it preaches, but in the fact that nobody genuinely believes in our society for which the children are being trained.' 'Nobody' is a pardonable exaggeration, as it is in the famous remark at the opening of *The Orators*: 'What do you think about England, this country of ours where nobody is well?' One answer is, so little that it's better to get out, to say *Goodbye to All That*, as Robert Graves did, or to emigrate, as John Nower's friend Dick does, in *Paid on Both Sides*. Another is, to stay and act as the priest and doctor, pointing out the ills of a society which can then set about mending itself.

This sounds improbably grandiose. Yet Auden, the son of a doctor with a 'mad Clergyman' streak, as he himself admitted, was also a keen student of Lawrence, of Blake and of Homer Lane, the American psychiatrist who taught that all physical illness was an expression of psychological upset or repression and that rather than being good in order to be happy we should be happy in order to be good. For Auden these three were 'once healers in our native land'; and in prose and verse alike he often sounds like an emanation of their collective spirit, wishing for an end to 'the liar's quinsy,/And the distortions of ingrown virginity', and pleading for 'New styles of architecture, a change of heart'. These phrases come from an early blank-verse sonnet that is in some ways a pastiche of Hopkins, which may explain why Auden later removed it from the canon. Yet 'Sir, No Man's Enemy' is full of stunning ideas and expression of the ideas. John Fuller suggests that the doctor in *Paid on Both Sides* who restores life to the shot spy is Auden's albeit-comic tribute to Homer Lane and is meant to suggest the rescue of the Id from the tyranny of the Ego. ('The conscious brain appears normal except under emotion . . .' the doctor says as he examines the spy. 'This advances and retreats and poisons everything around it.') Fuller's suggestion seems entirely probable, and here I have to say that I disagree with both Allan Rodway, who thinks Auden tried on ideas as one tries on hats, and Tom Paulin, who argues that Auden's 'fascination with politics and psychology was a voracious quest for an intellectual structure that would satisfy him long enough to write a poem. Once the poem was written he either jettisoned the structure or tacked on a new idea.'[7] Nor do I share John Fuller's view that during the 1930s Auden began to change his mind, so that 'August for the People', his marvellous poem to Christopher Isherwood, 'consciously, even programmatically divid[es] early Auden from the Auden of the late 'thirties'.

This is not to argue that Auden did not try out different ideas, and Tom Paulin is of course right to say that Auden doesn't have a consistent ideology. It would be tedious as well as perverse to try to reduce his thought to a system, or try to pin individual poems to some sort of ideological template. (Just as knowing about Yeats's system doesn't get you very far with the poems themselves.) Auden is not a philosophical poet. He has, however, a mind that moves among ideas with ease and delight, and my own view is that what he does is to provide himself with a loose, elastic and therefore adaptable set of ideas, all of which he can handle with a fine dexterity.

The dexterity is partly one of manner. I do not wish to go as far as

Graham Hough when, in the essay I have already referred to, he suggests that 'Auden is like Byron in that he is always at his most serious when his manner is most uncommitted. Slapdash, parody, self-parody, are his weapons in a real engagement; and the fanciful indulgences always have a moral in attendance.' It is however true that the sheer variety of Auden's approach – through ballads, pastiches of popular song, lyrics, riddles, monologues, irregular odes and so on – have persuaded some readers that he either isn't serious or that he can't make up his mind how serious he wants to be, or that he lacks a sustaining centre, is no more than the clever undergraduate, thumbing his nose at complex issues he is too impatient or callow to try to understand. My point is that by not settling for an earnest, utilitarian manner – the manner that looks so awful in the work of Stephen Spender and C. Day Lewis – Auden gives himself the necessary freedom to work out his attitudes to his own ideas.

Yet he is remarkably consistent in holding by some of these ideas. England *is* a country where nobody is well; physical illness *is* an expression of, or may be used as a metaphor of, psychological ills; romantic love *cannot* be a way out of the deep dilemmas and difficulties that face all who have to live in a rotten society (even though such love is frequently on offer as a calming drug, a repressive tolerance); liberal values *are* ultimately egotistic and therefore likely to be destructive. True, the later Auden turned against most if not all of these positions and as a result had to jettison some of his finest work; but this does not alter the fact that during the 1930s he used subversive wit and intelligence in order to retain his position as the enemy within. In particular, it seems to me, he has a great gift for mimicry, so that he will often take on the language and tone of those he detests in order to appear as one of them. To take an obvious example: Auden makes brilliant use of public-school slang, but always sardonically, even though he may disguise his true intentions.

On occasions, of course, he broke cover. The glee of 'Get there if you can' is part of its meaning:

Perfect pater. Marvellous mater. Knock the critic down who dares –
Very well, believe it, copy, till your hair is white as theirs . . .

When we asked the way to Heaven, these directed us ahead
To the padded room, the clinic and the hangman's little shed.

Like Isherwood's *The Memorial*, Auden's poem is steeped in contempt for an older generation – the social and cultural establishment. It also welcomes the possibility of overthrowing the society in which such an establishment still rules. 'Or, in friendly fireside circle, sit and listen for the crash/Meaning that the mob has realized something's up, and start to smash.' It is fascinating to see this last phrase turn up two years later, in a review Auden contributed to *Scrutiny* (on books about education):

> But, good God, what . . . is a useful citizen just now? . . .
> Education is a dope to allay irritation. If he is poor, now that
> you no longer want him very much on the land but in mass-
> production plants, better give him something to think about lest
> he sense the absurd inadequacy of the operations he is made to
> do, and start to smash.

Auden is taking on protective colouring here. He presumably knew about the Leavises' detestation of mass civilization, and his own prose comes near to a pastiche of Lawrence. Yet 'start to smash'. Well, why not?

> Consider this and in our time
> As the hawk sees it or the helmeted airman:
> The clouds rift suddenly – look there
> At cigarette-end smouldering on a border
> At the first garden party of the year.
> Pass on, admire the view of the massif
> Through plate-glass windows of the Sport Hotel;
> Join there the insufficient units
> Dangerous, easy, in furs, in uniform
> And constellated at reserved tables
> Supplied with feelings by an efficient band
> Relayed elsewhere to farmers and their dogs
> Sitting in kitchens in the stormy fens. ('Consider this')

I agree with those commentators who say that after this opening the poem rather goes off. But what an opening! Brilliant in its use of cinematic devices, as though a lens is suddenly zooming in on details whose signifiance we must deduce for ourselves; but in fact marvellously sure in the way those details are selected. The cigarette-end 'smouldering on a border', for example. Is the border a flower-border, or does it imply a border between two countries? (Auden often uses the device of being 'on the frontier' to suggest dangerous movements between states: political, emotional, psychological.) Here, the thrown down cigarette-end feels somehow menacing, one of those clues that brings to mind the 'spies' career' and may even be a telltale sign that someone who had been spying on the garden party has hurriedly left. Then, the party of the rich at their reserved tables, where the pun on 'reserved', taken up in the next line, suggests not only their ability to order a life but that such a life is identified with stiff-upper-lip civility and boredom. 'Easy, in furs' implies both the classy insolence of the wearers and also that they are bought by the men in uniform (are women of easy virtue, in the old cliché). This is the café society of Tilly Losch and her kind. And because the men are in uniform and are 'insufficient units' you have the feeling that time is running out for them, that they will soon be projected into a violence they will be unable to control. (Has the spy left to alert others that now's the time to attack?) No matter the 'efficient band', pumping out the music that became so regular a feature of late evening BBC listening during the 1930s – the sense of the Long Weekend, of temporariness, closes in; the music always must play, perhaps, but in the stormy fens the menace of the future has virtually arrived.

In later sections the poem adopts a hectoring style and the menace becomes weakened by the pulpit tones that take over. 'The game is up for you and for the others/.... It is later than you think'. And although a connection between the insufficient units and the public-school ethos is suggested – 'far other than that distant afternoon/ Amid rustle of frocks and stamping feet/They gave the prizes to the ruined boys' – the wonder of 'Consider This' is its opening section, before the sense of menace becomes dissipated.

Menace is an important element in much of Auden's 1930s poetry. It may be offered as the kind of rumbustious knockabout of 'O for doors to be open', where the six beggared cripples' dream of Cockaigne, of dining with 'Lord Lobcock and Count Asthma at platinum benches', owes everything to Auden's exuberant imagination, his love of word games. Yet the poem isn't at all trivial. On the contrary, it's a perfectly proper expression of outrage at the exclusion of the many from the riches of the few. Allan Rodway's excellent account of the poem draws attention to the 'far from noble and selfless desires' of the beggars; and it is worth adding that the hint of violence about the poem suggests not only Pabst's *Threepenny Opera* but early Buñuel. Rodway suggests that the 'silent statue' to which the beggars address their fantasies may be a bow in the direction of de Chirico, and may equally suggest the repressive Ego. But to my mind the statue suggests a set of values associated with social and political orthodoxy: with Royalty,

Militarism, Statesmanship. The beggars are in a town square, and the kinds of statues you find in such squares stand precisely for a world of authority and possession that mocks the beggars' wishes.

Such wishes are understandable and were part of the popular culture of the 1930s: of Hollywood 'dream-factory' songs and visions of small hotels, blue rooms, people who live on the hill; of a world somewhere over the rainbow. Auden makes mocking use of such dreams in the opening stanzas of the fine ballad 'As I walked out one evening', where he hears a lover sing of how 'I'll love you, dear, I'll love you/Till China and Africa meet/And the river jumps over the mountain/And the salmon sing in the street'. But more touchingly they reappear in the poem where a daydreamer finds 'a crack in the tea cup opens/A lane to the land of the dead'. It is hardly surprising that people should wish to escape, through dream if by no other route, from the years where there has been

> a boom in sorrow;
> The presses of idleness issued more despair
>   And it was honoured,
> Gross Hunger took on more hands every month,
> Erecting here and everywhere his vast
>   Unnecessary workshops. . . . ('Here on the cropped grass').

This is the condition of the 'policed, unlucky city', where all – or nearly all – must suffer, where nobody is well.

Moreover, the just society cannot be built on the promises of those in power. Such promises are, in fact, part of a world of menace, since they can't be trusted and are almost certain to lead to betrayal. This is the ultimate meaning of Auden's great ballad, 'The Quarry'. It is set in Scotland in the eighteenth century and is about betrayal: of the Scots by the English and of the Highland Scots by the Lowland Scots. The man who speaks, calmly and reassuringly, as it seems, is either a plant to lead the soldiers to his girl friend's hide-out, or – if he's innocent – is anyway out to save his own skin. At one level the poem is about rape, and the last stanza again uses a kind of cinematic device to focus on the horror of the soldiers as they close in on the girl.

> O it's broken the lock and splintered the door,
>   O it's the gate where they're turning, turning;
> Their feet are heavy on the floor
>   And their eyes are burning.

We are made to share her appalled vision as the men burst in on her. (She sees them turning in at the gate after they've broken down the door.) At another level the poem is about inexplicable but certain betrayal. (I have been told that on at least one occasion Auden said in conversation that you could read it as Judas's betrayal of Christ.)

> O where are you going? Stay with me here!
>> Were the vows you swore me deceiving, deceiving?
> No, I promised to love you, dear,
>> But I must be leaving.

John Fuller says that the male speaker is 'an honest rebel, for whom the cause of continued resistance is more important even than the girl he loves. The rebel's scale of values is not approved by Auden, however, and the poem is thus an important political comment appropriate to his developing emphasis on love and individual values.' This seems to me quite wrong and in a sense has to proceed by finding proof in the poem for a 'developing emphasis' which is supposed to be elsewhere but which only the poem supplies and then only if it's misread. For if the man is an honest rebel why can't he tell the girl the truth? He begins by pooh-poohing her fears, so that in reply to her covertly anxious 'O what is that sound which so thrills the ear?' he says 'Only the scarlet soldiers, dear.' He sounds like any would-be reassuring voice, trying to calm understandable worries which either he shares or he's at first too obtuse to understand. The point is rather that the girl's growing panic is proper: she senses the soldiers are after her and, perhaps, him; or that he's in league with the soldiers. (For why should he go on reassuring her when it's becoming increasingly clear that they mean trouble?) 'The Quarry' is a great poem because it so exactly captures the sense of growing distrust that comes to people who wish for reassurance but fear they are being lied to; and although it is set in Scotland you can't read it without sensing how it's also about Europe in the 1930s. The wonder is that it anticipates so much: the cover-up over Abyssinia, Britain's and France's non-intervention policy in Spain, Munich. I know of no other poem which so powerfully evokes the mounting sense of despair and panic over the systematic betrayals of democracy by the so-called liberal democratic governments of Western Europe during the 1930s.

Given the scale and persistence of these betrayals Auden was perfectly justified in acting as the enemy within. As we shall see, he was also entitled to feel that the 'love and individual values' which

Fuller claims he began to swing towards in the latter part of the 1930s were not much use – their action no stronger than a flower – given the forces directed against the societies of the time.

III

> Christopher sends off letters by air,
> He longs for Someone who isn't there,
> But Wystan says: 'Love is exceedingly rare.'
>
> ('Passenger Shanty')

Certainly Auden was suspicious of the claims made for romantic love. What was it but at best a temporary drug against the pains of the contemporary world, or at worst an invitation to turn your back on the unjust society? Everyone may want love, but that does not guarantee its worth. 'Be Lubbe, Be Hitler, but be my good/Daily, nightly' ('Easily, my dear'). Auden's point is that the drive of love can blind you to moral, social or political considerations. It can also blind you to the inevitable fact of mutability:

> Into many a green valley
>   Drifts the appalling snow;
> Time breaks the threaded dances
>   And the diver's brilliant bow. ('As I walked Out One Evening.')

This is one of the most heart-rending evocations of time having its way that I know. Time as blind fury, Atropos, snaps apart the threaded dances and the diver's bow. 'Threaded' is marvellous, suggesting at once the lovely intricacy of the social dance and how it is threaded on the years; and it links forward in a subdued manner to 'bow', which initially suggests the effortless, athletic grace of the diver, (the 1930s was a decade that saw the installation of sports lidos in many towns, mostly open air), but which picks up the suggestion of a ribbon which, like the dances, will be sliced through by Time's shears.

Auden, then, is anti-Romantic, anti-individualistic. This comes out in his complex, dense little fable 'Our Hunting Fathers'. In the first of the poem's two stanzas Auden considers the liberal-humanist tradition which imagines that love is a liberating, humanizing force. The second stanza casts a cold eye on the tradition. The first half of the stanza seems clear enough. Auden rejects love as a power that will give us 'the rightness of a god'. On the contrary, love may be linked to neurosis, can feed on ills rather than curing them. The difficult second half of the stanza suggests that love may make it 'his mature ambition/To think no thought but ours,/To hunger, work illegally,/ And be anonymous.' The following passage, from Auden's review of a biography of T. E. Lawrence, helps us to understand the meaning of these lines.

> To the problem of human relations [Lawrence] has an equally important contribution to make. Different as they appear on the surface, both he and his namesake, D. H. Lawrence, imply the same, that the Western-romantic conception of personal love is a neurotic symptom only inflaming our loneliness, a bad answer to our real wish to be united to and rooted in life. They both say 'noli me tangere'. It is at least doubtful, if in our convalescence sexual relations can do anything but postpone our cure. It is quite possible that the way back to real intimacy is through a kind of asceticism. The self must first learn to be indifferent; as Lenin said, 'To go hungry, work illegally and be anonymous'.

Auden's brilliant if obscure little fable is thus deeply subversive. The hidden quotation from Lenin with which it ends is an invitation to turn love outwards towards politics and social concerns. Since this poem was written some two years after 'The Quarry' it will be obvious that John Fuller's argument about Auden there coming down on the side of love and individual values can hardly be sustained.

There are many other poems where Auden works at this anti-romantic argument, ranging from the comic 'Some Say that Love's a Little Boy' ('Does its odour remind one of llamas?'), to more serious poems. One of the finest of these is the lyric 'May with its light behaving'. It's a magical poem, both celebrating the compulsions of sexual love and, as is so typical with Auden, turning from mere lyricism towards wit and argument. The opening line is of course a deft pun. 'Light behaving' suggests that May is the appropriate time for love and that this May is behaving properly, and yet also implies that during the Maytime of the year light behaving is to be expected, but that such lightness – with the sexual overtones of promiscuity or of impulses beyond control – is not to be trusted. Besides, 'The real world lies before us', with its terrible complications, where 'The unjust walk the earth'. The last stanza runs:

> And love that makes impatient
> The tortoise and the roe, and lays
> The blonde beside the dark,

Urges upon our blood,
Before the evil and the good
How insufficient is
The endearment and the look.

Insufficient but pardonable. For the poem is not censorious. On the contrary, it beautifully allows for the impersonal drives that lay 'the blonde beside the dark', although even there we notice Auden's witty recognition that 'choice' in these matters is hardly likely to be according to the dictates of 'racial sense'. The poem was written in 1934 and I am pretty certain that from then on Auden repeatedly introduces moments into his poems that with the utmost decency stand out against the kinds of Hitlerian, Mosleyite nonsense that were beginning to infect Europe. Auden the endomorph was in favour of 'the dumpy and the tall' and against the mesomorphic fantasies of Fascism. (In this context it is worth noting his witty put-down of health fads, in the 'Letter to Lord Byron'; 'And death is better, as the millions know,/Than dandruff, night-starvation, or B.O.'.)

On other occasions Auden saw romantic love as part of a social process that, in one way or another – love being one way – tried to escape from 'the sixteen skies of Europe'. In 'Here on the cropped grass' he has a passage which brings together varieties of escape:

> I hear arising
> From lanterned gardens sloping to the river
> Where saxophones are moaning for a comforter,
> From Gaumont theatres
> Where fancy plays on hunger to produce
> The noble robber, ideal of boys,
> And from cathedrals,
> Luxury liners laden with souls,
> Holding to the east their hulls of stone,
> The high thin rare continuous worship
> Of the self-absorbed.

This kind of panoramic survey reminds me of a certain kind of documentary film of the 1930s, especially those which take delight in studying the leisure habits of different classes in different places. The connection between such films and the 1930s novel is of course a close one, for many of the novels of the decade similarly set out to explore and record the life of the times. You might even think of them as one-person Mass-Observation Units. (Mass-Observation was founded in 1936.) And this brings us to another important point.

Auden's vision is, as I have said, insistently social. He loves considering this and in our time; and his brisk habit of docketing what he sees, of filing it under different headings, strikes me as very much that of the novelist *manqué*. There is an outstanding example of this in 'August for the people', his poem to Isherwood. Auden has typically seen off love as a curative to society's ills: 'Surely one fearless kiss would cure/The million fevers'. But no: 'Louder today the wireless roars/Its warnings and its lies . . .'. And what we see is

> Scandal praying with her sharp knees up,
> And Virtue stood at Weeping Cross,
> The green thumb to the ledger knuckled down,
> And Courage to his leaking ship appointed,
> Slim Truth dismissed without a character,
> And gaga Falsehood highly recommended.
>
> Greed showing shamelessly her naked money,
> And all Love's wondering eloquence debased
> To a collector's slang, Smartness in furs,
> And Beauty scratching miserably for food,
> Honour self-sacrificed for Calculation,
> And Reason stoned by Mediocrity. . . .

If this owes something to Shakespeare's Sonnet 66 ('And Captive Good attending Captain Ill') it owes still more, I think, to that allegorizing tendency which Auden shares with certain novelists of the period and which makes him address Isherwood as one whose art can 'warn us from the colours and the consolations', can 'Make action urgent and its nature clear'.

To ask for this is undoubtedly to ask for a great deal. It is certainly to ask for more than Isherwood was capable of or prepared to provide. (Which may be one reason why Auden dropped it from the canon.) Yet Auden seems to have been serious. At all events, I think we have to believe him when in the 'Letter to Lord Byron' he says that in his opinion 'novel writing is/A higher art than poetry altogether'; and I think we have equally to believe him when in his sonnet 'The Novelist' he compares the poet, 'Encased in talent like a uniform' with the protean novelist, who 'if he can,/Must suffer dully all the wrongs of Man'. Is Auden writing himself off? For after all in his poetry we are not going to find him suffering all the wrongs of Man. And yet in a sense we are. For the abstraction 'Man' reminds us of Auden's Augustan habit of generalization, of his passion for allegory. And it also reminds us that his social vision makes him

place Man within history, which in his case means the history of the
1930s or, as he says at the end of 'August for the people', 'the
dangerous flood/Of history, that never sleeps or dies'. History as
flood is something I shall return to. History as danger – as menace:
this is everywhere in Auden, as we have already seen. But I want to
note its presence in poems which I haven't so far commented on but
which do, I think, bear out my contention that Auden can work as a
kind of novelist *manqué*.

Or perhaps as the short-story writer. For what is 'Certainly our
city' if not a tiny, compact and tense, short story? Here is the first
stanza:

> Certainly our city – with the byres of poverty down to
> The river's edge, the cathedral, the engines, the dogs;
> Here is the cosmopolitan cooking
> And the light alloys and the glass.

It could be the eye of a camera or of a born story-teller, scanning the
scene, picking out the details: this is a modern, impoverished,
industrial city. It is 'ours' because 'built by . . . us'. It is thus both a
real city and an expression of cares and fears that have produced an
emblem of capitalism in seedy, aggressive decay. Into this city comes
'the malice of death'.

> For the wicked card is dealt, and
> The sinister tall-hatted botanist stoops at the spring
> With his insignificant phial, and looses
> The plague on the ignorant town.

He is very like the character of 'Gare du Midi' who arrives on 'a
nondescript express' and 'Clutching a little case,/He walks out to
infect a city/Whose terrible future may have just arrived'. These
menacing figures may to some extent remind us of Conrad's
Professor in *The Secret Agent*. They may equally well remind us of
early Graham Greene, who was of course deeply indebted to
Conrad. Moreover, they have contemporary significance. Fear of
germ warfare deepened as the 1930s progressed. In addition, the
character in 'Gare du Midi' has about him a sinister anonymity that
suggests a terrifying 'purity' of intention that could be Lenin's just as
much as Hitler's. ('To hunger, work illegally,/And be anonymous.')
But the major point I want to make is this: that Auden's way of
working, in these and a number of other poems, is radically new in
the way it sees the city as a complex of forces. Of course the 'seeing'

implies, as it must, a good deal of foreshortening, of as it were notation. No doubt it was this that made Auden speak out for the novel. For in the novel notation can be replaced by careful exploration, by detailed study of the lives and phenomena he hastily – but wonderfully – sketches in. Auden makes us see, not merely 'the cosmopolitan cooking/And the light alloys and the gas', but far, far more. 'Certainly our city' ends:

> Under their shadows the pitiful subalterns are sleeping;
> The moon is usual; the necessary lovers touch:
> The river is alone and the trampled flower,
> And through the years of absolute cold
>
> The planets rush towards Lyra in the Lion's charge. Can
> Hate so securely bind? Are They dead here? Yes.
> And the wish to wound has the power. And to-morrow
> Comes. It's a world. It's a way.

'They' are yet again the would-be healers in our native land: Lawrence and, in this instance, Proust and Kafka. I am not concerned with whether Auden is telling the 'truth' about what he sees. Of course he isn't, in any absolute way. But what the poem does achieve is a hauntingly precise sense of the fear, despondency and small compensations that we associate with so much prose fiction about urban life of the 1930s: of, for example, *Coming Up for Air* or *Hangover Square* or *A Gun For Sale*. And in addition, Auden provides that extraordinary sense of history as the dangerous flood, the inescapable element to which all lives are forfeit, and which he identifies through the unique blending of small detail and generalization so as to produce a panoptic vision typical of much of his 1930s poetry. I grant that there are occasions on which this can lapse into the 'mad Clergyman' aspect that some commentators – his later self included – regard as a deep flaw in his work. (The stanzas in 'Certainly our city' which deal with the 'Healers' are of this kind and not, it must be admitted, very satisfactory.) My own view is that it is the price to be paid for Auden's willingness to speak out about his society; and after all the 'mad Clergyman' may be one more disguise for the enemy within. At all events, I think Auden's habits of generalization, which are derived from the fact that he is within the situations about which he writes, are more satisfactory and more understandable than Eliot's. I trust Auden on the city far more than I trust Eliot, and if other commentators have thought differently, as they undoubtedly have, one good reason for this is simply their

sharing of prejudices with Eliot. His conservative elitism finds a
natural home in the academy. Auden's radical curiosity, his delight
in the phenomena of industrialism but detestation of its economic
arrangements and social consequences is, by contrast, more uncomfortable to have to come to terms with, if only because it refuses
to let anyone off the hook: 'Certainly our city', he says, and that
opening phrase feels like a rebuke directed at someone who has been
denying any responsibility for the society in which he lives.

This brings me back, yet again, to the note of menace. It can
sometimes come near to the feeling of 'Waiting for the end boys,
waiting for the end', to use Empson's famous jibe. Yet Auden is not a
prophet of doom in the manner that marks out *The Waste Land*, let
alone the approving criticism of that poem. It is *history* which is
Auden's concern, that sense of being caught up in a process. I
suppose this is why he makes so much of being on the frontier or on a
border: it dramatizes his awareness of being between two states.
True, these states may sometimes be seen in psychological terms, of
being 'poised between shocking falls'. But they also and perhaps
more importantly point to Auden's keen sense of living in the long
weekend, of knowing that you can't step into the past and of fearing
the future into which you must step. This informs the fine poem
'Dover', a town identified through its comings and goings, above
which

> expensive and lovely as a rich child's toy,
> The aeroplanes fly in the new European air,
> On the edge of that air that makes England of minor importance;
> And the tides warn bronzing bathers of a cooling star,
> With half its history done.

The European air is 'new' I take it because of the ways in which
boundaries were being redrawn, countries appropriated (the poem
was written in August 1937); and although at first glance the
aeroplanes might seem merely airliners, as they were then called, it is
equally possible that Auden is allowing for a more chilling frisson.
For by this time the Luftwaffe's strength was known to be
formidable and bombing raids were, it was feared, likely to destroy
England's previous invulnerability to attack from overseas. (People
already knew, from the events at Guernica, what Hitler's air force
was capable of.) The poem ends with Auden commenting that the
people of Dover do not 'Control the years. Some are temporary
heroes:/Some of these people are happy'. I think he means that they

are happy to be heroes, though they know it can't last. They aren't fooling themselves.

When E. M. Forster wrote his famous essay 'What I Believe', he imagined his aristocracy of the 'plucky, the considerate and the sensitive' saying to each other 'come along, let's have a good time while we can'. 'What I Believe' undoubtedly had an influence on Auden's 'September 1, 1939', especially on the 'ironic points of light', which flash out 'wherever the just/Exchange their messages', which comes from Forster's 'unquenchable lights of my aristocracy'. Yet influences can work both ways, and in his essay Forster seems to me to be echoing or aligning himself with the kind of stance that Auden strikes in several poems where, facing the horrors to come, he nevertheless refuses to panic. And so, in the marvellous lyric, 'Look Stranger', written in November 1935, he adjures the stranger to 'Stand stable here' and watch as

> Far off like floating seeds the ships
> Diverge on urgent voluntary errands;
> And the full view
> Indeed may enter
> And move in memory as now these clouds do,
> That pass the harbour mirror
> And all the summer through the water saunter.

I do not think you can read this without falling in love with the sheer beauty of its sound effects. And they help you to stand stable. For beneath the tranquil, delighted surface are ominous hints: 'here' isn't going to last. The ships 'like floating seeds' imply a world of autumn, and their 'urgent voluntary errands' suggests that such voluntary ways are under threat and/or that they 'diverge' with messages for help or to offer it. Hence 'urgent'. So the 'full view' may have to live in the memory because the future will obliterate the present peaceful amplitude of harmonious vision. In short, this is another frontier or border poem. The physical setting is a cliff, a meeting-place of land and sea.

But why does Auden tell the stranger to 'stand stable here'? And who is he? I think Auden is talking to himself as much as to anyone else, for the cadences of the poem suggest a kind of internal monologue or at most a murmuring voice. And Auden may fairly regard himself as a stranger in the sense that he both identifies with England ('Certainly our city') and feels an undoubted alienation from it. The poem is intensely mysterious and will not yield to a rational analysis, but I feel certain that it is at least partly about coming to terms with the complexity of being his kind of Englishman at this point of time.

> Stand stable here
> And silent be,
> That through the channels of the ear
> May wander like a river
> The swaying sound of the sea.

I find these lines extraordinarily suggestive, although in a way that will hardly convert to prose. ('I know if you don't ask me', St Augustine said when somebody asked him the meaning of time.) But the swaying sound of the sea may suggest some vast, ominous force that the ear can cope with – can humanize, perhaps – only as it converts it 'by ear' into something altogether more gentle, the windings of a river. Is this folly or is it courage? At all events it's a matter of standing stable.

In Auden's moralized landscapes rivers are linked to valleys and to the notion of the good society, of lit houses, friendship and hospitality. (See, for example, 'Taller today' and 'From scars where kestrels hover'.) The sea is altogether more threatening, violent. It is tempest-ridden, destructive. In the poem's second stanza

> the chalk wall falls to the foam, and its tall ledges
> Oppose the pluck
> And knock of the tide,
> And the shingle scrambles after the suck-
> ing surf, and the gull lodges
> A moment on its sheer side.

That phrase 'falls to the foam' feels more than merely literal; and indeed the language of the stanza is the language of warfare and siege. (The 'tall' ledges heroically resist the courageous battering of the tide, but the shingle defects to the seductive wiles of the enemy. For a moment a gull lodges – but does not make a home – on the sheer 'side' that's soon, maybe, to fall.) Yet I don't want to moralize this landscape into a heavy-handed allegory. That would be to ruin the poem's wonderful deftness, its delight in balance, in finding a way to stand stable.

I would say that a similar deftness is on show throughout the great 'Letter to Lord Byron', which manages the almost inconceivable feat of equalling the qualities that make *Don Juan* one of the great poems of our language. Above all, Auden's poem has about it the kind of gaiety that can't be separated from courage (intellectual, moral, psychological). It outfaces panic even though it strongly suspects that force is the ultimate reality, that 'The dragon rises from his garden border/And promises to set up Law and Order'.

But the poem that matters most in the context of my discussion is 'Out on the lawn'. One of its starting points is a mystical experience which Auden many years later described as having occurred on a summer's night in 1933 when he and three colleagues were sitting on a lawn and suddenly felt an intense, loving calm invade them. The first part of the poem re-creates that experience: 'Equal with colleagues in a ring/I sit on each calm evening/Enchanted as the flowers'. This feeling of peaceful harmony is as beautifully evoked as in 'Look Stranger'. But it would be quite wrong to say that Auden is merely trying to recapture a unique experience. More to the point is the fact that what he evokes is a little world of friends, contained in a sort of 'retreat' from the bigger world. And Auden's insistently social vision means that history presses in on the retreat. The *hortus conclusus* becomes a symbol of inevitable selfishness, of privilege, in which 'we' who share in it do not 'ask what doubtful act allows/Our freedom in this English house,/Our picnics in the sun'.

What we have here is a compact and withering critique of the tradition and champions of the country house. As we saw in chapters three, five and six, the country house was long associated with all that its defenders and champions thought to be best in English manners, values and customs. What is so new about Auden's poem is that he writes in one sense from within the tradition and at the same time refuses to exculpate it. (Another reason, I suspect, why certain critics have been ill at ease with him is that what he is saying here makes the protected world of Oxford look distinctly shaky. Beyond the walls are not merely Judes a-plenty, but a world that is hardly likely to be appeased by blithe endorsements of the country-house tradition as all that's best about English life.)

> The creepered wall stands up to hide
> The gathering multitudes outside
>   Whose glances hunger worsens;
> Concealing from their wretchedness
> Our metaphysical distress,
>   Our kindness to ten persons.

Got it in one, I want to say of this mordant, incisive stanza. This is the enemy within, writing with unerring accuracy about the limitations of the society which it feels so seductively important to be invited to join.

> Soon through the dykes of our content
> The crumpling flood will force a rent
> And, taller than a tree,
> Hold sudden death before our eyes
> Whose river-dreams long hid the size
> And vigours of the sea.

Here, sea and river are moved into the open opposition that in 'Look Stranger' remains muted. Auden's point is that there is very little that can justify this life of privilege and exclusivity, except for loving kindness. The just society, when it has rightly wiped out the enclaves of cultured selfishness, must therefore include that:

> But when the waters make retreat
> And through the black mud first the wheat
> In shy green stalks appears;
> When stranded monsters gasping lie,
> And sounds of riveting terrify
> Their whorled unsubtle ears . . .

Any revolution or social upheaval is bound to produce some odd features – one says in dull paraphrase of what Auden so vividly evokes. The stranded monsters may stand for all the ignorant armies that inevitably come into positions of influence during such periods. They are like the holiday crowds of wreckers in *Barnaby Rudge*. But they are much more reminiscent of the 'Grass' of Clare's 'The Flitting'; and Auden's 'few' then belong to and with 'Where castles stood and grandeur died'. In saying this I do not mean to imply that Auden knew Clare's great poem. I *do* however mean to suggest that more than any other English poet of the twentieth century Auden imaginatively grasps the experiences out of which that poem was made. Although his social circumstances are entirely different from Clare's – he writes from within the privileged social grouping which Clare rightly saw as having the power to propose and dispose – Auden recognizes that a community which proclaims at one and the same time its exclusiveness *and* its absolute cultural and moral merits is a malign contradiction, an insult to the very 'Englishness' it pretends to embody. It must go.

And in its place? The poem can only gesture towards that, in the 'sounds of riveting' which wittily takes up the Conradian symbol of constructive energies – in this case to refloat the ship of state. 'We' are at the border again, because 'soon' our exclusive happiness will be overwhelmed by the tides of history. Rightly so, the poem says. What matters then is to find a way of standing stable, which here means wishing the just society to possess the values of affiliative love that for the moment remain the possibility of the few. The radical generosity of this vision is remarkable both for its refusal to panic in the face of what it foresees and in its social and political commitments.

IV

Why then did the later Auden turn away from all this? For it can hardly be denied that he did. As we have seen, John Fuller tries to suggest that by the mid-1930s Auden was already moving in the direction of 'individual values', but as I have said this seems to me quite wrong. Typically, when Fuller discusses 'Out on the lawn' he does not mention the poem's sense of menace. What is true is that when the change came, it did so with the kind of suddenness that implies conversion. 'Poetry makes nothing happen', Auden says in the famous elegy to W. B. Yeats, and many commentators have been happy to agree with him. They are the ones who want poets to be golden birds. Yet in the same month that he wrote the elegy (February 1939) Auden was writing 'Voltaire at Ferney'. To be sure, Fuller suggests that Auden is somehow criticizing Voltaire and that the poem's ending 'Overhead/The uncomplaining stars composed their lucid song' apparently offers 'a bland and limiting comment on [Voltaire's] purely secular efforts to achieve the Just Society', but this seems to me a misreading of a line that, as so often with Auden, offers a contrast between the world of 'a cooling star', and one where 'we are left alone with our day', as he says at the end of 'Spain 1937', and in which therefore we have to take responsibility for the lives we live, the society we compose.

The point is that 'Voltaire at Ferney' precisely rejects the Horatian withdrawal which Fuller and others take it as endorsing. It starts with Voltaire as the true Horatian. 'Perfectly happy now, he looked at his estate.' But the happiness does not last. The second stanza runs:

> Far off in Paris, where his enemies
> Whispered that he was wicked, in an upright chair

A blind old woman longed for death and letters. He would write
'Nothing is better than life.' But was it? Yes, the fight
Against the false and the unfair
Was always worth it. So was gardening. Civilize.

Cultivating his own garden was what Auden later became famous
for, and there is no denying the Horatianism of much of his poetry of
the 1950s and 1960s. But in 'Voltaire at Ferney' he is still the enemy
within. Or rather, he presents Voltaire as such an enemy, and I do not
see in this presentation the kind of criticism that John Fuller claims to
detect.

Cajoling, scolding, scheming, cleverest of them all,
He'd led the other children in a holy war
Against the infamous grown-ups . . .

Out of context this may look like criticism, but then 'History to the
defeated/May say alas but cannot help or pardon.' Voltaire, the child
of the enlightenment, is not naïve but cunning. And looking back to
the society he thinks to have withdrawn from he cannot be happy.

Yet, like a sentinel, he could not sleep. The night was full of wrong,
Earthquakes and executions. Soon he would be dead,
And still all over Europe stood the horrible nurses
Itching to boil their children. Only his verses
Perhaps could stop them: He must go on working.

I will allow that the tensions in the poem have to do with the possible
hopelessness of the case. How on earth can Voltaire's verses (or
Auden's) prevent the horrors that threaten Europe? But through
Voltaire Auden is aptly dramatizing his own commitment to the
fight: '*Sentinel:* A person assigned to keep guard.' I do not think
Auden lightly invokes that word, and even in the much maligned and
certainly unsatisfactory 'September 1, 1939', he claims that 'All I
have is a voice/To undo the folded lie'.

But by then of course Auden was writing from America. I am sure
that he soon felt deep shame for making that move at that time, such
a rush from standing stable. It is this, I am certain, which explains the
hectoring tone of 'At the Grave of Henry James', where Auden
speaks of art as a turning away from the 'Resentful muttering mass,/
Whose ruminant hatred of all that cannot/Be simplified or stolen is
yet at large'. That mass had previously been the 'gathering multi-
tude'. Now it is simply – very simply – dismissed as of no relevance to
the artist, who must apparently be concerned only with 'those formal

rules that help a child to play'. Again, I can see from this why later Auden will appeal to formalist critics, just as later James does. But the unpalatable truth is that his new stance led to his becoming, as Randall Jarrell remarked, 'a rhetorical mill grinding away at the bottom of Limbo . . . an automaton that keeps making little plays on words, little rhetorical engines, as compulsively and unendingly as a neurotic washes his hands'.

Of course, this is not the whole story, as Jarrell himself confessed, as soon as he read 'The Shield of Achilles'. For this great, sadly wise poem is a most authoritative statement about the horrors of a world controlled by powers which can prove by statistics 'that some cause is just', and which do unending harm to moral feeling and the capacity for love. Nor is this the only fine poem that Auden produced after the 1930s. 'The Fall of Rome', the wonderful 'In Praise of Limestone', which is both a masterpiece of the 'moralized' landscape and a witty, poised and judicious statement of principled liberalism: these and several more are clearly the work of a man whose Horatianism did not necessarily or always mean a turning away from urgencies to such an extent that he was left with nothing to write about. And there are a number of more minor lyrics whose grace and charm give the lie to any suggestion that after 1939 Auden became a kind of extinct volcano, in which you poked about and found only petrified stone. I have especially in mind such poems as 'Hunting Season', 'Deftly Admiral, Cast your Fly', 'The Willow-Wren and the Stare', 'Our Lonely Betters' – with its bow in the direction of Robert Frost, whose contained stoicism worked its influence on much of later Auden – 'The Truest Poetry is the Most Feigning' and 'Goodbye to the Mezzogiorno'.

Nevertheless, I think that Auden was at his greatest in the 1930s. The problem with becoming Horatian is that your position becomes defined for you. Horatianism is an all too plausible way of identifying with that cultural orthodoxy which recommends detachment from the wide world and a cultivation of private graces. It is fatalistic and, I will add, fatally compliant. Uncle Wiz may be a lovable figure but he is too often a tame magician. (Though one, we should remember, who made some wickedly stupid remarks by way of defending the American presence in Vietnam.) 'There are many whose works/Are in better taste than their lives', he wrote in 'At the Grave of Henry James'. True, but that does not seem to me the crucial issue. Good taste did, however, become a crucial issue for later Auden and led to *About the House*, over which there hangs such an air of cosiness that it suggests an uncritical endorsement of 'metaphysical distress/Our kindness to ten persons'. The great Auden knew why that would not do.

Further Reading

Apart from the books mentioned in this chapter, there is Samuel Hynes's *The Auden Generation*, which I think overrated, Geoffrey Thurley's *The Ironic Harvest*, and D. E. S. Maxwell's *Poetry of the 1930s*. Two more general approaches are offered by: Bernard Bergonzi in *Re-Reading The Thirties*; and a collection of essays I edited, *The 1930s: A Challenge to Orthodoxy*.

Auden's poetry of the 1930s is now available in *The English Auden*, edited by Edward Mendelson; the later poems may be read in *The Collected Poems*, both Faber. A book of some general interest is Graves and Hodge's *The Long Weekend: Britain Between the Wars*; and I also recommend in this context Margot Heinemann and Noreen Branson's economic and social history of the decade. Stan Smith's outstandingly good *W. H. Auden* (1985) appeared too late for me to be able to profit by its highly sophisticated reading of the poetry, but it is an essential companion to Auden's work.

- 8 -

Healers in our Native Land?

I

By common consent, Auden was not only the great poet of the 1930s, his voice was so persuasive that more minor poets found it difficult to escape its influence. Nevertheless, the 1930s was a decade rich in good poetry, and in Geoffrey Grigson's *New Verse* it had the ideal 'little' magazine for the publication of good new work. In a different kind of survey I would want the space to discuss the work of William Empson, Bernard Spencer, Kenneth Allott and Dylan Thomas, all of whom appeared in Grigson's magazine, and all of whom are poets of worth. Of these, Thomas is the odd one out, in the sense that his roots lie in the bardic tradition of Welsh poetry, rhetorically mannered and rather grand: very different from the clipped or matter-of-fact tone adopted by the others. After being underrated in the 1960s, Thomas is now once again being overpraised, especially in America; but only a handful of his poems seem to me of any worth.

Like Auden, Thomas was a dazzler, and once Auden was in America Thomas became the dominant voice among English poets. Although Welsh, he spent most of his time during the 1940s in London, and it was there, and especially in and around the Soho pubs and drinking clubs, that he would hold court. Among those who listened and were impressed was Louis MacNeice. This is odd because MacNeice had managed not to be overwhelmed by Auden, with the result that he seems to me, after Auden, the finest of the 1930s poets. I do not suggest that his meetings with Thomas led to his decline; but there is no doubt that his work becomes duller during the latter part of the 1940s and recovers only with his final, posthumous volume, *The Burning Perch* (1963); and the recovery is far from total. Perhaps his work with the BBC drained off energies that might have been better directed towards his poetry; and possibly his remarkable gifts for writing radio drama began to take precedence over verse.[1] Whatever the explanation, MacNeice is at his best during the 1930s and early 1940s.

The previous chapter began with a reference to an anecdote from MacNeice's undergraduate days and suggested that there is about it something of the heartless aesthete. MacNeice was at school at Marlborough and there met and became friendly with Anthony Blunt. Aesthetes together, they both later moved towards political commitment, although MacNeice never became a communist and Roy Campbell's tag of MacSpaunday does not make a great deal of sense. On the other hand I cannot agree with Derek Mahon's account of MacNeice as the tourist. This is not to say that he lacked the gift of acute observation with which Mahon credits him, the relish for what he calls 'the existential tingle of the passing minute'. But it is to say that the poet who, in his essay on modern poetry, can say that 'I would have a poet . . . a reader of newspapers, informed in economics . . . involved in personal relationships, actively interested in politics, susceptible to physical impressions', is clearly either fooling himself or wishes to be more than a mere tourist.[2]

MacNeice wrote this essay in 1935. He had already established himself as a poet who specialized in a kind of rapid notation that often seems near to inspired journalism, as in these lines from 'Birmingham',

On shining lines the trams like vast sarcophagi move
Into the sky, plum after sunset, merging to duck's egg, barred with mauve
Zeppelin clouds, and Pentecost-like the cars' headlights bud
Out from the sideroads and the traffic signals, crême-de-menthe or bull's
blood,
Tell one to stop, the engine gently breathing, or to go on
To where like black pipes of organs in the frayed and fading zone
Of the west the factory chimneys on sullen sentry will all night wait
To call, in the harsh morning, sleep-stupid faces through the daily gate.

There was a good deal of what we might call 'factory poetry' during the 1930s, but MacNeice's poem stands out because it doesn't go in for the kind of clumping moral or political reflections that wreck the kinds of poems written by Spender and Day Lewis. If anything, I suppose there is a kind of fatalism under the zesty lines: 'To call, in the harsh morning, sleep-stupid faces through the daily gate'. This is really a verbal equivalent to key scenes in many documentary films of the period. It also implies an unchanging world of work, of drudgery; and this, and what it portends, is present in the melancholy of 'Sunday Morning', which ends with church bells ringing 'To tell how there is no music or movement which secures/Escape from the weekday time. Which deadens and endures'.

I cannot here enquire into whether this melancholy has anything to do with MacNeice's origins and upbringing. Obviously the particular nature of his Irishness would have to feature – perhaps largely – in any full account of his work. But in the space I have available I want to concentrate on what I see as his enviable ability to 'stand stable', even while knowing how the world presses in on him. It is an ability which is first shown, I think, in the verses he called 'Postscript to Iceland', written out of the experiences he and Auden shared during their famous trip there in 1936.

> Holidays should be like this,
> Free from over-emphasis,
> Time for soul to stretch and spit
> Before the world comes back on it,
>
> Before the chimneys row on row
> Sneer in smoke, 'We told you so'
> And the fog-bound sirens call
> Ruin to the long sea-wall. . . .
>
> Our prerogatives as men
> Will be cancelled who knows when;
> Still I drink your health before
> The gun-butt raps upon the door.

One might perhaps object against this that MacNeice is rather piling the gloom on, especially since he did not have to endure the chimneys, row on row, and even given the condition of England in 1936 it was hardly likely to turn into a police state. But this is to be unfairly literalistic. In his account of MacNeice as 'profoundly superficial' because in love with surfaces, Mahon quotes Camus's 'He made love and read the newspapers'. It is in accord with some of the recommendations for the poet that we have seen MacNeice offering in 'Modern Poetry'. But the lines I have quoted, and many more in MacNeice's work, may be more justly aligned with another remark of Camus's: 'It's too damn silly living only in and for the plague'. This remark comes at the moment when the chief protagonists of Camus's great novel, Dr Rieux and Tarrou, go for a swim together, 'for friendship's sake'. MacNeice is a much finer poet than Mahon allows for, and the major reason for this is his ability to find relish in the actual no matter how the storm clouds build. *This* kind of existentialism is altogether more substantial than the one Mahon offers; and it also makes MacNeice a far better poet than most of those who come after him, who tend to endorse gloom or seek to avert it by the kinds of extremism that are the very opposite of standing stable. Mahon's account – and that of several others – makes too much of the side of MacNeice famously present in what is perhaps his best-known poem, 'Snow', where he responds to 'The drunkenness of things being various'. It is a marvellous phrase and certainly you can apply it to much of MacNeice's work. But to make it definitive is to end up, as Mahon does, thinking of MacNeice's career in terms of the Man Whose Pharynx Was Bad. So Mahon says 'It must have been clear to him, in his last years, that the things he valued were being daily outnumbered by the things he feared. Trying, for example, to find a seat in a renovated London pub throbbing with pop music can't have been much fun.' Perhaps not, but a music-loud pub can hardly have been worse than the possibility of the 'gun-butt at the door', or the certainty of another war against Germany, which matters are present in much of MacNeice's 1930s poetry. If you persist in making him a type of the tired aesthete whose ennui Wallace Stevens records in his famous poem, 'spouting new orations of the cold', you have no room for MacNeice's finest work.

Some of it, as with the celebrated 'Bagpipe Music', uses an almost manic high-spirited quality to outface the worst.

> It's no go my honey love, it's no go my poppet;
> Work your hands from day to day, the winds will blow the profit.
> The glass is falling hour by hour, the glass will fall for ever,
> But if you break the bloody glass you won't hold up the weather.

On other occasions, MacNeice's formal skills become an essential expression of resilience. 'The British Museum Reading Room', 'London Rain', 'Chess': these and several more could well take as their epigraph Luther's famous remark, 'And though I knew the world should end tomorrow, I still would plant my apple tree'. One of the best of these poems is 'The Sunlight On The Garden', with its brilliantly adroit interweaving of repeated phrases and rhymes. 'We are dying, Egypt, dying', the poem says at the end of the third stanza, and continues into the fourth and last:

> And not expecting pardon,
> Hardened in heart anew,
> But glad to have sat under
> Thunder and rain with you,

> And grateful too
> For sunlight on the garden.

It is not clear whether this poem is addressed to a particular woman. Probably not, and certainly the first lines of the poem's second stanza – 'Our freedom as free lances/Advances towards its end' – suggests a more general context. But what might otherwise have been wry stoicism becomes altogether more forceful because of a gratitude which has to do with writing poems, itself a kind of love affair for MacNeice; and which in his case, is linked to that special gratitude for sexual love, given and received.

MacNeice is in fact a very fine love poet, whether he is writing about love lost or frustrated, as in 'June Thunder', love achieved, as in 'Trilogy For X', or – more typically perhaps – love as providing the existential tingle of the moment, which becomes the more poignant simply because it must pass. Of all the poems that fall into this category I think 'Meeting Point' is the most beautiful even though or perhaps because it is perilously close to the kind of sentimental brief encounter that you find in films and plays of the period. Indeed, the restaurant scene, two people seated at a table sharing looks and cigarettes, is something of a cliché. Or would be, were it not for the quality of MacNeice's writing, the joy he takes in redeeming cliché:

> Her fingers flicked away the ash
> That bloomed again in tropic trees:
> Not caring if the markets crash
> When they had forests such as these,
> Her fingers flicked away the ash.

Poems such as this create or encapsulate the kinds of epiphanic moments in which MacNeice seems to have found his chief pleasure. (Perhaps for this reason he took a fairly glum view of love through the years, as in 'Les Sylphides', which ends with a wife waking beside her husband and wondering whether 'It was really worth it and where/The river had flowed away/And where were the white flowers'. This rather anticipates Larkin's 'Love Songs in Age' and 'Talking in Bed.')

When MacNeice is not involved in or responding to the actualities of the moment, he becomes more Auden-like in seeing people as caught in a history they cannot control. 'Christmas Shopping' for example, moves from the observation of shoppers 'spending beyond their income' (and again the poem in a sense anticipates Larkin's 'cut-price crowd') to a meditation where the camera's eye, as it were, zooms up to take an aerial view:

> The little firtrees palpitate with candles
> In hundreds of chattering households where the suburb
> Straggles like nervous handwriting, the margin
>   Blotted with smokestacks.
>
> Further out on the coast the lighthouse moves its
> Arms of light through the fog that wads our welfare,
> Moves its arms like a giant at Swedish drill whose
>   Mind is a vacuum.

MacNeice's sapphics here offer themselves for comparison with Auden's 'Dover'; but there is no doubt that Auden's is by far the better poem. For, there really *is* something journalistic about the ending of 'Christmas Shopping', about, for example, the suburb that 'straggles like nervous handwriting', an image which, though it may at first seem clever does not repay attention (*whose* handwriting, *why* is it nervous?); and which then requires or anyway leads to the 'margin/Blotted with smokestacks'. (It's smoke not the stacks that blots, but anyway the notion of margin is plain silly.)

To say this is to say that MacNeice lacks Auden's genius for overseeing a peopled landscape and feeding in a history and a guessed-at future. What MacNeice *is* excellent at is travelling through such a landscape and commenting on what he sees. This is the newspaper reader-cum-journalist able to speculate with extraordinary incisiveness; and the triumph of this mode is undoubtedly *Autumn Journal*. It is a quite remarkable piece of work, and I greatly regret not having the space to discuss it in some detail.[3] Yet this perhaps matters less than might at first seem to be the case, if only because it is so obviously good. Loosely linking events in MacNeice's personal life with the public world – of Spain, the gathering threat of Hitler, unemployment, the problems of Ireland – the poem is the verse commentary of an exceptionally intelligent, observant man who, while never merely the tourist, is never so trapped by one particular point of view or emotion that he loses his ability to stand stable. And this is so, in spite of the ever-present threat to stability. The poem opens with one more renovation of that dream of England which we have had occasion to note in earlier chapters, but here the sense of an ending is deftly caught: this is a peopled Adlestrop, although the county referred to is actually Hampshire, and the people described have stepped out of *Howards End*, or the novels of Elizabeth Bowen.

> Macrocarpa and cypress
> And roses on a rustic trellis and mulberry trees
> And bacon and eggs in a silver dish for breakfast
> And all the inherited assets of bodily ease
> And all the inherited worries, rheumatism and taxes,
> And whether Stella will marry and what to do with Dick . . .
> And the growth of vulgarity, cars that pass the gate-lodge
> And crowds undressing on the beach
> And the hiking cockney lovers. . . .
> But the home is still a sanctum under the pelmets,
> All quiet on the Family Front,
> Farmyard noises across the fields at evening
> While the trucks of the Southern Railway dawdle . . . shunt
> Into poppy sidings for the night. . . .

This could even be Metroland. But MacNeice does not share Betjeman's lamentably uncritical endorsement of a small segment of English society offered for our unquestioning approval. MacNeice may not be the enemy within but he is certainly not a lapdog. Instead, these lines have about them a tart awareness of the bland self-confidence with which 'the lives of retired generals and admirals' can be thought by some to stand for a heart of England.

When war was declared MacNeice happened to be in Ireland. 'Spent last Saturday drinking in a bar with the Dublin literati,' he notes in his Journal. 'They hardly mentioned the war but debated the correct versions of Dublin street songs . . .' That this was not MacNeice's reaction is evident not merely from the many poems which, as we have seen, are acutely aware of the approaching menace, but from a sequence he wrote at the time, called 'The Closing Album'. It isn't among his finest work, but I mention it because in the fifth and last poem MacNeice, brooding on the outbreak of war, asks himself:

> And why, now it has happened,
> Should the atlas still be full of the maps of countries
> We shall never see again?
>
> And why, now it has happened,
> And doom all night is lapping at the door,
> Should I remember that I ever met you —
> Once in another world?

It is typical of him both to balance the public against the private and to affirm the conditional rights of personal relationship even at a time when it feels impossible for them to exist. 'Under the delight that glitters on the surface', John Montague wrote of MacNeice, 'there is always the hidden ice.' I disagree, because it seems to me that Montague's somewhat inept metaphor ignores one of MacNeice's great strengths: his balancing of contraries. To speak of hidden ice is to suggest that MacNeice somehow submerged or kept under what he most feared. But at his considerable best he is a sane and bracing poet because he shows and names the fears, does not underestimate them, and yet nevertheless refuses to give way to them.

II

You cannot sensibly compare English poets of the Second World War with those of the First. Nor, for that matter, can you compare them with such American poets as Randall Jarrell, Howard Nemerov and, above all, Louis Simpson, for all of whom it was the first war on a world-wide scale in which America had become fully and continuously involved. The English poets of the 1940s knew about Owen, Sassoon and Thomas. They also knew that the idealism, heroism and horrified protests of the First World War could not be repeated. The characteristic material of Second World War poetry is therefore regret at parting, quizzical observation of foreign habits and landscapes, or wry commentary on the more outrageous absurdities of military life. Of all the poets who fought in and wrote about the war, probably the best are Keith Douglas and Alun Lewis,[4] and had they lived they might have developed into important writers. War did not make them poets, for the very good reason that both were writing before it began. Of the two, Douglas's voice is the more detached, sardonic, Lewis's engaged, warm, but also rather clumsy and fadedly poetical. His best poems appear to be deeply indebted to Edward Thomas, as these lines from 'All Day It Has Rained' show:

> And we talked of girls, and dropping bombs on Rome,
> And thought of the quiet dead and the loud celebrities
> Exhorting us to slaughter, and the herded refugees;
> – Yet thought softly, morosely of them, and as indifferently
> As of ourselves or those whom we
> For years have loved, and will again
> Tomorrow maybe love. . . .

In fact, his poem 'To Edward Thomas' shows an awareness of Thomas's dark side, although he rather overdoes it when, in the last line, he says 'Till suddenly, at Arras, you possessed that hinted land', for that suggests a death wish on Thomas's part unopposed by any contrary pull. It was Lewis himself who committed suicide in India, in March 1944.

Keith Douglas was killed in the Normandy landings, on 9 June of the same year. He was 24 years old and had been writing since at least the age of fourteen. Some of his juvenilia is astonishingly precocious and assured, and his war poems are clearly the work of a gifted writer. His best known and probably best poems are 'Egypt', 'Vergissmeinicht', 'How to Kill', 'Behaviour of Fish in an Egyptian Tea Garden' and one known either as 'Aristocrats' or 'Sportsmen'. This last poem – which exists in at least two versions – seems to me to typify Douglas's mixture of cool sardonicism and social awareness. It is about the officer-gentleman class which Douglas was born into, knew well, and which he calls 'this gentle obsolescent breed of heroes'. In the version I prefer the poem ends:

> These plains were their cricket pitch
> and in the mountains the tremendous drop fences
> brought down some of the runners. Here then
> under the stones and earth they dispose themselves,
> I think with their famous unconcern.
> It is not gunfire I hear, but a hunting horn.[5]

This is good but I do not think that it will bear up under the more extravagant claims that have been made for it. The target is, after all, an obvious one.

However, Douglas's manner anticipates some of the poetry that was to develop after the war. (Lewis's more sonorous but padded voice is Welsh in a way that links him to Dylan Thomas and Vernon Watkins.) Its posture is that of the wry, almost dry commentator; its language is chaste, neither dazzling nor eclectic, as with Auden and MacNeice. Above all, its perspectives are limited. It would be unfair to make too much of these matters, for Douglas's early death means that we are dealing with a poet comparatively inexperienced, and one who might have changed much that survives and have gone in quite different directions. Nevertheless, Douglas does seem to point towards the future, especially as that was to be embodied in poets who became known as the Movement.

I do not know whether these poets, and that pre-eminently means Philip Larkin, were aware of Douglas; but since they were mostly Oxford poets, and he had left Oxford in 1940, it seems probable. On the other hand I have no wish to argue that Douglas was a direct influence on them. It is more likely that his characteristic traits were in the air and as such would be picked up by writers coming after him. Certainly, they admired those traits in a poet who during the 1930s had been almost invisible but whose reputation during the 1950s rose to extraordinary heights.

For the duration of the 1930s Robert Graves had been living abroad. While the war lasted he was back in Britain, but as soon as it finished he returned to his home in Majorca. He did not however return to the anonymity which had previously marked his poetry. (The prose is a different matter: *Goodbye to All That* was widely known, as were his historical novels.) Graves became a hero for several young poets of the 1950s, a poet to model yourself on. It is easy to see why. In the first place his language was severely chaste. Although given to extremely bardic pronouncements, Graves did not write like 'mad Dylan', and in fact his almost blanched vocabulary could be used as a way of sternly reproving the neo-Romantic excesses of Thomas and his followers, notably George Barker. Thus Donald Davie's *Purity of Diction in English Verse*, published in 1952, and arguing for the merits of a number of later Augustan poets, fitted very well with Gravesian practice, even though Graves had always shown a contempt for Augustan poetry. (His strictures are very old-fashioned and seem to come straight from the then Oxford orthodoxies of Arnoldian pronouncements about Pope as a classic of prose, not poetry.)

Graves also becomes seen as a model of 'Englishness'. This is difficult to pin down, perhaps, but has much to do with the notion of 'good form'. Graves's clipped, military manner of speech, his use of traditional metrics – at which he is greatly skilled – his decorum: all these things could be offered as very English, as ways of not making a song-and-dance about poetry. Moreover, while Graves was prepared to make very large claims for 'true' poetry, he also turned his back on what, in one of his professorial lectures on poetry at Oxford, he called 'the foul tidal basin of Modernism'. And in the Clark lectures, which he gave at Cambridge in 1954–5, he delivered lengthy and for the most part incoherently silly attacks on Yeats, Pound and Auden. The Clark lectures, the Professorship of Poetry at Oxford: these are indications of the extent to which Graves had been brought in from the cold. The fact that what he stood for could be so unhesitatingly proclaimed as valuable also tells us about the shrinking horizons and ambitions of many English poets during the

1950s. For Graves's vocabulary, procedures and interests are all linked to the private and personal. Or rather, they are quite incapable of nourishing a poetry which tries to confront or comment on social and political matters. Poets who followed Graves were committed to a tone of voice in which the quizzical, the self-deprecatory, dominates, or in which discretion is always the better part of ecstasy.

'The Cool Web' is typical of Graves's work and is exactly the kind of poem to appeal to his admirers. It is about the constraints of language, and at first seems to be mourning the loss of immediacy of the child's eager, impassioned responsiveness to the world. But having spoken of the 'cool web of language' that 'winds us in', the poem ends:

> But if we let our tongues lose self-possession,
> Throwing off language and its watery clasp
> Before our death, instead of when death comes,
> Facing the wide glare of the children's day,
> Facing the rose, the dark sky and the drums
> We shall go mad no doubt and die that way.

The neat ironies, the carefully laundered rhythms, the unemphatic rhymes: these modest virtues become the stuff of much poetry of the 1950s. So too does the rueful sense of the inevitability of constraint, of let-down. At the end of 'Questions in a Wood', Graves, having argued a case against sexal love – and this is a preoccupation of his – concludes:

> Yet, if from delicacy of pride
> We choose to hold apart,
> Will no blue hag appear, to ride
> Hell's wager in each heart?

This gimmick of concluding a poem with a question or with a statement that reverses expectations is a device very much favoured by 1950s poets. 'Watching oneself being clever being clever', as John Wain ironically put it, and by so doing made a further claim for ironical cleverness. It can be found at the end of Donald Davie's poem, 'The Preacher'.

> If, when he plays upon our sympathies,
> I'm pleased to be fastidious and you
> To be impressed, the vice in it is this:
> Each does us credit, and we know it too.

And the quizzical ending of Graves's 'A Slice of Wedding Cake' –

> Has God's supply of tolerable husbands
> Fallen, in fact, so low?
> Or do I always over-value woman
> At the expense of man?
> Do I?
> It might be so.

is echoed again and again in the endings of poems by Amis, Larkin, Wain and Davie.

Here I must make two points. One is that at his best Graves is undoubtedly a very fine, though minor, poet. I would say that such poems as 'Questions in a Wood', 'Theseus and Ariadne', 'Never Such Love', 'End of Play', 'The Sea Horse' and the entirely magical 'She Tells Her Love While Half Asleep', are all fully achieved, exact and searching poems on the attractions and repulsions of sexual love. They are rarely impassioned, and with the exception of 'She Tells her Love' and some stanzas in the other poems, are rarely even lyrical. If they remind me of anyone it is of Landor, for Graves shares the earlier poet's pure, almost marmoreal, respect for form and language. He does not often go beyond that, but when he does as in, above all, the wonderful 'To Juan at the Winter Solstice', his most eloquent statement about his muse, the eternal witch, queen, White Goddess, the effect is uniquely memorable,

> Dwell on her graciousness, dwell on her smiling,
> Do not forget what flowers
> The great boar trampled down in ivy time.
> Her brow was creamy as the crested wave,
> Her sea-blue eyes were wild
> But nothing promised that is not performed.

Graves only very rarely attains this pitch of amplitude, but in 'To Juan' and a few other poems he shows himself to be more than a trim technician.

Yet having said this, I come to the other point, which is my strong sense that Graves's influence was not a good thing. He can't of course be blamed for this, for no poet writes in order to be imitated or to found a school. Moreover, Graves's virtues are real and desirable. But where I think matters go wrong is in the fact that his admirers, who were by and large a group of poets known as 'the Movement', were as much influenced by his vices as they were by his virtues.

Was no one embarrassed by his ignorant and shallow attacks on the great Modernist poets? Did no one think that his little-England posturing was not far removed from Podsnappery? Not Kingsley Amis, at all events. One of his more infamous pronouncements of the decade was to the effect that 'Nobody wants any more poems about foreign cities – at least I hope nobody does'. And this may be linked to Philip Larkin's scornful dismissal of the three Ps: Parker, Pound and Picasso. Little-Englandisms thus become the token for a narrowness that eventually mutates into a blinkered, almost parodic reactionariness, with Philip Larkin's admiration for Mrs Thatcher and Amis's role as a blend of Norman Tebbit and Colonel Blimp. Little-Englandism also explains, I think, the dull shallowness of so much poetry of the 1950s, the retreat into academic, self-imposed and self-contented indifference to those larger concerns which had engaged Auden and, to a lesser extent, MacNeice. Little-Englandism further explains the undervaluing of Charles Tomlinson, *not* on the grounds of a rather chilled aestheticism, which is where I think he is vulnerable, but on the grounds that he admired such great American modernists as Wallace Stevens and William Carlos Williams.

To speak plainly, I think that a number of poets of the 1950s betrayed the trust placed in them by readers who, like themselves, came from the kind of social environment which was outside the orthodoxy. As we have seen, that orthodoxy had, in its thoroughly debilitating way, offered to nourish much twentieth- century English poetry and had failed to do so. The new poets began to write in post-war England, where the massive, heartening parliamentary victory of the Labour Party in 1945, and the rapid opening-up of education – especially higher education – to large numbers of people who had previously been excluded from it, gave a unique opportunity for a radical realignment of writer and reader. For like their readers, most of the poets came from provincial, lower-middle-class backgrounds; and they were therefore in a position to speak for and from an England not commonly met with in poetry. At first it looked as though they would seize this opportunity. Soon, however, their scholarship-boy ambition to achieve a certain classlessness led them to identify weaknesses as strengths, to overvalue Graves, and to turn their backs on history, including the history of their own times. What resulted was poetry of unimaginable timidity.

There was also a good deal of self-parody in the way they presented themselves. Some see this as an engaging modesty. I think it argues for bad faith. If you imagine the typical poet of the 1950s you are likely to picture a young man in a belted mackintosh, which he wears over a shapeless tweed jacket and corduroy trousers. The trousers may well be tucked into his socks or snared by bicycle clips. One hand cups a smouldering Woodbine cigarette, the other grasps a copy of the latest Fabian pamphlet. When he speaks it is in a defiant, prickly manner, and his accent is that of the midlands. Of course this is parody, but my point is that it is a parody the poets themselves encouraged and conspired to produce. They liked to think of themselves as rebels – for this was the decade of the Angry Young Men and of apparent contempt for Establishment values – but only in so far as it did not damage their chances of joining the metropolitan Establishment, which in practice most of them soon did. They became upholders of 'good' English, in love with a mistily imprecise past where England was characterized by devoted peasantry, red-brick farms and thatched cottages (the links between the Movement's political and social views and those of Alfred Austin are truly alarming); and they enlisted as Cold War warriors. Their natural home was *Encounter*, and just how appalling *that* is becomes apparent the moment you try to imagine the intelligentsia of just about any other country in the world agreeing to write for such a fatuously shallow, cliché-ridden journal. No wonder they hastened to endorse the Gravesian dogma of 'inspiration'. No need now for hard thought, no need to worry about the betrayals: the Poet could appeal to his Muse to preserve him from other pressures.

Two reactions against this parochialism deserve mention. One is Donald Davie's *Articulate Energy*, of 1955, a critical study of poetic syntax which argues the case for Pound. (An argument that Davie was to develop, qualify, and enlarge over the next decades.) The book predictably earned Davie the scorn of the little-Englanders, and this scorn was fully returned when in 1973 Philip Larkin brought out his old-fashioned and in some ways amateurish *Oxford Book of Twentieth-Century English Verse*. The second reaction came in 1962, with the publication of A. Alvarez's Penguin anthology, *The New Poetry*. In a combative, not to say tendentious introduction, called 'Beyond the Gentility Principle', Alvarez argued that what English poetry needed was a dash of extremism, a readiness to face the horrors lurking beneath the surface of everyday life. Accordingly, he began his anthology with selections from the work of Robert Lowell and John Berryman, because these American poets upheld the Alvarez cause by making poems out of breakdown, madness and emotional disorder. Poetry should take risks, Alvarez proclaimed. (He also, very stupidly, suggested that poets themselves should take risks: 'poetry is a murderous art', he announced).

According to Alvarez the only English poet who answered to these prescriptions was Ted Hughes. Behind much that he has to say about Hughes lurks, I think, the figure and indeed the poetry of D. H. Lawrence, about which Alvarez had already written. In 'Beyond the Gentility Principle', Alvarez contrasts Larkin's lovely poem, 'At Grass', with a far less successful poem by Hughes, in order to argue that it is Hughes's poem which is breaking new ground, because it is Hughes who is tapping the dark, psychic, violent forces latent in modern life.

Today's violence is, however, tomorrow's *Grand Guignol* and I have to say that, re-reading Hughes's early poetry, I am struck by how badly much of it has worn. I shall return to this, but before I do so I want to insert into my argument some remarks from an essay that appeared in the *London Magazine* for February 1985. The essay, which is called 'Macaulay's Children', is by M. G. Ramanan, and is concerned with the lasting imprint of the English on Indian life. Ramanan ends by suggesting some of the ways in which Indians may look at post-Imperial English literature. He says:

> Indisputably the loss of the jewel in her crown was a traumatic experience for Great Britain. We can show that this resulted in an insecure and embattled mental condition which in turn led writers to become more and more insular, more and more concerned with the English landscape, with the pikes, otters, hawks and crows of England, with merry England gone.
>
> Is it any wonder that a very English and very insular poet like Betjeman is Poet Laureate, and that all English poetry after the war seems to take its bearings from Betjeman's disciple, Philip Larkin, and from Ted Hughes, who in violent desperation attempts to impose his myths on us and to wrest an identity for England? Indeed, it has been argued that Larkin and Hughes make up what one might call a composite British poet, if such a creature were possible. One is soft, Norman French, concerned, nostalgic: the other is tough, Anglo-Saxon, assertive, imposing. One represents British gentility, the other British 'masculinity', virtues appropriate to the Imperial character. What Larkin in his neutral and modest way seems to be saying is that it is a pity the soldiers could not be maintained and had to be brought home from their duties abroad. What Hughes seems to be saying is

that this is no time for self-pity or nostalgia. This is the time to assert ourselves as we did in the good old days of empire.

Hughes's violent imagery is closely aligned with authoritarian politics, while Larkin's poetry is aligned with that other side of British society – the side which says 'keep England British'. Together these poets are saying in their different ways the same thing.

Clearly, this was written before the appointment of Ted Hughes as Poet Laureate in succession to Betjeman. But Ramanan might well have added a further point: that such an appointment, under such a government as Mrs Thatcher's, may be taken as further proof of the authoritarian nature of Hughes's politics, which will chime very well with the progressive loss of civil liberties, the malign farce of the Falklands campaign and the almost hysterical, bullying aggression which is an essential element of Thatcher's England.

Unfair? Yes, of course. But by no means absurd. For there is something about Hughes's poetry which, both at its best and worst, testifies to a preoccupation with violence. 'Thrushes' begins with the 'Terrifying . . . sleek thrushes on the lawn', who

> Overtake the instant and drag out some writhing thing.
> No indolent procrastinations and no yawning stares,
> No sighs or head-scratchings. Nothing but bounce and stab
> And a ravening second.

Hughes may call the thrushes 'terrifying' but the term feels overloaded, especially when set against the last three lines, which suggest what contempt he has for the merely human. 'Indolent procrastinations': what can he mean by the phrase? Moral choice as self-indulgence, perhaps? This feels to me dangerously Lawrentian in its scorn of ordinariness, its Nietzschean endorsement of power. Of course, you can argue that Hughes is entitled to write a poem such as 'Thrushes' because through it he can explore the lust for power and violence which is part of the story of twentieth-century (and perhaps all human) experience. Certainly, 'Hawk Roosting' is about the egotism of single-minded concern with a violence that seeks no justification for itself:

> The sun is behind me.
> Nothing has changed since I began.
> My eye has permitted no change.
> I am going to keep things like this.

There is a sense in which Hughes's hawk is close to the 'ragged urchin' in Auden's 'The Shield of Achilles', for whom it is axiomatic that 'Two boys knife a third and girls are raped'. But: 'Nothing has changed since I began'. The absurdity of this entirely solipsistic view is not challenged from within the poem because the consciousness of violence comes to us unmediated. It is all seen from the hawk's point of view. (Whereas in 'The Shield of Achilles' Auden both sees the violence and comments on its place in history.)

But it isn't only the egotism of violence which interests Hughes. Violence as pure expression of spirit, violence as assertion of identity: these seem to be at the heart of much of his poetry. And it is here that Ramanan's remarks begin to bite. Consider the ending of one of Hughes's best-known poems, 'Pike'. The pond where he fished was

> . . . as deep as England. It held
> Pike too immense to stir, so immense and old
> That past nightfall I dare not cast. . . .
>
> Owls hushing the floating woods
> Frail on my ear against the dream
> Darkness beneath night's darkness had freed,
> That rose slowly towards me, watching.

The dream which is as 'deep as England' is expressed through the rapacious pike. It is a dream of violence. This is not without justification. The English have always been a great deal more warlike and belligerent than they like to believe, and the imperialism which both proves and is a self-condemnation of such belligerence is perhaps as near to the heart of England as the sweet dream of Adlestrop. But the point I want to make is that here, as elsewhere, Hughes's fascination with what Ramanan calls his 'masculinity' amounts to an endorsement of it. In their ruthless predatoriness the Thrushes, the Hawk and the Pike all say 'there is no alternative'. Hughes can be very skilful at handling this, as in 'Pike', whose slow-paced muscular rhythms and heavy vowel and consonant patterns combine to create an atmosphere tense with a hidden, withheld menace.

Yet there is surely something very suspect about this use of birds and fish to explore issues as complex as the history and use of power and violence. Time and again, however, this is precisely what Hughes does. In 'Thistles', for example, he describes the plants as 'like pale hair and the gutturals of dialects./Every one manages a plume of blood'. The Thistles become a metaphor for England's Viking inheritance: all weaponry and warriordom. And again, nothing has changed since they began.

> Then they grow grey, like men.
> Mown down, it is a feud. Their sons appear,
> Stiff with weapons, fighting back over the same ground.

This kind of apprehension of a violence latent in English history is more justifiably approached in 'The Warriors of the North', where Hughes has the Vikings thawing out over the 'red and black disgorging of abbeys,/The bountiful, cleft casks,/The fluttered bowels of the women of dead burghers/And the elaborate patient gold of the Gaels'. It is an adroit summary of the main features of Viking culture; and Hughes is both imaginative and plausible when he writes that the culture produced 'the gruelling relapse and prolonguer of their blood/Into the iron arteries of Calvin'. Dread and destruction are undoubtedly close allies. But notice the 'fluttered bowels of the women of dead burghers', and how that line may be linked to the implicitly violent sexuality of the 'bountiful, cleft casks'. This seems to me crude cliché. Women feel sexually attracted to the muscled killing-machines who destroy their husbands – those soft burghers. (The contempt in this echoes the contempt shown for 'indolent . . . head-scratchings'.) Ramanan is surely right when he says that Hughes is deeply identified with the 'masculinity', the 'tough, Anglo-Saxon, assertive, imposing' cast of thought – or consciousness of identity – that is a key to one side of post-Imperial English poetry.

It is for this reason that, as I suggested earlier, much of Hughes's early work has worn badly. Its habitual concern with violence not only becomes monotonous, it is also limiting. This is not to dispute Hughes's great gifts as a maker of memorable images and taut, packed lines; but it is to say that his reading of history feels insistently reductive. 'In the end', he seems to suggest, 'it all comes down to war, to a struggle for survival, to the blood instinct of rapine.' To which I answer, 'perhaps, but between the beginning and end ought to be a long way'.

Of course, this is not the whole story. In a fuller assessment I would want to pay homage to Hughes's empathetic powers: to his fine account of the 'Jaguar', for example; and I would want to speak in praise of his sense that the world may not be fully apprehensible in terms of a rationalistic positivism. 'Ghost Crabs' and 'Wodwo' are brilliant poems that touch on, explore, evoke, a feeling for hidden mysteries which may legitimately run 'deep as England'. And against the strictures I have offered must be set the poem 'Wilfred Owen's Photographs', which isn't about Owen at all – or rather never mentions him – but is about the kind of blimpishness and love of disciplined violence that made the Great War inevitable. Hughes, that is to say, is a more complex poet than my account makes him out to be.[6] Nevertheless, there is a good deal to be said for Ramanan's argument, and I think Hughes needs to be approached in a more critical manner than is usually the case.

What of the other side of the coin? In some senses Philip Larkin obviously is as Ramanan describes him: concerned, nostalgic. At its least acceptable such nostalgia shows itself in the poem 'Homage to A Government', where Larkin writes about our abandonment of Empire and of worldly responsibilities. This is mere sentimentality. 'Going, Going' is not much better. It is about the disappearance of a presumed, pastoral England; and I can imagine the shade of Alfred Austin nodding approval over its lament for 'The shadows, the meadows, the lanes,/The guildhalls, the carved choirs'. But at least both these poems show that Donald Davie was less than fair when he accused Larkin of being prepared to put up with the second-best, or of simply being anaesthetized against ugliness. The problem with this argument, which Davie advances in *Thomas Hardy and British Poetry*, is that in what I think are Larkin's uncharacteristically worst poems he takes up a position that is identical to Davie's. At his finest, he does not so much accept the second-best as speak for a kind of decency of acceptance, which is more truly Hardyesque than his famous 'authority of sadness'. Larkin undoubtedly likes Hardy for those dark poems where the earlier poet speaks of the inevitability of time passing, of 'long perspectives/Open at each instant of our lives', as he puts it in the sad-sombre 'Reference Back'. And as everyone who begins to read Larkin comes to understand, death is an obsession of his. Some of the poems that deal with this subject are extraordinarily fine. When you come across 'Next, Please', with its haunting last stanza:

> Only one ship is seeking us, a black-
> Sailed unfamiliar, towing at her back
> A huge and birdless silence. In her wake
> No waters breed or break.

When you read 'Dockery and Son', whose syntax slowly, insidiously uncoils to the poem's final line where we confront 'age, and then the only end of age'; or 'The Building', the marvellous, bitter poem about a hospital, which ends with people bringing 'Wasteful, weak, propitiatory flowers' – and what a master of the last line Larkin is; or the great and quite unique poem, 'The Old Fools', which ends:

> Can they never tell
> What is dragging them back, and how it will end? Not at night?
> Not when the strangers come? Never, throughout
> The whole hideous inverted childhood? Well,
>   We shall find out.

– in all these and some other poems it is obvious that you are reading the work of a major poet. The poems are technical and imaginative triumphs: the wonderfully inventive metaphors, the cunning rhythms, the dramatic use of line-endings (look, for example, at the trick that is sprung in the last line of 'The Old Fools', after that apparently innocent 'Well'); these are matters that belong with and to high art. They also do not lack for praise.

But the poetry of acceptance is different. It also puts Larkin nearer to MacNeice than any other post-war poet. Indeed, like MacNeice he can often look like a tourist travelling through England. I think, for example, of how many poems of his are set on trains. I think, too, of his use of brand-names, something which he surely takes from MacNeice. And against MacNeice's 'Christmas Shopping' we might place 'The Large Cool Store' and 'Here', poems which make use of shops and shoppers, in order to give the flavour of contemporary England. It is a flavour further enhanced by those poems in which both poets talk directly about work: as in MacNeice's 'Sunday Morning' and Larkin's 'Toads' and 'Toads Revisited'.

However, I do not wish to give the impression that Larkin in any way borrows from or is improperly derivative of MacNeice. The fact is rather that his uniquely accurate recording eye is like MacNeice's in the sense that both poets have a relish for the actual, and do not withhold their approval from the world of the 'cut-price crowd', as Larkin puts it in 'Here'. But this is to speak in a pompous and un-Larkin way. The point can perhaps be more accurately made if I say that Larkin's modes of acceptance come into focus once we recall Hardy's insistence that beautiful scenery is unimportant compared to the wear of a foot on a threshold or Auden's remark that 'Art's subject is the human clay,/And landscape but the background to a torso'.

And yet even here we have to make distinctions. Larkin is

undoubtedly more in the grip of a deep melancholy than MacNeice and his sadness can often seem more enervate than Hardy's. I do not choose to spend time on this point because it seems to me both obvious and irrefutable. I do, however, want briefly to enlarge on his modes of acceptance, both because Donald Davie's position needs to be exposed and because I think that it is acceptance which most fully substantiates Larkin's right to be considered as a major poet.

To say this may seem strange. After all, Larkin's interests can seem limited and as limiting as Hughes's, very different though they are. But without wanting to put the point too emphatically, I suggest that Larkin often writes out of a much more complex set of feelings than he is commonly credited with, even if he is sometimes surprised into them. Yes, the misogyny exists, as one mode of expression. Yet the man who wrote 'A Study of Reading Habits' ('Get stewed:/Books are a load of crap') also wrote 'For Sidney Bechet', which is far and away the best poem about jazz that has ever been written, witty, tender, loving, even exuberant. Like many of Larkin's best poems it is so densely packed with specific references to the moment out of which it was born that I suspect future generations will need an almost endless supply of footnotes to understand it fully; but that is part of its genius, its proper use of the contemporaneous. It ends:

> On me your voice falls as they say love should,
> Like an enormous yes. My Crescent City
> Is where your speech alone is understood,
>
> And greeted as the natural noise of good,
> Scattering long-haired grief and scored pity.

The Crescent City is New Orleans, and Sidney Bechet who, like many of the greatest jazz musicians, came from there, was pre-eminently a master of the soprano saxophone, with a wonderfully thrilling, wide vibrato, and a unique way with glissandi. Larkin has been saying that anyone listening to Bechet's music will conjure up an 'appropriate falsehood', an image of New Orleans apposite to his idea of happiness: of sexual licence, a free-and-easy community, and so on. For Larkin himself, Bechet's music dispels, while it lasts, life's abounding and constricting sadnesses. It blows away Niobe's tears.

But in fact the last line is a dazzling pun, because in the 1950s 'long-hair' was a phrase applied to musicians who played classical music, and 'scored' pity suggests their music, in opposition to the improvised and unscored music of the great jazzmen. 'For Sidney Bechet' is scrupulous in acknowledging the subjective nature of the interpretation of the music, and at the same time passionate in its affirmation of what such music means to Larkin. And its richly idiomatic language is altogether more vital than Hughes's literariness. ('Attent' is the kind of word Larkin would never use.)

This comes out in 'An Arundel tomb', where the magical writing about the stone effigies of Earl and Countess and their endurance through a time when 'A bright/Litter of birdcalls strewed the same/Bone-riddled ground', yields to the final, utterly authoritative stanza:

> Time has transfigured them into
> Untruth. The stone fidelity
> They hardly meant has come to be
> Their final blazon, and to prove
> Our almost-instinct almost true:
> What will survive of us is love.

The jolt on 'Untruth', where again Larkin shows himself a master of the use of enjambement; the cunning ambiguities of 'stone fidelity' and 'blazon'; above all the hesitancies and siftings of the penultimate line and the line that issues out of it: these matters provide for a most beautiful, quiet flush of acceptance.

Of course, the negatives are also there, as in 'Mr Bleaney', with its necessarily chill sense of a life lost in the blanknesses of the city. Yet if you compare Larkin's writing about Bleaney with Eliot's writing about typist and clerk Larkin surely comes off better.

> But if he stood and watched the frigid wind
> Tousling the clouds, lay on the fusty bed
> Telling himself that this was home, and grinned,
> And shivered, without shaking off the dread
>
> That how we live measures our own nature,
> And at his age having no more to show
> Than one hired box should make him pretty sure
> He warranted no better, I don't know.

This does not condescend to Bleaney, nor does it write him off. Its rueful, slightly appalled-cum-bewildered tone is in fact a tactful way of both recognizing the bleakness of a life that may be horribly incomplete and a refusal to judge it so: 'But if . . .' The poem's last phrase, which has been arrived at by a stunning technical achievement as the sentence unwinds itself over two stanzas, says, with a shake of the head, that this is the pity of it. There is nothing aloofly Olympian about such a moment, and the use of that worn phrase in fact locks the poem into a shared awareness of how anyone's life can go wrong. It is the kind of thing anybody might say. Indeed, it is the kind of thing they *do* say. This is in short a properly imaginative use of the common language.

I know that there are dangers in this position. One is that Larkin will become fatalistic about lives whose inner strengths he may not know or share. Where this happens you could argue that he is moving towards the Eliotic position. (As, for example, in the damp 'Love Songs in Age' and 'Afternoons.') The other is that he will simply settle for a cataloguing of the dailiness of things, as a way of suggesting that it is by cluttering yourself with phenomena that you get through a life. Consider, for example, the inert listings in the Betjemanesque and truly awful 'Show Saturday'.

> Broad beans (one split open), dark shining-leafed cabbages – rows
> Of single supreme versions, followed (on laced
> Paper mats) by dairy and kitchen; four brown eggs, four white eggs,
> Four plain scones, four dropped scones, pure excellences that enclose
> A recession of skills.

Given the customary inventive accuracy of Larkin's 'swivel eye', these lines feel particularly dead.

But the point is that Larkin is capable of a discreet visionariness that can be almost Hardy-like in its ability to redeem the deadliness of the phenomenal. I think, for example, of the beautiful ending of 'At Grass', with its almost pagan suggestion of life slipping into the shadows: 'Only the groom, and the groom's boy,/With bridles in the evening come'. I think, too, of 'The Explosion'. Here, Larkin writes with a kind of intense, rapt calm about a colliery disaster and its aftermath, and imagines the lives of a community with a rare, unforced generosity. It's a marvellously compact narrative, and part of its power depends on the way Larkin cuts abruptly from the tremor that heralds the explosion to the words of the preacher in the chapel, conducting the men's funeral service. (A lesser poet would certainly have wanted a stanza about the explosion itself, and perhaps its effects on the community.) The tactful imaginativeness of the ending is dense and subtle: it is as though the men stand for a kind of heroism associated with commemorative coins or perhaps the figure of Christ, seen in the chapel's East window, towards which the women will be facing, his nimbus behind his head. The men can thus become 'larger than in life' – which is a hauntingly discreet use of the cliché 'larger than life' (not really believable, in other words, but enviable). And the last line equally hauntingly and discreetly suggests unimpaired sexual potency offered as a love gift. 'The Explosion' imagines ordinary lives with the kind of generosity that is very rare in post-war poetry.

But the finest of all these poems is 'The Whitsun Weddings', and I will close my account of Larkin with a few words about this much-discussed and deservedly famous poem.[7] It is about a train journey through England, but unlike Thomas's 'Adlestrop' or the opening of MacNeice's 'Autumn Journal', to both of which it may owe something, 'The Whitsun Weddings' has a wider, more inclusive sense of England. It is not only that Larkin offers a much-peopled landscape; it is that the journey allows us to see England in such a way that sequence becomes simultaneity, so that all of England feels to be on view, and the different glimpses are blended in the solvent of Larkin's observant eye.

> Wide farms went by, short-shadowed cattle, and
> Canals with floatings of industrial froth;
> A hothouse flashed uniquely: hedges dipped
> And rose

There is no heart of England in 'The Whitsun Weddings', no wished-for penetration into a 'real' secret place that nurtures a mystic identity. Instead, the insignia of rural, suburban and in-dustrial are alike held in view, and none is seen as more or less valuable than any other. There is no hierarchical ordering, no attempt to turn the observations into a 'prospect'.

On the other hand, Larkin does present himself as a fastidious observer of the human scene, as a 'disinterested' and condescending outsider, looking down – in both senses of the phrase – at the marriage parties who come on to the station platforms. To put it this way is not to suggest that Larkin is like Eliot's Tiresias, but it is to say that I think he deliberately presents himself as the aloof com-mentator on human folly. At first his response to the parties is that of the man who thinks in terms of the mocking tale or jibe, as he notes 'girls/In parodies of fashion, heels and veils'. But this note is progressively invaded by another, warmer and livelier, stanza by stanza, as the newly married couples board the train and the journey moves towards its end. Larkin has to be discreet about this, for to parade his quickening responsiveness would be self-regarding. But I think it heartening and lovely, the way he sees the marriages in the context of ordinariness – of the details glimpsed from the train-windows – so that the scenes beyond the windows and those within blend together to form the emblematic image of a society that may not be written off by the poet cocooned in his superior sensibility and taste.

> They watched the landscape, sitting side by side
> – An Odeon went past, a cooling tower,
> And someone running up to bowl – and none
> Thought of the others they would never meet
> Or how their lives would all contain this hour.

This is neither a picturesque nor a blighted landscape. It has value and meaning conferred on it by the fact that the lovers on the train come from it and will return to it. They are not sealed off from it, and nor can the poet afford to be; sneers about the picture house as a 'cheap drug' are out of order once he has come to recognize the fact that it is part of the world these people belong to. They are perhaps enclosed in their own dreams, but the poet is enabled to see them as part of the larger society for which he can now come to speak, positively and expansively:

> I thought of London spread out in the sun,
> Its postal districts packed like squares of wheat [. . .]
> And as the tightened brakes took hold, there swelled
> A sense of falling, like an arrow-shower
> Sent out of sight, somewhere becoming rain.

This marvellously turns London into the pastoral world of natural riches which earlier poets had identified in opposition to the city, and very often to people. The wonderful last lines testify both to the inevitable regret that this hour of transient harmony is coming to an end – a glimpsed social ease and richness – and to the certainty of renewal. For the ending supplies the right hint of further harvests, further riches. Larkin's vision is intensely democratic.

III

The ending of Larkin's great poem, and particularly the image of the 'arrow-shower', importantly calls to mind an image from which this book started out, Clare's grass, which 'eternal springs'. Both poets humanize a moment of energy in order to suggest how it can usher in

the promise of a generous future. Clare's is of course the more
avowedly political, for the grass will spring at and overwhelm castles
and grandeur. Yet there is a politics implicit in the ending of 'The
Whitsun Weddings', and for all the aggressive, snobbish, or merely
nostalgic little-Englandism that Larkin has increasingly displayed,
the vision with which he brings to an end 'The Whitsun Weddings' is
anything but that.

Laments for the death of castles and grandeur undoubtedly
abound in much post-war English poetry. I think, for example, of
Charles Tomlinson's 'On the Hall at Stowey', which mourns the
decay of a country house and the way of life that went with it.

> Five centuries – here were (at least) five –
> In linked love, eager excrescence
> Where the door, arched, crowned with acanthus,
> Aimed at civil elegance, but hit
> This sturdier compromise, neither Greek, Gothic
> Nor Strawberry, clumped from the arching-point
> And swathing down, like a fist of wheat,
> The unconscious emblem of the house's worth. . . .

But the tendentiousness of the properties Tomlinson here introduces,
and especially the 'fist of wheat' – with its presumably unintended
suggestion of shadowy bullying – show how literary this poem is. It
comes out of a tradition of country-house poetry and really makes
sense only in terms of that tradition. It is utterly empty of living
human reference. (It is also badly, clottedly written). It is, in the
worst sense, a poem smelling of books.

Or consider Geoffrey Hill's sonnet sequence, 'An Apology for the
Revival of Christian Architecture in England', from his volume
Tenebrae. Like Tomlinson, Hill comments on the passing of a
tradition which can be resurrected only through a language that
already feels dead:

> Autumn resumes the land, ruffles the woods
> with smoky wings, entangles them. Trees shine
> out from their leaves, rocks mildew to moss-green;
> the avenues are spread with brittle floods.
>
> Platonic England, house of solitudes,
> rests in its laurels and its injured stone,
> replete with complex fortunes that are gone,
> beset by dynasties of moods and clouds.

The echoes of Pope ('And laughing Ceres reassumes the land'), of Tennyson, of Yeats (the 'brittle floods' recall Yeats's 'brimming water', and although Hill changes 'brimming' to 'brittle' in order to suggest how under sentence of immediate death this dream of England lies, it nevertheless feeds on a tradition which in his own poem comes to feel merely self-reflexive): these and other echoes are ultimately debilitating because so persistently nostalgic. Moreover, the attempted reviving of cliché where the house 'rests in its laurels' fails – rather ridiculously – because the cliché isn't properly used. 'Injured stone' suggests some unfair hurt. I prefer to think of the grass springing in spite of the injuries that had been done to it by precisely the 'house of solitudes', whose passing Hill sonorously mourns.

Set against the literary pastiches of Tomlinson and Hill, Larkin's language and vision feel liberating and altogether worthwhile.

Further Reading

Louis MacNeice's *Collected Poems* are published by Faber. There are two full-length studies of his work: D. B. Moore, *The Poetry of Louis MacNeice*, Leicester University Press, 1972; and Robyn Marsack, *The Cave of Making: the Poetry of Louis MacNeice*, Oxford, 1982. For poets of the Second World War see the Penguin anthology by Robert Blythe, called *Components of the Scene*. Desmond Graham has edited the poems of Keith Douglas and has written a biography of him. For Alun Lewis, see *Selected Poetry and Prose*, edited and introduced by Ian Hamilton, published by Allen and Unwin, 1966, and *Selected Poems of Alun Lewis*, selected by Jeremy Hooker and Gweno Lewis, 1981. John Pikoulis's *Alun Lewis: A Life*, was published by Poetry Wales Press in 1984. See also Robert Hewison, the *Nineteen Forties*, and G. Thurley, *Poetry of the Forties*.

Robert Graves's *Collected Poems* are published by Cape. See also *Swifter than Reason: The Poetry and Criticism of Robert Graves*, Oxford, 1963, and the biography by Martin Seymour Smith, *Robert Graves: His Life and Work*, Sphere, 1983.

For the Movement see Blake Morrison, *The Movement: English Poetry and Prose of the 1950s*, Oxford, 1980. Both Philip Larkin's and Ted Hughes's poems are published by Faber. See also David Timms, Philip Larkin, Oliver and Boyd, 1973, and Andrew Motion, *Philip Larkin*, Methuen, 1983. There is a full-length study of Ted Hughes by Keith Sagar.

See also Calvin Bedient, *Seven Contemporary Poets*, Oxford, 1974. For more generous accounts than mine of Hill and Tomlinson see Merle E. Brown, *Double Lyric: Divisiveness and Communal Creativity in Recent English Poetry*, Routledge, 1980. David Trotter's *The Making of the Reader*, 1984, provides extremely sophisticated readings of a number of poets and poems with which the present study has been engaged.

Notes

Chapter One, pages 9–21

1. For a full account of the relationships between Clare, his patrons and his editors, see *John Clare: A Life*, by J. W. and Anne Tibble, revised edn. 1972. Unfortunately, the Tibbles take just about everyone's side against Clare, not understanding the enormity of their condescension towards him. As to the matter of texts: the Tibbles, like everyone else, took it upon themselves to emend, to re-punctuate, standardize spelling, etc. Now at last matters are beginning to mend. Although the new Oxford edition promises to be horrendously expensive, the Selected paperback, edited by Robinson and Powell, is splendidly full and sensitive.
2. For this see my essay 'The idea of the provincial' in *Romantic to Modern*, 1982.
3. I owe my discovery of this to Piers Gray's excellent *T. S. Eliot's Intellectual and Poetical Development, 1909–1922*, 1982.
4. Mark Storey, *The Poetry of John Clare*, 1974, pp. 143–5.
5. Keith Thomas, *Man and the Natural World*, 1983, p. 66.

Chapter Two, pages 22–49

1. Donald Davie, *Thomas Hardy and British Poetry*, 1973.
2. Tom Paulin, *Thomas Hardy: The Poetry of Perception*, 1976. (The best book on Hardy's poetry.) See also my *The Literature of Change*, 1977, for the chapter on Hardy's women.
3. In the special issue of *Agenda*, edited by Davie (vol. 10, nos. 2–3, 1972).
4. Douglas Brown, *Thomas Hardy*, 1964. Thom Gunn's essay may be found in the special issue of *Agenda*.

Chapter Three, pages 50–69

1. There are several important monographs on Lutyens, perhaps the most substantial being A. S. G. Butler's *The Architecture of Sir Edward*

Lutyens (3 vols), 1950. See also Mark Girouard, *Life in the English Country House*, 1978.

2. Mark Girouard, *Sweetness and Light, The 'Queen Anne' Movement, 1860–1900*, 1977.

3. Doughty's *Dawn of Britain* goes even further back. But although Edward Thomas read and admired it, I do not think of it as an influential work, rather as a curiosity.

4. I owe a good deal of what follows to my former student, Allan Chatburn, whose lively interest in the role of the clerk – in literature and life – did much to prompt this discussion.

5. 'Uranian' poetry is discussed by Paul Fussell in his *The Great War and Modern Memory*, 1982.

Chapter Four, pages 70–102

1. See Davie's essay in Dominic Hibberd (ed.), *Poetry of the First World War*, 1981.

2. Jon Silkin, *The Penguin Book of First World War Poetry*, 1979.

3. Edna Longley (ed.), *Edward Thomas, Poems and Last Poems*, 1973. Stan Smith's essay, 'A language not to be betrayed' first appeared in *Literature and History*. It is largely reprinted in his *Inviolable Voice*, 1983.

4. Helen Thomas, *Time and Again*, 1978, p. 111.

Chapter Five, pages 103–129

1. Evelyn Waugh's *Diaries* reveal just how cynical and horrible the 'bright young things' of the 1920s were; and how they defended their behaviour on the grounds that there was no society and no cause left for them to believe in. See also Martin Green's *The Children of the Sun*, 1976, for a full study of the Waugh generation.

2. For a brilliant account of Yeats's 'invention' of himself see Ian Fletcher and D. J. Gordon, *Images of a Poet*, 1961.

3. Elizabeth Cullingford, *Yeats, Ireland and Fascism*, 1980. Cullingford's book is a detailed rebuttal of Conor Cruise O'Brien's charge that for most of his adult life Yeats was a fascist.

4. For the reception of *Cathleen ni Houlihan* see Richard Fallis, *The Irish Renaissance*, 1978.

5. In an *Observer* review of 18 May 1985, O'Brien claims that the rhetoric of the play 'involving the glorification of past insurrections, etc – was mainly about pushing out people whom you expected to leave anyway. . . . The nationalist excitement was genuine, but all the more enjoyable in that no real violence was expected.' This seems to me disingenuous.

6. Raymond Williams has of course covered some of the same ground in his *The Country and the City*, 1973.

7. There is a good account of the Elegy in Dudley Young's *Out of Ireland*, 1975.
8. Poggioli's essay is to be found in *The Mind and Art of C. P. Cavafy*, Athens, 1985.

Chapter Six, pages 130–150

1. In later years Leavis turned away from Eliot, complaining that among other failures, Eliot had a deep 'blankness' about England's past. See, for example, remarks and essays in *The Common Pursuit, Lectures in America* and *Nor Shall My Sword*. I imagine that Leavis began to smell a rat when Eliot trained his sights on Lawrence, in *After Strange Gods*; and that he rightly saw Eliot's ready incorporation into metropolitan London literary life as a betrayal of integrity. But my point is that the betrayal is always to be expected, given Eliot's desire to become an insider and also given the fact that he lacked James's by no means complete ability to distance himself from all that is softest and worst about such a life.
2. See, for this essay, George Seferis, *On the Greek Style*, London, 1967.
3. Michael Hamburger, *The Truth of Poetry*, 1969 (reprinted by Penguin), an indispensable study of what Hamburger calls 'tensions in modern poetry from Baudelaire to the 1960s'.
4. Evelyn Waugh's *Diaries* and Martin Green's *Children of the Sun* (op. cit.) suggest the kinds of cynical exploitation of sex that Eliot – and Leavis – may have had in mind. In some ways *The Waste Land*, and especially some of the cancelled passages, reads as a candidly disenchanted account of the doings of the 'beautiful people' of the 1920s, although that will not make it as deeply diagnostic a poem as Leavis believed it to be. See also an essay by John Heath-Stubbs in the special *Agenda* number devoted to Eliot (vol. 23 nos. 1–2) in which he points out that the poem's epigraph from Petronius is taken from the *Satyricon*, most of which (as we have it) gives 'a scarifying picture of a society obsessed with sex and terrified by the fear of impotence. That Eliot sees analogies between this society and that of post-war Europe is clear enough.'
5. This argument is more fully worked out in an essay I wrote in conjunction with William Myers, and which may be found in *Essays in Criticism*, April 1969.
6. Lucy McDiarmid, *Saving Civilization: Yeats, Eliot, and Auden Between the Wars*, 1984.
7. See, for example, Helen Gardner and Hugh Kenner, as listed under *Further Reading*.
8. Hans Meyerhoff, *Time in Literature*, California, 1960.

Chapter Seven, pages 151–178

1. Mahon's essay is to be found in Brown and Reid (eds), *Time Was Away: The World of Louis MacNeice*, 1974.
2. In Stephen Spender (ed.), *W. H. Auden: A Tribute*, 1974.
3. In Ronald Carter (ed.), *Thirties Poets: The Auden Group*, 1984.
4. John Fuller, *A Reader's Guide to W. H. Auden*, 1970.
5. In his essay in Graham Greene (ed.), *The Old School Tie*, 1984.
6. Unless otherwise indicated, poems will be identified by their opening lines.
7. I am thinking especially of his account of Lady Queenie Paull, and her ruthless self-destruction and willingness to destroy others.
8. However, both Rodway's *Preface to Auden*, 1985, and Tom Paulin's essay in *Ireland and the English Crisis* are excellent.

Chapter Eight, pages 179–205

1. Tom Paulin suggests that MacNeice's work at the BBC was partly responsible for his decline as a poet. See his *Ireland and the English Crisis*, 1984.
2. Louis MacNeice, 'Poetry' in *The Arts Today*, ed. Geoffrey Grigson, 1935.
3. See 'Further reading'.
4. There have been attempts to make a case for Sidney Keyes, but they do not impress me. However, Keyes's poetry can be read in Ronald Blythe's anthology for which see 'Further reading'; and although out of print his volumes of poetry are in good libraries.
5. The text comes from the standard edition of Keith Douglas's poems, edited by Desmond Graham, 1979.
6. See 'Further reading'.
7. See 'Further reading'.

Index

Page references to major discussions of individual poets appear in bold type.